GOD GOES TO MURDERER'S ROW

Other Works by Rev. M. Raymond, O.C.S.O.

Burnt Out Incense
Trappists, The REDS and You
Three Religious Rebels
The Family That Overtook Christ
The Man Who Got Even With God

Booklets

Is Your Home Like This?
Running Off With God
Life Is Someone
Are You?
FIAT! Remake Your World
Life Is a Divine Romance
Set the World on Fire
For Your Own Defence
What Are You Doing to Jesus Christ?
Doubling for the Mother of God
Whispers From the Wings (Sequel)
Do You Want Life and Love?
A Startling Thing for You
Have You Met God?
Facts About Reason, Revelation and Religion
To Mothers Whose Sons Are in the Service
A Message From Those Killed in Action
The God-Man's Double
What's Wrong?
Help God Be a Success
You Are Leading a Dangerous Life?

God Goes to

Murderer's Row

BY

REV. M. RAYMOND, O.C.S.O.

THE BRUCE PUBLISHING COMPANY
MILWAUKEE

Nihil obstat: Fr. Maurice Mulloy, O.C.S.O. } Censores
           Fr. Paul Bourne, O.C.S.O.
Imprimi potest: Rt. Rev. Dominique Nogues, O.C.S.O., Abbas Generalis

Nihil obstat: John A. Schulien, S.T.D., Censor librorum
Imprimatur: Milwaukiae, die 6a mensis octobris, A.D. 1951

/s/ ✠ MOYSES E. KILEY
ARCHIEPISCOPUS MILWAUKIENSIS

Grateful acknowledgment is made to the editors of *The Christian Century* for their kind permission to use the poem "Upon a Hill," by Miriam Crouse.

My Vindication

THE impossible has happened: I have become what I always despised — and glory in the actuality. I, who have always detested ghost writing, am writing for a "ghost" in the strict sense of that word in its relation to literature. For the man of whom I now write drew his last breath at Eddyville, Kentucky, on the morning of February 26, 1943, at exactly 1:22 a.m. He was sitting in the electric chair of Kentucky's State Prison.

That day most of the papers in the nation, and all the papers in the state, carried a gross misstatement. They told how Tom Penney, the convicted murderer of Marion Miley and her middle-aged mother, had paid with his life for the crime committed, September 28, 1941. But that was far from the truth; for the man in the electric chair that bleak February morning was not Tom Penney the murderer.

I do not mean to startle. I simply intend to state facts. Tom Penney the murderer had died fourteen months earlier — on a Sunday afternoon, December 21, 1941 — in Fayette County Jail at Lexington, Kentucky; and there had been buried. That is why I say the body through which the electrocutioner sent four fierce shocks on February 26, 1943, belonged to a man far different from the scar-faced Tom Penney who, with Bob Anderson, had entered the Lexington Country Club early that Sunday morning in late September, 1941, to come forth with guns almost empty, a paltry $130 in their hands, while behind them one woman lay dead and another dying.

To tell who it was from whom the State exacted the supreme penalty that February morning is only one of the purposes I

now write for a ghost. But that revelation alone would be justifica-
tion enough for the bounding joy I feel in my change of attitude
and vindication enough for my rupture of Trappist silence; for
Tom Penney the murderer had once confessed that to him "God
was only a three letter word, and as far as any practical bearing
on his life was concerned, those three letters might just as well
have been x-y-z." Whereas the man who entered Eddyville's
Death House in the company of big Jess Buchanan, the prison's
warden, had but recently written: "My only peace is in God
and with God. Until I am with Him, His Mother, and all His
saints, I am miserable." The man strapped into the electric chair
this February morning had said again and again: "I know that
death is the only way to God, and I am very impatient to be on
my way."

On behalf of this one who was so impatient for death I speak,
but it is the miracle story of his rebirth that I tell; and I tell
much of it in his own words. Those words I have before me in
two hundred and twenty-one letters, two poems, two thirds of a
thumbnail autobiography, and a last will and testament. The
letters, all but fifteen of them, were written in those fourteen
months that stretched between the time Tom Penney the murderer
died and the dark February morning when four severe shocks sent
life out of the body of the man who sat in Eddyville's electric
chair. Though each bears the signature of Tom Penney, I ask
you to decide whether or not so much as a single line was written
by Tom Penney the criminal.

But there is a deeper purpose to this "ghosting" of mine. I
write not to tell you merely of the value of the soul of him who
died in the electric chair, but to tell you that your own soul and
the soul of every human being is of infinite worth. And the book
world of our day has made my writing necessary for, although our
bookshelves literally bend under the weight of testimonies to
God's grace, most of them are by or about the literati. We have
biographies and autobiographies, magazine articles and clever
symposia telling brilliantly of the conversion of the learned. They
run the full gamut: from the *Confessions* of St. Augustine and

the *Apologia* of Cardinal Newman down to *Now I See* by Arnold
Lunn and *The Seven Storey Mountain* by Thomas Merton.
Marvelous though these testimonies be, they may lead some to
forget that every soul is so infinitely precious to almighty God
that He will spare no pains to save the least and the worst of us,
stalking us even to the death house to save us from hell. But if
His stalking is to be successful we must see as did this man at
Eddyville.

This book, then, is written only for those who want the revelation of truths that are soul-deep and of souls that are deep in
Truth. All others can turn back to their Sunday supplements,
comic strips, and tabloids.

Since this is to be a revelation of God for God's glory, let me do
as did my father St. Bernard, who pointed out that on the
Friday afternoon we now call "Good" one was saved on Calvary's
top — and only one. *"One,"* he says, "so that none of us may ever
despair; *only* one, lest any of us ever presume." And that aspect
of Calvary was re-enacted at Eddyville on the night of which I
speak; for three men died, but only one . . . Let Miriam Crouse
speak for me. She says:

> Three men shared death upon a hill,
>   But only one man died;
> The other two —
>   A thief and God Himself —
> Made rendezvous.
>
> Three crosses still
>   Are borne up Calvary's hill,
> Where Sin still lifts them high:
>   Upon the one, sag broken men
> Who, cursing, die;
>
> Another holds the praying thief,
>   Or those who penitent as he,
> Still find the Christ
>   Beside them on the tree.

Three men shared death at Eddyville, but only one . . . Well, let me begin the story of this soul's salvation where the story of every soul's salvation — even that of the very Mother of God — began: at Gethsemani.

It is America's, not Palestine's, Gethsemani of which I speak. But those two are so closely knit in Time and for Eternity that he who stood hesitant in the doorway this afternoon in late October, 1941, could just as well have been the Apostle John as one of his twentieth-century successors — Father George Donnelly. He was trying to decide which way he would go back to Covington. On what gave every appearance of being a whim, he decided to go home through Lexington. It was that decision which brought death to Tom Penney the murderer and sent a far different man to the electric chair at Eddyville. For what Father George took to be a whim was actually the will of God, and while it is true that it was Father George's hand on the wheel and his foot on the accelerator, it is even truer that Jesus Christ did the driving that day.

As the priest sped through the October afternoon he was conscious of a great sense of peace. His short retreat at the gray-walled City of God called Gethsemani, had brought him close to the Source of the beauty he now found all around him. His cigar was drawing perfectly; his machine purred as it ate up the miles; small wonder that he himself was aglow with the realization that life is good. With the woods around him full of color, the world above and below washed clean by yesterday's rain, and the rich tang of autumn in the air, he drove on never dreaming he was heading for the leading role in a drama that would end not in the dark room of death of Kentucky's State Prison, but in the blinding white light of Heaven's High Halls.

That sounds mysterious; but we are dealing with mysteries — deep ones. And as Father George sped through the brilliant autumn countryside toward Lexington, Austin Price, chief of the Lexington Police Department and Guy Maupin, his superintendent of identification, were facing another deep mystery — that of Tom Penney the murderer.

CONTENTS

CHAPTER ONE

Chief Price Is Uneasy

GUY MAUPIN trotted down the steps of the Fayette County Jail and swung jauntily along Short Street. A few dozen strides brought him to the City's Police Headquarters, where he pushed through the door, swept along the corridor, and quite airily entered the office of the Chief of Police. He found Austin Price with the morning *Herald* spread out before him.

"Any bouquets for the Detective Department today, Chief?"

Price's large head came up; his nod was both greeting and an invitation to be seated. "Newspapermen know only one language, Guy. They are not complimenting us this morning or any other morning."

"Well, after the roasting they gave us for about ten days, I thought they might be decent enough to — "

"Decent?" Austin Price was almost sneering. He sat back. "What I'd like to know is why they picked on the City Police for a job that belonged to the County Patrol, and why they singled me out as a target and overlooked the Sheriff. We cracked the case, Guy, but it really didn't belong to us."

"Of course it didn't. The Lexington Country Club is fully three miles from the city. But I'm not sorry we did the job."

"Neither am I," rejoined the Chief. "But why do the papers ride us so?"

"Wish I knew." Maupin pushed his hat far back on his head. "What stops me completely is their silence on the speed with

1

which we cleaned up the mess. Think of it: We are pulled from our beds on Sunday morning, September 28, to find Marion Miley nationally known golf star, sprawled out in her pajamas, on the floor of her apartment at the Country Club with a bullet in her back and another through her brain. Down the road her mother, Elsie Ego, has just crumpled with three slugs in her stomach. By Wednesday she's dead. And what have we got to go on besides the two bodies? A messed-up bedroom, three slugs from a .32 automatic in a mattress, and two buttons from a man's coat."

"That was about all, wasn't it?" said the Chief.

"The smart newspaper boys tell the world it was an 'inside job.' You were smarter. You told us it was 'local' and set me thumbing the files. In two days we knew exactly whom we wanted. Before the week was out we had teletyped his description to every state in the Union. If the busybodies in the papers and on the phones had left us alone we might have had him sooner."

"They gave us the tip on the car," objected Price quietly.

"Tip!" snorted Maupin. "We were told a newsboy had seen a two-toned Buick sedan parked at the Club Sunday morning. Big help that was! It set us on the wrong track completely. It had us watching for a green Buick sedan two ex-cons had stolen in Parrot, Georgia. No, Chief, the fact is you had nothing to go on but your own good gray matter. Yet the papers squawked as if the murderers had handed us their calling cards and we were refusing them an interview."

"The local boys got sore because I established Press Conferences," said Price quietly. "I was only trying to play square. . . ."

"Yeah, and they played square with you after that, didn't they? Headlines: *'Local Police Still in the Dark'* and *'FBI May Be Called In.'* Then silence for two full days."

A slow smile stole across the Chief's face. "That hurt worse than the headlines, Guy. It was the old army game of killing a man by ignoring him. . . ."

"Well, we soon made them recognize us, didn't we?"

"God gave us a break."

"I suppose He did. But if so, it is only another proof that God helps those who help themselves. Look at the facts: September 28 a crime is committed. October 1 you have nothing but two corpses on your hands. Yet, by October 9 you have the criminal and his confession — "

"Oh, not so fast, Guy. Not so fast. We got the call from Fort Worth, Texas, October 9, saying they had picked up a man answering the description we sent out. . . ."

"Come on, Chief. It said more than that. It said they had picked up two men in a 1941 two-toned Buick sedan bearing Kentucky license plates. It said one of them was from Lexington — the man we wanted: Tom Penney. It said the other, Leo Gaddis, another ex-con, had worked in Louisville recently. It said a shell from a .32 automatic and a pair of women's sport shoes had been found in the rear of the car. Why, that call gave us everything but the confession."

"You'd never think so if you had gone to Fort Worth with me," said the Chief as that same slow smile crossed his features.

"You never did tell me how you got the confession, Chief. Was it hard to make Penney talk?"

Price shook his head. "It's never hard to make Tom Penney talk, but to make him tell the truth is another story. He had been talking to — and laughing at — the police and newspapermen at Fort Worth for two days and two nights when I arrived there Saturday, October 11; but he had told them nothing. They had picked him up with Leo Gaddis and some woman on the ninth. The girl and Gaddis were soon discharged. Penney was held for me. He had denied all knowledge of the Country Club affair and given a reasonable account of his actions since leaving Louisville, October 1. But it was what he had been doing just prior to the first that interested me."

Price rocked on his swivel before going on. "I slept Saturday night. After early Mass Sunday I arranged to see Penney alone. They shut us in a room at nine o'clock. It was not quite one when I came out. For me the probe of the Miley murders was over, but a greater mystery had begun."

"Yeah?"

"Yes. Remember I had set you and the boys checking on Bob Anderson the minute we learned his was the car Penney had been driving when picked up? You found him at 'The Cat and Fiddle,' his night club in Louisville. He swore he hadn't left the place in weeks. But we knew he had been charged with vagrancy at Newport, our next door neighbor, just over a month ago because he had been driving that Buick of his around with an ex-con and some shady characters as companions. Before I left for the South I ordered you to watch him. Sunday afternoon I told you to arrest him."

"Joe Hoskins did the job, Chief — and found Anderson as cool as a cucumber."

"He's one boy we'll never break."

"We don't have to. Penney squealed; so did Baxter."

"Yes, I suppose you can call it squealing. But it was only after Anderson had dealt as mean a double cross as I've ever seen. He told Penney to take his car to make his getaway. Then reported the car as stolen."

"What a rat!"

"Very appropriate! He'll fight this case to the last ditch, giving us plenty of trouble."

"With what? We've got the whole thing sewed up. Penney confessed to you in Texas, naming Anderson as the murderer. He confessed to us here in Lexington after you brought him back, telling how Skeeter Baxter, the greenskeeper at the Club, had hatched the whole plot. . . . We picked up Baxter that very day — last Friday it was. In less than four hours we had his confession. It tallied perfectly with Penney's. Saturday Penney took us to where the guns were buried. We unearthed two automatics — a .32 and a .38. Yesterday I got word from the FBI's that the markings on the slugs we sent and the slugs taken at the Club are the same. So we've got the guns and the gunmen. What chance has Anderson got?"

"Penney's been quite helpful, hasn't he?"

The question had been asked casually, but Maupin knew his Chief. Price was noted for being a good listener. He seldom broke in on anyone. The Identification Head caught all that had been unsaid in the query, and wondered. He reached for his pipe and, while filling it, slowly said, "I was with Joe Harrigan from eight o'clock last Thursday night until seven o'clock Friday morning. For almost eleven hours we questioned Tom Penney. Thank God the boy finally decided to tell the full truth, otherwise we'd still be there asking him questions and getting anything from a laugh to some of the cleverest and most cutting sarcasm I ever heard. That boy has a brain, a tongue, and very little love for officers of the law."

"Is it true, Guy, that the slug you took from the floor of the Country Club was from the .38?"

"Uh-huh."

"And Penney claims he had the .38?"

"Uh-huh."

"Then it looks to me that he will build his case on the fact that the only bullet he fired struck neither of the women. He showed me a letter he had written to his mother last Monday morning. In it he said something like this: 'Don't believe everything that is printed in the papers. As usual, they try to convict a person before he is tried. I can tell you one thing, Mother, that may make you feel better: I am not guilty of murder. I have definite proof of that now.' "

"What does he mean?" Maupin removed the pipe from his mouth.

"What you've just told me. He fired his gun, he admits; but you've proved that its bullet went into the floor of the Country Club. . . ."

"That won't keep him from the chair," said the Detective as he crossed his legs and smiled somewhat pityingly. "The law takes care of that. Tom Penney may not have killed either of the Mileys, but he'll be found guilty of complicity — and that's enough. Why, Chief, I could prosecute this case myself and get the same verdict and same sentence for all three. They're going to ask for separate trials, you know."

When the Chief merely took off his glasses and polished them,

Maupin went on, "That will be a help to Jim Park in the prosecution and to whoever helps him. I suppose it will be Harry Miller. They'll be able to use Penney and Baxter against Anderson, and Penney against Baxter if necessary."

Price cleared his throat a bit noisily. "I wonder if those two will promise Tom a life sentence for his testimony."

"They had better not. This town is hot over the case. Hot enough for a lynching. Marion Miley was not only pretty, she was popular."

The Chief's eyes narrowed.

Maupin's guttural chuckle was pleasant to hear. "No attempt will be made, Chief. Penney's in Fayette County Jail; but Fayette County Jail is in the city of Lexington; and we're fairly civilized here. But tell me, what's on your mind? You're not yourself. It's not the wife, is it?"

"She's all right," replied Price, cooled and calmed by the query. "The operation was only a minor one and she's in the best hands possible. Sister Mary Laurentia, you know, is her blood sister."

The detective stood up. "So that nun up at St. Joseph's Hospital is your sister-in-law, eh? I met her and a few others when I went there about Mrs. Miley. She impressed me deeply."

"She does everyone, Guy. I'm going up early this afternoon to see the Mrs. — Sister called me an hour ago to say everything was fine."

"What's on your mind, then?"

"Tom Penney."

"He's as good as dead."

"That's precisely why I can't forget him."

"But look at the record he's had!"

"That's exactly what makes me worry."

Maupin pushed his hat further back on his head, took the pipe from his mouth, and spread his two hands on the edge of the Chief's desk. Leaning toward Price, he said: "I've never known you to go soft on any criminal, Chief. Why should this boy bother you? He's a bad actor. We've had him on our hands at least ten times, and five of them have been after his term at Frankfort.

He's a confirmed criminal. The city, state, and society will be benefited by his removal."

Price's large head shook slowly in the cup of his two hands as his elbows straddled the paper on his desk. "I wonder what it is," he mused. "It can't be heredity. That boy's father was a professor of English. His mother has something fine about her. She's run a rooming house ever since Tom's father died. It can't be environment. Not everyone in the same neighborhood, or even in the same gang, goes wrong. As for education . . . the only place youth gets educated into crime, it seems, is in our Reform Schools. It was there Tom met Anderson. . . . "

"Yes, Chief," objected Maupin, "but that was not Penney's first time up. He had been sentenced to three years in 1926 for grand larceny. He served only two of them. When he met Anderson in 1934, he was supposed to be doing a twenty-year stretch for robbery and assault in 1930. He shot and wounded two men in that grocery-store holdup. Anderson was doing only a five-year stretch for storehouse breaking."

Maupin's pipe was out. He puffed vigorously before reaching for a match. As he lit up again, he squeezed his question at Price. "What's the story, Chief? You admit the boy's bad. You know he's going to die. You know he deserves it. Yet you're sad."

Chief Price rose from his swivel chair and began to pace his office. "Guy, what's the most important moment of life?"

"Huh?"

Price stopped pacing and faced his friend. "The most important moment in life is the *last*." The Chief's knuckles struck his desk.

"I've just gone over Tom Penney's record in the files. He was found guilty of grand larceny when he was fifteen years old. That was in June, 1924. From then till this day, the only years not marked with some criminal act are those he spent in prison. He was in our hands in '24, '25, and '26. We sent him to the Reform School that year. He stayed until 1928 or '29. But, as you say, in 1930 we had to send him up for twenty years. They let him out in '37. And we've had Tom Penney in here five times in the past five years. . . . No, it's all too obvious Tom Penney has not lived right — but I'm going to do all in my power to see that he dies right!"

"What are you going to do?" asked Maupin in wonderment.

The Chief slumped into his large swivel chair. "That's my mystery. I don't know what to do. Anderson will take care of himself. Baxter is a hop-head. Can't do much for them. But Penney . . . I've known him since he was a child. How can I touch Tom Penney's heart?"

Guy Maupin knew when he was beyond his depth. This had been one of the strangest conversations he had ever had with Chief Price. Obviously, his superior was deeply concerned about a man who held little more interest for the Police Department. What should he say to ease himself out of a talk that was beginning to bewilder him? He decided to be blunt.

"Aw, forget him, Chief. Leopards don't change their spots. Once a criminal always a criminal."

Austin Price's head turned swiftly. His eyes were sparkling behind his horn-rimmed glasses. "Did you ever hear of Dismas?"

"Have we got his prints?"

"I doubt it, though he was a criminal with a pretty bad record."

"Well, what about him?"

"He ended the way I want Tom Penney to end."

"How was that?"

Chief Price spaced his words deliberately. "Dismas was convicted and sentenced to death. . . . He died. . . . But it is where I want Tom Penney to die — at the side of Jesus Christ. How can I get him there?"

CHAPTER TWO

God Gathers His Instruments

It was almost midafternoon before Austin Price reached the hospital. He hurried along the corridor, but checked his pace as he neared his wife's room; for the half-opened door allowed him to hear a merry chuckle. Sister Mary Laurentia was visiting Mrs. Price, her sister. A taunt was on his lips as greeting, but died there when he pushed the door farther open and discovered Sister Robert Ann standing at the foot of the bed.

"Oh, come in, Mr. Price," she called. "We were just telling Birdie she must hurry home and take care of you."

"Discharged?" queried the Chief as he bent to kiss his wife.

"Yes, but I don't think I'll go home until tomorrow."

"She likes it here," put in Sister Mary Laurentia from the other side of the bed. "It's like old times when we fight every day, isn't it, Sis?"

Mrs. Price smiled at her sister and asked her husband: "How's little Jackie?"

Austin Price's eyes opened wider as he whistled: "Glad you asked, honey. I promised the kid I'd take him for a ride this very afternoon. He and his mother must be waiting downstairs right now." He turned to Sister Robert Ann. "That's the youngster who came all the way from Seattle to see your Dr. Rankin, you know. He and his mother are staying at our house."

"But how is he?" broke in Mrs. Price insistently.

"Don't know, hon. — Dr. Rankin had not finished all his tests the last time I saw him."

"Well . . . " A knock on the door interrupted Mrs. Price and Sister Mary Benigna, Superior of the hospital, entered.

"What have we here — a family meeting? How are you, Mr. Price? I'm very glad to see you. And you, Mrs. Price? They tell me you're going to leave us — "

"Not until tomorrow, Sister."

"Oh, that's fine. Get some good rest before going back to slave for this big husband of yours. It's a man's world, isn't it, Chief?"

"Not this little corner of it," laughed Price as he swept the four faces with a glance. "Did you come downstairs or up, Sister?"

"Up."

"Did you happen to see Jackie Regan and his mother?"

"Dr. Rankin's patient? Yes, he's sitting in the lobby."

"Then I ought to be on my way."

"Wait," cut in Mrs. Price. "Sister Benigna, wouldn't it be grand to have Sisters Robert Ann and Mary Laurentia go out for a nice drive with the Chief and the little fellow? I've been after them every day to get out for fresh air; but they pay as little attention to me as does the Chief when he's on a hot case."

"I'm obeyed no better, Mrs. Price," said the Superioress as her hands played with her beads. "I tell every Sister in the hospital to get as much fresh air as possible, but — "

"The air in the hospital is much more safe. Think of all the disinfectant, the antiseptics, the utter sterility," cut in Sister Mary Laurentia.

"Go on with you," replied the Superioress. "You and Sister Robert Ann chaperon the Chief as he takes the little boy and his mother for a ride. I want to talk to Mrs. Price alone. Go on now." She turned to the Chief. "You'll have Mrs. Price the rest of your life. I'll have her only these few hours."

"Not much of a visit, hon," said Price to his wife as he swept his hat from the bed, "but I'll be back in no time. How soon will you be ready, Sisters?"

"Oh, they'll be at the door before you," replied Sister Benigna.

"I know that pair." And she waved the two nuns out of the room.

Ten minutes later, as the Chief swung his car out the main drive, Jackie, sitting beside him on the front seat, pointed to the car radio. "Can we get Police Calls on this, Mr. Price? How do you send those calls out anyhow? Will you show me before I go back to Seattle?"

"No, Jackie, you won't get any Police Calls on that radio. This is Mrs. Price's car and she hears enough Police reports and Police Calls without any special equipment. But if you really want to see how we send them I'll take you down to the Station after we stop at the jail."

Sister Robert Ann lifted an inquiring eyebrow to her companion in the back seat. "That means the County Jail!" Her voice was filled with real consternation.

"I hope you're right. I've always wanted to see that place," was the only comfort she got from the older nun.

But ten minutes later Sister Mary Laurentia experienced a qualm herself when she saw the Chief actually drawing up before the Fayette County Jail. But quickly she decided to be as big a child as Jackie and see what she could see in this curious place. She felt a pronounced tremor in Sister Robert's arm as she helped her from the car. And what was this tingling in her own veins? Sisters of Charity had been in jails before, she told herself; but then just as quickly told herself they had not been Sisters of Charity of Nazareth, nor had the jails been the Fayette County Jail. Then she saw the challenging light in her brother-in-law's eye. If he thought he was frightening nuns, she'd show him!

"Now let us see all of it, Chief," she demanded as he locked his car.

"From bottom to top." Price laughed as he started for the steps.

After the main office had been thoroughly examined, the Chief showed the Sisters the storerooms and the huge kitchen. The order and cleanliness impressed the nuns.

"Could we see some cells and prisoners?" asked Jackie, who had as much interest in steam cookers and heating tables as the Sisters would have in roller skates and hockey sticks.

"Up we go," said the Chief and led the way to the cell blocks on the second floor. Out of the corner of his eyes he studied the nuns. Sister Robert Ann did look a little frightened, but Sister Mary Laurentia was walking along with all the calm and assurance she displayed on the floors of the hospital. Austin Price suddenly wondered if there was any way he could shock this sister-in-law of his.

Before any idea suggested itself to the Chief, she shocked him with the quiet question, "Is Tom Penney here?"

"Uh-huh. Would you like to speak to him?"

For a split second Austin Price thought he had found his answer, for the slightest shadow of alarm seemed to start in Sister Mary Laurentia's eyes. But she quietly replied: "Love to!"

"Tom!" called the Chief and strode toward a central cell. From the far end a tall blonde sauntered forward. As soon as his eyes saw the religious habits they fell and his head lowered. The Chief thrust his hand through the bars and shook the prisoner's hand. "This is my sister-in-law, Tom, Sister Mary Laurentia. And this is her companion, Sister Robert Ann." Penney flashed a look at each nun and bowed his head in greeting. "They are from St. Joseph's Hospital."

"I know," came the quiet reply. "I have seen the Sisters from St. Joseph's before. I have worked there."

"So?" said Sister Robert Ann, stepping nearer the bars. "Well, I want you to know the Sisters at St. Joseph's are praying for you, Mr. Penney."

"Thank you," was the somewhat embarrassed response.

"Do you know the 'Our Father,' Tom?" asked Sister Mary Laurentia.

"I'm afraid I've forgotten it, Sister."

"Well then, just say often: 'My Jesus, mercy!' "

"Yes, Mr. Penney," put in Sister Robert Ann, "no sin is too great for Him to forgive, you know. And He loves you!"

Austin Price was studying the prisoner as the Sisters talked. Never had he seen Tom Penney so intent on anyone's words. It was a concentration totally different from the alertness which characterized him while on his guard under questioning. Now he appeared anxious to catch the full import of the little speeches.

"Thank you, Sisters. And I'm very grateful to you for coming. And to you, Mr. Price, for having brought them."

"I have a young man here, Tom, who wants to see you. This is Jackie Regan from Seattle. And this is his mother."

"Hello," said Jackie, and held out his hand.

"Hello, yourself," said Penney taking the hand.

A trace of a smile lighted his scarred face. Then the party moved on.

Tom Penney turned back to his bunk. Squatting on the edge of it he put his head in his hands. "My Jesus, mercy!" he mumbled, then frowned. "I wonder how the 'Our Father' goes anyhow."

Before any answer came, Tom Penney was smiling twistedly. Cynically he lit a cigarette and as he snapped the match into the far corner wondered what Bob Anderson and the rest of the boys would think of him going religious. He blew a scornful puff of smoke toward the ceiling and stretched full length on the bunk.

Staring at the juncture of the bars and the ceiling, he went over the events of the past few weeks. Soon he twisted in disgust and muttered: "What rotten breaks!" He was thinking of the last Saturday in September. He and Anderson had no intention of shooting when they entered the Club. Baxter had told them there was just one old lady there and that it would be like taking candy from a kid to gather in ten grand.

Ten grand! . . . He hadn't got a hundred dollars out of the whole stinking mess.

He sat on the edge of the bed and shook his head in anger telling himself he should have known better. Everyone knew Baxter was a hop-head. . . . Still his story had made sense; for a free-spending crowd frequented the Lexington Country Club, and with the Saturday Night Dance as an extra, it seemed plausible that there would be between five and ten thousand dollars in the place.

The prisoner arose and began to pace his cell. He was trying to dispel the memory of what had actually happened inside the Club that fatal night. Why had he ever taken that gun from Anderson? They had been in once utterly unarmed. The lights of a passing car had halted them. They had come out to see if the car had passed on. It was then they took the guns. But why had they done it? They had pulled the switch of the main control, cut the telephone wires, and were sure no man was around the place. Why had he ever taken that gun from Anderson?

"Hell!" he growled and tamped a fresh cigarette. "I don't suppose it'd make much difference now anyhow, since I was with Bob when he turned loose with his gat."

Over on the bunk again he stretched out, blowing clouds of smoke ceilingward and marveling at the courage and strength of Marion Miley. He could not recall ever having seen the girl in his life. But from what the papers said he was sure it was she who had come from her room and not only grappled him — a long six feet of bone and muscle — but actually knocked him down! It was then that his gun went off.

Penney was breathing hard as he reviewed this event, but now he drew in a long inhale and, while letting it out, said within himself: "Thank God they found one bullet in the floor!" Soon he was sitting up thinking: Why can't my lawyer make a case of that? Let him grant that I was there. That I went there to rob. That I was armed with the .38. That's all true. But there's the unquestionable evidence that I committed no murder: the bullet, the only bullet from my gun, the only .38 in the place, was found in the floor, not in either of the bodies!

With his elbows on his knees and his head in his hands he wondered how Bob Anderson felt about it all. The FBI bullet experts had proved the slugs in the bodies and Mrs. Miley's bed were all from Bob's .32. And still Anderson maintained his innocence, denying all connection with the crime.

"That guy's an iceberg — or crazy!" whispered Penney somewhat fiercely and flicked gray ash to the floor. "I involved him. Baxter involved him. The guns involve him. And now the slugs.

Yet the guy goes on denying it all. Whew! How does he expect to get away with it? Of course he's got money and mouthpieces. But even so . . ."

Flinging himself back on the bunk he asked himself if he had really "ratted" on his pal. He gritted his teeth as he thought of how he had been taken. A traffic light . . . a lifeless signal would now most likely mean three lives! It was at Fort Worth, Texas. He had been driving all over the South for ten days, and nothing had happened. He had been to Florida, came back through Georgia and Alabama, had crossed Mississippi and Arkansas without the slightest trouble. Had even telegraphed Anderson for more money and received it within a few hours. But then, down deep in Texas, a traffic light turned against him — and that light might yet mean the electric chair.

With a chuckle that was like a growl he swung his long legs down on the floor and sat on the edge of his bunk with his huge hands spread wide on each side of him. Again he gave that hard, harsh chuckle. "That's what I get for obeying the law!" But suddenly he was sitting bolt upright. His gray-blue eyes narrowed and a glint, as cold as steel, leaped from them. Rat? he thought. Rat? Why it was Anderson who ratted on me! Reporting his car as stolen after giving it to me for a getaway. If it wasn't for that, those dicks in Fort Worth would never have given me a second glance. Wait until I see that guy again!

Then the three days and two nights of constant questioning at Fort Worth came back to him. The corner of his mouth lifted in a sneer as he thought of how they had badgered him, bullied him and all but beaten him in a fruitless effort to worm a confession out of him. Had he to deal only with such dicks he'd be a free man today — or at most a suspect auto thief. But Chief Price had come down from Kentucky.

Tom Penney rocked a bit on his bunk as he faced a real puzzle. He knew he should be hating Austin Price with all the hate of his being; and yet, far from hating him he found himself almost liking the fellow. He had been decent. He had talked to him like a human being; had treated him like a man. For four hours they had been together that Sunday, yet never once had the Chief raised his voice. Quietly, almost considerately, he had put question after question; and even more quietly noted down Tom's replies.

As he rocked back and forth now, Penney could hear the calm voice of Austin Price: "Tom, you're contradicting yourself." Even more clearly he could hear his own voice — a voice that was not near so calm; a voice that was harsh with a false bravado and resonant with a confidence that was assumed. It was a resonance that spoke to the trained ear of guilt. "Pu-fff! Do you think I'm going to confess to a double murder?"

With a start Tom Penney sat up. "There's where I made my mistake," he told himself. "If I had kept on answering instead of asking. . . . " But then he shrugged his shoulders and comforted himself with the thought that they would have pulled it out of him finally anyhow. No man could face the grilling Chief Price administered without tripping up somewhere.

He ground the stub of the cigarette under his foot as he concluded he had not "ratted," but had been trapped into an admission. But the fact that he had been captured at all was Anderson's fault. So if blame there be for the mess they were in, let that double-crosser take it! If he hadn't reported his car as stolen . . .

Tom Penney stood up and stretched. This kind of thinking would do no good, he told himself. It was crying over spilt milk. Let the cat lap such stuff up.

Late that evening, just as he was thinking of retiring, Penney heard his name called. Looking up he found Detectives Harrigan and Gravitt at the door of his cell.

"No more questions!" he growled. "I've told you bulls all I know. I've told you all I intend to tell you — "

"Not s' fast, Penney. 'S a friendly visit this time."

"Friendly!" Penney sneered. "Officer Harrigan speaking. How kind of you! Friendly! That's the way you bulls always begin."

"No, no, Tom," put in Gravitt. "You've got us wrong this time."

"Wrong? I've had you guys right from the time I was a kid."

"If you won't take our words, at least take your cigarettes."

The prisoner looked at the oblong package the detective held out to him, then flashed a suspicious eye at the two men.

"They're yours, Tom," Detective Gravitt assured him. "Joe and I saw them lying on the desk as we came by and thought we'd bring them up to you. What kind of a day did you have?"

Penney took the carton from Harrigan's hand, read the return address on the upper left-hand corner, smiled, and tossed the package on the bunk. Then he answered Gravitt. "Not bad at all. Ate well. Slept well. Saw the morning and evening papers. Even had some visitors. I'll call it the end of a perfect day if you two won't fire questions at me all night."

Joe Harrigan relit his cigar. "Questions ended. Chief gave orders to leave you alone. Seems to like you, Penney. Glad you had a good day. Hope you have a nice night. See you later."

Tom smiled as the two men swung down the cell block. He took the carton and reread the return address. He fished a pencil from his pocket, reached for a piece of paper, and sat down to acknowledge the gift to his cousins. Five minutes later he sealed the envelope, placed it on the thin ledge between the bars, took another piece of paper, and wrote:

Lexington, Ky.
Oct. 22, 1941

Dear Chief:

You will never know just how much I appreciated your visit this afternoon. I never knew that an Officer of the Law could be so human before now.

Isn't it strange how one learns such things too late — and the price one has to pay for them! It is not of myself I think. My suffering is nothing compared to Mother's, my brothers and sisters, and all my friends.

What hurts so bad is to think what I could have been had I chosen the right road instead of the wrong. If I could only tell the world the story of my life, it would be sure to help someone.

Chief, honestly I have told you all I know and it is the truth. I told them the other night that I wanted you present; they said you were sick and wanted me to tell them. They were all very kind and considerate; and Mr. Price, if there is nothing that you can do for me, I at least know you are sincere on my behalf, and I want you to know that I hold no malice against anyone on earth and that I have the deepest respect for you and the Force. I also think Mr. Maupin, Harrigan, and Gravitt deserve a lot of credit in this case. They certainly stuck with it to the end without rest. I am not throwing bouquets for sympathy. I really mean this from my heart. I just want to say something to show my appreciation of their and your kindness. For all the hard things I have said and thought in regard to Officers of the Law, I am sorry. Very sorry. I see them differently now.

If you feel — Oh, I don't know how to express myself, but if you feel bad about having to crack this case, please don't. I know it is your duty.

Mr. Price, I would like very much to know the names of the Sisters who were with you today. God bless them. They are always the same: so kind and sympathetic. I always felt a sort of security to be in their presence.

Well, Chief, I won't take any more of your time. Try not to think too badly of me. And remember I honestly am sincere in all I've said. To you and yours best of health and good luck.

Respectfully,

Tom Penney

The prisoner read his letter over. For a moment he was tempted to tear it up. It sounded crawling. He did want to thank Price, but somehow these lines did not ring with the gratitude he wanted them to have. He had said some pretty nasty things about cops both at Fort Worth and here in Lexington. But now he felt differently toward them. Price was O.K. So were Maupin, Harrigan, and Gravitt. He owed each an apology and he owed the Chief some real thanks. But this letter sounded . . . Then his eyes fell on the paragraph about the nuns.

Were those few sentences the real reason for this long letter? What was it they had said? . . . "They were praying for him." For what could they be praying? He had been caught. He had confessed. His days of crime were over. If he didn't get the chair he'd surely get life. So for what could they be praying? For what?

The question finally had him folding his letter and addressing it to the Chief. If nothing else came from it he might get the names of those nuns and write to them to find out what they were praying for.

"Surely not for my life," said Penney as he prepared for bed. "And I know they wouldn't be praying for my death." But a few moments later, as he pulled the blankets up under his chin he admitted that they might be praying just for that. He hadn't lived right. The Sisters at St. Joseph's Hospital might very well be praying that he die right.

The thought disturbed him. Did he know anything about dying? He remembered well the impulse that seized him when the cops had recognized him at Fort Worth by means of his long facial scar. He was tempted to force them to pull their guns and kill him there at the wheel. He could not now tell himself just why he had denied that impulse. It would have saved him so much trouble. The questionings. The publicity. The long ride back and the shameful return to his home city. Then the weeks that lay ahead with the trial . . . Why hadn't he done it? Was it because of the others in the car at the time: Leo Gaddis and that woman they had picked up? Stupid how chivalrous he was toward all women no matter how little worthy of chivalry they might be. As he turned on his side he told himself that was the very reason he had not forced the cops to open fire — a skinny, hard-faced prostitute.

But then his eye caught a solitary star in the heavens and he wondered if there was not something more to it than his own false chivalry. Suddenly he realized that every letter he had written from Fayette County Jail had had a "God bless you" in it. Even this latest to Price had a "God bless them" in it for the nuns. Yet at Fort Worth he had laughed into the teeth of one of his questioners who had asked: "Doesn't God mean anything to you?" "God?" he had laughed. "To me that is only a three-

letter word. And for all practical purposes those three letters
might just as well be x-y-z!"

Then why was he writing of God to his mother, his cousins,
and even to the Chief?

The stars slowly marched across the sky above Lexington that
night, silvering even some of the bars in the Fayette County Jail.
They were majestically calm and peaceful. But Tom Penney slept
a light and troubled sleep beneath them, never dreaming that He
who had set those stars in their courses had been gathering instruments to bring him back to the orbit traced out for man. At Fort
Worth the questioner with his question about God had been one
small instrument. The curiosity of Jackie Regan about jails had
been another. But it was only as Penney fell asleep that God
had gathered His four main instruments: two nuns up at St.
Joseph's Hospital, and down at the Price home two men who were
discussing the man they knew would be convicted as a murderer.

"I know he's going to die for this crime. I want you to go to see
him," said Price doggedly.

"Okay, Chief. I'll go. You pray that I say the right thing when
I do." And Father George Donnelly smiled as he saw relief in
Price's eyes.

The object of all this heavenly and earthly concern stirred in
his sleep as he dreamed of his mother. . . .

CHAPTER THREE

"Most Likely I'll Burn"

MRS. PENNEY waited until the postman had gone down the front steps before she moved from behind the protecting overdrapes. It was not like her to hide, or let the postman pass without a greeting, but she did not feel up to meeting anyone just yet. Perhaps tomorrow or the next day . . . She opened the door hastily and grabbed the little pile of letters. Quickly she closed the door and stood breathing heavily in the hall. But there was something more than the fear of neighbors that set her heart pounding now. There on the very top of the pile was the bold, graceful sweep of a handwriting she loved to see and a handwriting she now dreaded to read. Staring at the clear calligraphy of her own name she suddenly found the characters shimmering and herself sobbing.

The bills, advertisements, and boarders' mail she placed upon the table in the hall. The one that had set her sobbing was taken to the kitchen. She felt more at home in the kitchen. Quickly she drew her rocker to the window, wiped her eyes and polished her glasses, then opened the envelope — which was postmarked Lexington, November 9, 1941.

My darling Mother:
    Hope this finds you much better. I am O.K. Just finished supper: fried chicken, cranberry sauce, tomatoes, celery, and devil's food cake. I still have fruit and candy to go. So you see I am not suffering from lack of food. Of course that came from outside; but the jail food is good, and plenty of it.

. . . Father Donnelly was here this afternoon. Said he came to see you Wednesday and was coming again. How do you like him?

How did she like this tall man with the very white skin and the silky white hair; hair that was so thin he seemed bald? How did she like this man whose kindly blue eyes were filled with so much genuine sympathy and real understanding? Yes, he had come on Wednesday. She had not known how to greet him, but he had been so gentle and had talked so friendly about Tom that she had loved him immediately. Yes, she could tell Tom that she loved this priest who was being so good to him — and to her.

The white head bent over the letter again: So the boy was thinking of becoming a Catholic! She frowned ". . . after all, it is God we are interested in, isn't it . . . regardless of how I've lived I assure you I'll die right. . . ."

Mrs. Penney looked up to the ceiling. Why was the boy writing so definitely of death? Had he given up all hope? Would not the lawyers prove that he did no murder? She rose, went into her bedroom, and from their place of security took a card and two letters, then returned to her kitchen with its better light and its rocker. The letters were unfolded when she arrived. There it was in the very first letter he had written from jail almost three weeks before. She knew its every syllable by heart, yet she must read it again:

Dear Mother:

I don't know what to write to inspire you. I know you are heart-broken. However, Mother, don't worry; it is not as bad as it seems.

Don't believe everything that is printed in the papers. As usual, you know, they try to convict a person before trial. I can tell you one thing that will make you feel better: I am *not* guilty of murder! I have definite proof of that. . . .

Leona Penney's eyes went to the window, but they saw not the bleakness of November. They saw nothing; for the mother was feeling again the surge of relief that had risen from the very depth of her being the night her son, Charles, had told her the one bullet from Tom's gun had been found in such a position that

it was evident he had killed neither of the Miley women. . . .
Then why was he thinking so much of death?

She turned the first letter's second page and read again those
earliest hints of death. "Please don't let it worry you, Mother,"
he had written, "for I am ready for whatever comes."

She picked up the picture post card which rested atop the
second letter. She glanced at its highly colored face and read the
legend: "Rock Garden in Cypress Gardens in Sunny Florida."
Then at its few words: "Mother, Will write later. Am O.K. No
address as yet. Lots of love. . . ."

How much more those words told her now than when she had
first read them. The card had arrived October 9. It held the first
word she had had from Tom since the Saturday morning of
September 27, when he told her he was going to Louisville to
look for work. He had gone to Louisville. But that night he was
back in Lexington with Baxter and Bob Anderson. That night
they had robbed the Country Club. . . .

She read the card again and remembered now how disappointed
and puzzled she had been when she first looked on the Florida
scene and thought her boy that far south. She now stared as her
eyes fell on the postmark for the first time and she read "Delhi,
Louisiana." He had been on the run, then; was dodging police;
worried sick no doubt by newspaper accounts. Yet he had thought
of her! Had managed to allay suspicions and banish fears. He
had reason to close with: "Lots of love." The mother looked at
the card and knew that no volume could tell the complete story
held in this little two-cent post card. But how soon the comfort
it brought had vanished. That very evening the papers had told
of Tom's capture at Fort Worth.

Quickly she unfolded the second letter that lay on her lap. It
was dated October 24.

Father Donnelly came to see me Friday night. Sent me some
books. Everyone has been so nice. Lorraine and Edith sent me a
carton of cigarettes. Jean sent me four packs. Everyone wants to
know if there is anything they can do for me. But no one can do
what I want done: stop you from worrying!

As she wept quietly, she forgot what he had said about becoming a Catholic in the remembrance of his filial love.

But there was one who could not forget, and he was on his way to Lexington from Covington that very moment. Father George Donnelly was driving rapidly and thinking faster than he was driving. He was living over again the events of the day he had first met Tom Penney — Friday, October 23. He had offered Mass at St. Joseph's Hospital on that morning; listened to Sister Mary Laurentia's account of her meeting with Tom as she led him to Mrs. Price's room. Sister's reaction to the man had impressed him. They had hardly greeted Mrs. Price when her phone rang. It was the Chief who wanted to tell of the letter he had just received from the prisoner.

"I never saw Austin like this before," his wife had said. "He has Tom Penney on the brain. He couldn't worry any more if the man were his own son. I don't understand it."

Neither did the priest. He had visited the Chief the night before and found him glum. It was only by solemnly promising to visit the prisoner that Father George had been able to bring anything like peace to Price's mind and a semblance of cheer to his countenance.

That afternoon, despite the elation evident in the call of the morning, the priest found the Chief more disturbed than ever. For he had sent two of the local pastors to visit Penney and nothing had come of the interviews.

"Then why should I trouble the poor fellow?" Father George had asked. "If these two good Fathers could do nothing with him, what chance have I? I have nothing more to offer."

The Chief had thumped his desk and said, "If you are my friend, go. You're different from those two. Maybe he'll open up to you." Father George went. But after forty-five minutes with Tom Penney he was quite convinced that the man would never open up to anyone. Not once had the cold, gray-blue eyes been off him. There was suspicion in their steady stare, and Father George thought he detected antagonism also. But he did not know just what Tom Penney was thinking.

When summoned, the prisoner had cursed under his breath, thinking it was some curiosity seeker; but as he ambled along the corridor he felt a vague hope arise; it might possibly be some friend. When he saw it was a priest, he knew a little anger. This was the third sky pilot today. He hadn't cared for either of the others. They did not have what he wanted. This one would hardly be different. But from the first quiet word and the warm handshake Tom Penney knew he was different. This man was genuinely friendly. No veneer. Just man to man.

Penney had repeated his name: "Donnelly, eh?" and said: "Good of Price," when the priest told him the Chief had sent him. When invited to sit, the prisoner had refused. "Been sitting all day." After that he had said little more than "Yah." "Uh-huh" and "Is that a fact?" as the priest talked on everything that could interest a man except the one thing Tom Penney expected from him. He brought up the late World Series between the Dodgers and the Yanks. At any other time and in any other place, Tom Penney would have made a lively conversation out of what was now little more than a monologue, especially when the priest expressed sympathy with the Dodgers for losing a game which they already had won when the catcher dropped the third strike on the third out in the ninth inning.

"Tough, all right," was all that Penney offered now. So the priest had to go on to the War. Tom wondered whether this Father Donnelly was a diplomat, an expert psychologist, a clever salesman, or something of that sort as he spoke of the Nazi drive on Moscow and predicted their repulse by Russia's winter rather than by Russia's army, then recounted Napoleon's defeat on the same terrain by the same unconquerable force.

"Such little things can cause such great disasters," said the priest. "Think of it: just tiny snowflakes falling from a Russian sky defeated the greatest military strategist history has ever known." Then as if mesmerized by the paradox, the priest went on to tell how tiny raindrops were the ultimate cause of a catastrophe Tom had heard about when a very small boy — the sinking of the *Titanic*. As the priest went on with other examples of little things causing great disaster, Tom was expecting him to end with: "And a tiny traffic light was your great undoing," or "The tiny pressure of a finger on a trigger can bring terrible trouble." But to his surprise and relief the priest had said: "But tiny things can cause great triumphs, too, Tom. St. Peter was converted by a look; St. Augustine, by the voice of a little girl. The Battle of Marengo turned on a drummer boy's not knowing how to beat 'Retreat.' You remember the story of the English King who watched a spider 'Try, try again,' don't you?"

"Uh-huh," was the only comment Penney supplied.

It was not very heartening, but Father George was determined to keep his promise to Price and do his utmost. He talked of the little thing that had turned the tide in the Duke-Colgate football game a few days previously; of the Kentucky Wildcats 21–6 victory over Xavier; discussed teams in the Southern Conference; and ended by saying that Center's Praying Colonels needed another Bo McMillin. Tom agreed, but that was all he offered to the attempted conversation. So Father George came closer home.

"Are they feeding you well, Tom?"

"O.K."

"Have you plenty of cigarettes?"

"Uh-huh."

"Do the guards allow you papers?"

"Oh, yeah."

Father George arose. His watch told him he had been three quarters of an hour with this man. His head told him he had accomplished nothing. His heart told him he must break through this cold steel of reserve behind which the man hid himself, if he were ever to do Tom Penney any good; but how to do that he did not know.

"Well, Tom, I'd love to be able to help you. Is there anything I can do? Anything that I can send in?"

"Naw. Nothing."

"I've got to be going, Tom. Just remember I'll always be praying for you, and if there is anything . . ." The priest held out his hand. Tom Penney did not take it. He was still staring at the priest with eyes that bored like blue flame. The priest did not know exactly what to do or what to expect. What happened was the last thing he could have expected after the experience of the past forty-five minutes.

"Will you sit down a few more minutes, Father?"

The priest sat.

"I'm in a tight spot. I want to talk to you about religion. Most likely I'll burn for these murders. I haven't lived right. I want to die right. I want to die a Catholic." Tom Penney sat on the edge of a chair and bent toward a priest whose heart was doing very odd things. "I don't know much about your religion. I ran around with a gang of kids who were Catholics when I was young. I used to sit in the back of the church while they went to Confession on Saturday afternoon. When I was at Frankfort we had to attend Chapel. I chose the Catholic service. But I didn't know what it was all about."

The prisoner paused. The priest found his eyes not exactly friendly but the piercing gleam had left them. He bent forward and smiled. "O.K., Tom. I think I can fix it so that you can receive instructions."

"What do you mean — with Chief Price?"

"I wasn't thinking of him, Tom. I don't imagine there'll be any difficulty there. I was thinking of one of the local priests. Father Sullivan, perhaps. . . ."

"Oh," said Penney and arose. There was both finality and disappointment in his tone. "If you can't do it, forget it."

"But, Tom, I'm stationed in Covington. That's eighty miles away."

"Oh, I didn't know. That's O.K. We'll forget it."

"Oh, no, Tom, I'll get Father Sullivan or . . ."

"If you can't do it, Father, I don't want anyone to do it."

Father George put out his hand. Penney took it. "If that's the way you feel, Tom, I'll do it. I'll fix it with the pastor here and my own boss. I'll be happy to do it." The priest felt the crushing grip of the prisoner's hand and tried to return the pressure as well as he could. "I was talking with Sisters Mary Laurentia and Robert Ann this morning. They told me about their visit. They are praying for you, Tom."

"I wonder, Father," said the prisoner slowly, "I wonder if they could ever come back."

"Oh I think so, Tom. I'll speak to them. . . ."

"Will you? What did you say their names were?"

"Sister Mary Laurentia is the older nun. Sister Robert Ann the other one."

"Mary Laurentia and Robert Ann," repeated the prisoner.

"Well, Tom, I'll be running along now. I may send you a book or two as soon as I get home. You can look for me early next week."

They parted. The priest's heart was singing: "How strange, O God, are Thy ways!" Penney went back to his cell feeling happier than he had felt since September 27.

The very next day a Special Delivery package arrived at the Jail. Tom opened it with mounting curiosity. There was no return address, but as soon as he glimpsed the title he knew the source of the present. *"Father Smith Instructs Jackson"* was on the outside, while the fly-leaf held the message: "You be Jackson; I'll be Father Smith. Best of luck and God's special blessings, Father George."

While now taking a turn on the road, Father Donnelly recalled rapidly the five visits he had managed to East Short Street those first two weeks and admitted he had received almost as many revelations as he had given to Tom Penney. On the very first visit Father George saw that he would not instruct Tom Penney half as much as Tom Penney would instruct himself. The prisoner had read the first part of *Father Smith Instructs Jackson* not only with a mind that was open, but with one that closed, as Chesterton says every open mind should close: "like an open mouth, over something solid and substantial." Tom had many questions to ask, but they were questions that showed he had read and reflected, had assimilated much and was now looking for amplification rather than elucidation.

"It all fits so perfectly," he had said the day they talked of Creation, of the purpose God had in mind when He made man — when He made Tom Penney. When the matter of the Natural Law came up, the prisoner said: "Anyone who denies the voice of conscience has not ears like mine, Father. I always knew when I did wrong. I believe everybody does. But, you see, we defend ourselves; we excuse ourselves. We blame Society." Then with a frown he added: "And we have some truth in our claim. A man with a record is outside the pale. Look at me. Just before this final trouble I tried to get a taxi license. I was denied it because the Police had my finger prints. If I had gotten that license, you would not be sitting here today." Then with a quick laugh he had concluded: "Maybe that wouldn't have been so good for me at that, Father. Now I think I have a chance to save my soul. I believe, Father George. I believe. This Catholic explanation is so simple, yet so all inclusive. It satisfies. It leaves out nothing; not even my tendency to sin. . . ."

As Father George now threaded through Lexington traffic he was asking himself the question he had asked after every contact with Tom Penney: What had this man done to win such graces — or who was winning them for him? It might possibly be his mother's prayers. He would have attributed them to the nuns, but he considered the nuns and their apostolic interest in the man as one of his greatest graces.

He smiled now as he thought of Sister Robert Ann's discussion of her first visit. "Oh, Father," she had said, "when I heard the click of the key that first day, my heart jumped — a nun alone with a murderer!"

"Alone? Wasn't Sister Mary Laurentia with you?"

"Yes, but there were only three chairs. She took the one nearest the door, and Tom sat facing me. So it was almost the same as if he and I were alone in the cell."

"Cell?"

"Oh, I know they call it the Visitors' Room, but it has an iron grating on the door and they lock you in, so it's a cell to me. But as soon as Tom starts talking I forget where we are. He has the heart of a child, Father."

As he stopped for a traffic light Father George thought in irritation of the man who a few days ago had more than hinted he would be using much better judgment if he stayed away from Fayette County Jail and the Miley murderers. The priest frowned now as he had then. Why would people so misunderstand? he wondered. Why would they forget that Christ had come for sinners? When would they remember that:

> He ate with them, drank with them;
> And died with two as company on a Hill?

The more he thought of it, the more his puzzlement and indignation grew. When would these self-complacent ones realize the truth Abraham Lincoln expressed when a better-than-thou Congressman looked his condemnation at a staggering inebriate. "There, but for the grace of God, goes Abraham Lincoln," the President had said. But Father George felt sure that the Congressman missed the wisdom in the remark, just as so many millions have missed the wisdom and truth in St. Augustine's query: "If these men and women can reach such heights of sanctity, why not I?" When would these moderns . . . But then Father George caught himself. He was really growing hot under the collar, and a man who wears a Roman collar must never do that. He shook his head though as he remembered the man who had told him he might be jeopardizing the fair name of the Catholic Church by his visits to Tom Penney.

"Gosh!" exclaimed the priest as he swung his car into the hospital drive. "I wish these people would read *The Hound of Heaven* and realize that God will follow us 'down the nights and down the days,' until He catches up with us — even if it takes Him to a prison cell."

He smiled as he locked his car and quietly reminded himself that people who talk to themselves this way end up in hospitals different from St. Joseph's. The grapevine had gone to work before he had climbed out of his car, so it was not to be wondered at that Sisters Mary Laurentia and Robert Ann were in his room almost before he hung up his coat.

"Why is Tom so sure he'll die, Father?" came the somewhat petulant query from Sister Robert Ann.

"Tell her, Father. She won't face facts."

"But what do his lawyers say?"

Father George shook his head. "I haven't spoken with them, Sister; but from what Tom tells me, they do not seem very hopeful."

"But — the only bullet from Tom's gun was found in the floor."

"I know it, Sister. He is very happy that he is not a murderer; and doubly happy to be able to tell his mother so. By the way, have you two visited her yet?"

"Oh, indeed!" said Sister Mary Laurentia. "For her sake I wish those lawyers could do something. . . ."

"Sentiment is too high, Sister," said the priest sadly. "The papers have played this thing up in such a way that I don't see how it will be possible to get an unprejudiced jury. . . . Of course it was a brutal thing. We can't deny that. . . . I'm afraid Tom has very little chance. . . ."

"I wonder if there isn't something we could do."

"I'm thinking, Sisters," said Father George carefully, "but I'm not worrying. God's hand has been so palpable in this entire affair that I am positive everything is going to work out for the best. Just look how each of us came into the case: I had no right to come back from Gethsemani through Lexington. You, Sister Mary Laurentia, in a way, had no right to be in St. Joseph's Hospital the time your sister was ill. You were a school teacher originally. You, Sister Robert Ann, are an Instructor of Nurses, not a nursing nun. Yet you two were in Mrs. Price's room when Austin arrived. Then think of God bringing Jackie Regan all the way from Seattle. . . . All these are parts of the puzzle. Each fits in to complete the picture. We have been like pawns on God's chessboard, or even like puppets who move to the jerk of the string in His hand. It's marvelous. That's why I don't worry even though I do think carefully. Why even the questions Tom asks and the answers that pop into my head seem to me to be heaven sent. That man is farther along after half a dozen instructions than most people are after half a year. It is that fact which makes me believe his time on earth is short."

"But look, Father," put in Sister Mary Laurentia slowly. "Tom has turned State's Evidence. Isn't there a possibility that he may get life instead of the chair?"

Father George's eyes narrowed. "Have you ever mentioned that to that brother-in-law of yours?" The nun shook her head. "Austin is the one man who could answer, Sister. I must confess I had thought of it. In fact, I mentioned it to Tom and tried to get him to use it in order to cheer up his mother. His answer was: 'I'm not going to kid myself, Father. Neither will I kid my mother. If we expect the worst and get something better, our joy will be all the greater. The Chief told me down in Texas that he could offer nothing. Maupin, Harrigan, and the other one — Gravitt — said the same thing here. So I don't expect anything from the State. But I'm going to go through one hundred per cent.' "

"Why?" broke in Sister Mary Laurentia.

"The very question I asked him, Sister. Can you guess the answer?"

"I can," Sister Robert Ann said happily. "He knows now what it means to please God."

"Close enough, Sister. He said he was never going to offend God again; that he had enough on his conscience already without adding so much as a little white lie."

"Isn't it wonderful to watch a man's soul grow!"

"And humiliating, Sister. Tom Penney is still only a catechumen. He is not a Catholic as yet. But how many Catholics, how many priests, how many religious are striving for perfection as he is?"

Sister Mary Laurentia laughed lightly. "Just like you to talk of 'striving for perfection.' But will you talk to the Chief about that State's Evidence angle?"

"I had planned to, Sister. But it's a delicate subject. This town is in an angry mood against Anderson, Baxter, and Penney; so angry that I feel sure we shall see a perfect exemplification of *summum jus, summa injuria.*"

"What in the world does that mean?" asked Sister Robert Ann.

"It means, Sister, that the Law will be applied in all its rigor. Baxter, you know, wasn't even in the Club. Tom's gun went off, but his bullet killed nobody. Yet all three men will probably die: one for the actual murders, the other two as accomplices. It's the Law. . . ."

"But doesn't State's Evidence always get a reward?"

"Usually, Sister. But, as I said, feeling is too high. Tom knows that. He keeps saying: 'Most likely I'll burn.' "

"Well, I'm going to pray that he won't," came the determined and somewhat defiant reply from Sister Robert Ann.

"We'll be with you, Sister," said Father George softly.

"In the meantime you speak to the Chief."

"I shall, Sister. But you know my immediate concern is bringing Tom Penney to birth by Baptism rather than to death by the chair or to life imprisonment. But, tell me, isn't it time for the trays?"

The two nuns laughed. "Don't worry about trays. Your place is all set in the priests' dining room. You were spotted before you got out of your car."

"You nuns ought to teach the detectives your technique. Nothing escapes your eyes."

CHAPTER FOUR

Sentenced to Birth

DINNER over and a few calls on the sick made, Father Donnelly hurried to his car, turned it down the drive and headed for Fayette County Jail. Signs of preparation for Armistice Day along the main streets set the priest thinking that it was something of a crime to celebrate such a day when most of the world was at war. But soon he shrugged his shoulders and summoned some of that buoyancy which keeps mankind facing life even though death be crowding in from all sides. He was himself by the time he locked his car; he turned and trotted up the dozen stone steps of the old building.

The Jailor was in his office and greeted the priest warmly. "I suppose it's Penney you want, eh, Father? Well, step into the Visitors' Room. I'll have him down in a minute."

"Sorry to be such a bother, Mr. Veal. Of course I could talk to Tom up in his cell, but — "

"No bother at all, Father. You're instructing Tom, aren't you? Well the Visitors' Room is the place to do it. Too many eyes, ears, and tongues up above. Baxter and Anderson are up there now you know."

"So I've heard. Tom promised to introduce me some day."

Soon the prisoner appeared, accompanied by a guard. He nodded to the Jailor. "Thank you, Mr. Veal." Then, "Thank you, Roger," he said to the guard who locked them in. In a flash he turned to the priest, grasped his hand and said, "Father George!

I've got a hundred and one questions to ask you. I know all the prayers you gave me: the Our Father, the Hail Mary, the Apostles' Creed. I know all the Acts of Faith, Hope, Love, and Contrition. And I've made up my own Act of Thanksgiving. I say them a hundred times a day. But let's get down to the other business, huh?"

"You're in a rush today, Tom. What's on your mind?"

"That next Article in the Creed, Father. The one you told me to study: 'From thence He shall come to judge the living and the dead' . . ."

"Well, what about it?"

"We're still talking about Jesus aren't we, when we say 'He'?"

"That's right."

"Then it's true that He'll be our Judge?"

"Uh-huh."

"Now see if I've got this straight. The God who is going to judge me is the same Jesus Christ who pardoned Dismas, the Good Thief, and promised him Paradise the very same day?"

"That's your Judge, Tom — and every man's."

Penney got up from his chair, and as he paced the room, he murmured, "It seems too good to be true!"

"What do you mean, Tom?" asked the priest quietly and kindly.

Tom turned, threw out both hands in a gesture of triumph and exclaimed, "Why, Father, it's a cinch! Jesus Christ, the One you told me brought the kid back to life and gave him to his widowed mother; the Jesus who wouldn't allow the Jews to stone the woman taken in adultery; the Jesus who took care of that street walker — what's her name? . . ."

"Mary Magdalen?"

"That's the one. The Jesus who protected and defended her against that gang at the banquet, remember?"

"Uh-huh."

"He's going to be my Judge? Why, Father, I'm ready to die now. Look. I'm going to trial soon. I'll stand before a man who doesn't know me from a hole in the wall. There'll be lawyers there.

Smart guys. They'll trip me up with clever questions; then turn and twist my answers until black seems white and white seems black. There'll be 'twelve good men and true' there, huh? And those twelve mugs, who don't know me from Adam, will listen to a lot of tripe some mouthpiece will spout and to the oratory of a Prosecuting Attorney who has his eye on a political position and his finger on the pulse of the mob; these mugs, I say, will pass judgment on me. They'll send me to the Chair, Father. They'll take my life. For what? For a crime I did not commit."

"But, Tom . . ."

"Oh, I know. I know. The Law says I'm guilty morally. I've talked it over with my lawyers. I know how the charge will read and how the trial will go. I even know the verdict and the sentence. But, Father, don't you see why I'm happy to have Jesus Christ as my *final* Judge? He knows everything! You told me He is God. I believe you. I believe Him. And I'm happy to know He'll be my Judge."

Father Donnelly's lips parted in a slow smile, but his heart was pounding. He seemed to feel God's grace pulsing in this room with its two solitary chairs and its iron-grated door. For the hundredth time since he had met Tom Penney he said within himself: "O God, how wonderful are Thy ways!" But to the bright-eyed prisoner whose enthusiasm and joy had transformed his hard, raw-boned face into something of beauty, he said: "You've got it, Tom. You've got the truth from the right angle. But I wonder if you've seen it from every angle. The Jesus who is to judge you, does know all. Our every thought, word, and deed from the moment we began to be, from the day we began to think and do, from the hour we first went off the beam down to the latest sin. . . ."

"You'd make a good lawyer, Father George. Yes, I've thought of all that. But it is that very angle that gives me confidence. See, Father, it's just as if Jesus was looking into my mind the night we were at the Country Club. He knows how much and how little — He knows absolutely *no* murder was in that mind. . . ."

"But, Tom, weren't there days when you had close to murder in your heart? And, after all, you did intend to rob the Club, and you actually carried out that intention — "

"Sure I did. . . . Listen, Father: don't get me wrong, and don't let me get you wrong. Didn't you tell me this Dismas guy, this thief who died next to Christ, was a pretty bad egg?"

"From all we know, Tom, he must have been. The Romans were putting him to death; and on the cross he admitted the sentence was just."

"Then he was really guilty of a capital crime?"

"I take it so."

"Then don't you see why I feel so free? What did Jesus say to *him?*"

"What do you mean?"

" 'This day thou shalt be with Me in Paradise.' Ah, Father, if all you've told me about Jesus is true; if all I've read is fact, I'm sold! I may be dumb, but I'm not so dumb as not to see that God is merciful. That was the first prayer the Sisters taught me: 'My Jesus, mercy!' Isn't that something like what this Dismas said to Christ on the Cross?"

"Yes, it is! But, Tom, most people fear the Judgment."

"Then they don't know God — or else I'm crazy. See if I have it straight, Father. God became a Baby for me, huh? That's what we mean by 'born of the Virgin Mary'?"

"Exactly."

"It's God though — the Baby in the cave, in the Crib at Bethlehem . . . it's God. He grows. He does wonderful things. Cures the deaf, the blind, the lame; cleanses lepers, the poor guy at the pool, you know. . . ."

"Uh-huh."

"And that old man they let down through the roof. He raised the dead: the little kid of the widowed mother; the twelve-year-old daughter of the ruler, and Lazarus. . . . What a job that was! This same Man took care of those women I spoke about. You know: the one taken in adultery and that street walker. He died on a Cross after promising Dismas, a bum like me, Paradise; and

after praying for the very brutes who murdered Him. He's to
be my Judge, eh? And you tell me people fear Him. . . ."

"Plenty."

"Something's wrong somewhere, Father. Either I've missed
something or people are a lot worse than I think they are. Why
do they fear?"

The priest hesitated to throw cold water on this heated enthusiasm, yet he wanted his pupil to know the full truth and see
the entire picture. So he reminded him of hell. He told him that
this same Christ, from whose hands and lips mercy had dripped,
was also the One who had hurled thunderbolts of "Woes!"
against Scribes and Pharisees; the Jesus who wept over Jerusalem
was the same God who allowed it to be destroyed; the Jesus who
prayed for the Jews as He hung on the Cross was the same God
who permitted the overthrow of that nation and set them wander-
ing over the face of the globe. He was a merciful Jesus, but He
was also a just God.

A deep frown cut into the forehead of the prisoner as he
followed every word of the priest with burning intentness. Father
George spoke at length on God's justice, and ended his exposition
with: "There is a hell, Tom. And some souls go there. For God
must be just if He will be God."

The prisoner's frown did not lift, nor did the light of puzzlement fade from his eyes, but his voice was quiet and held overtones of firm conviction as he said: "That doesn't scare me,
Father. It gives me hope. It actually gives me joy. It was just
this Justice that you talk about that gave me so much confidence.
I want to be tried by a Just Judge — by One who knows
everything."

"But, Tom, you know you've done some very wrong things. . . ."

"More than I can count, Father! More than I want to count.
But think of that Dismas guy. What did he do but plead for
mercy, and get it? I can do the same. So can everyone else with
any brains. And if all you and the Sisters have told me is true,
then God's very Justice will force Him to be merciful. If I throw
myself on the mercy of the Court here in Lexington, what will I

get? The Chair. But with God . . . Ah, no, Father; you can't fool me. Maybe it's heresy, as you say, or blasphemy, but I still feel that His justice will make Him merciful. How about it?"

Father Donnelly's mind was groping in his memory. Where, had he heard or read something just like that before? Was it from Fulton Sheen? No. It was further back and more authoritative. St. Augustine maybe. Sounded like him. Was it in the Breviary? Somewhere someone had said something just like this prisoner had said: "God's justice will make Him merciful." He looked closely at Tom Penney.

"Tom," he said slowly and tapped the prisoner's knee, "I won't call it either heresy or blasphemy. I'll call it the truest statement of truth I've ever heard. Where did you get it?"

"It stands to reason, Father. Or maybe it was something I picked up from the Sisters. In their short visits they teach me much more than they ever realize. Sister Robert Ann told me of the Prodigal Son. He made a comeback. Or rather, he had guts enough to walk back; and his father was all father, wasn't he? He forgave the little tramp everything. Wined him. Dined him. Turned on the music. Sister told me God is just like that. He is our Father. Isn't that the way we begin the Lord's Prayer: 'Our Father . . . '? Sister Mary Laurentia told me of the Good Shepherd and the Good Samaritan. . . . I hope I'm not all wet. But this Article of the Creed, which you say scares people, is the one that has given me most joy."

Father George had come prepared to cover this one Article and expected a rather difficult time. He had conjured up a situation where he would have to stress the mercy of God without slighting His justice in order to reassure the prisoner. Now he found the tables turned, and was forced to stress the justice without slighting the mercy. He did so. But Tom surprised him again with the statement that God's justice would force Him to be merciful. The priest looked at his watch. It was nearing five o'clock. How speedily this hour and a half had flown! He sat back with his thumbs in his vest pockets.

"O.K., Tom. Study the next Article. I'll be here Thursday or Friday. Now how about introducing me to Bob and Baxter?"

Tom Penney's face changed. The light that had danced in his eyes as he talked of Christ and Judgment faded. Even his voice changed.

"Bob's not ready yet, Father. I'll bring him to you when he's set. Trust me."

Two weeks later when the last Article in the Creed had been covered, Tom said: "I'm sending Bob down this afternoon, Father. . . . Let me warn you — Bob's a cool customer. But I've been praying and the Sisters said they'd pray."

When the priest asked how much he had seen of Anderson, Tom replied: "Perhaps too much." Then Father George learned of all that had transpired upstairs since the three men had been housed under the one roof. There was a trace of bitterness in Penney's tone as he told of the lawyers Anderson had been able to hire. He and Baxter had to take what the court offered. But Bob had the services of W. Clarke Otte and S. Rush Nicholson of Louisville. From notes Anderson had sent him, it was evident to Tom what line of defense these attorneys were preparing to follow. He, Tom Penney, was the key to the whole situation, and plenty of pressure was being brought to bear, directly and indirectly, to have him turn in their direction.

He looked a bit worried as he said: "We'll be tried in about two weeks. And I'm to be the main witness."

"The papers say you'll have separate trials, Tom."

"That's right. And I'm sure Park, the Prosecuting Attorney, will use me against Bob, then against Baxter, finally against myself. It's not a pleasant spot to be in, Father. I hate rats as much as anyone. Both Anderson and Baxter will think I'm letting them down; that I'm squealing; that I'm a rat. But, don't worry, Father; the only one I'll really let down is myself."

The priest looked puzzled, so Tom quickly added: "I won't let God down; and that's all that matters, isn't it?"

"That's all, Tom."

"Well, pray, Father, that I'll have a clear head on that stand. I'm in for a beating from all the lawyers — both Bob's and the State's — so pray. I'll send Bob down now. One of the books you gave me says we write our own final sentence, and God merely pronounces what we have written. I'm afraid Bob's not writing the right way, Father; so do all you can. . . . O.K., Roger," he called to the guard outside the door, and the key was turned.

Five minutes later there entered a smooth-shaven, rather well-groomed, chunky man. He said suavely: "This must be Father George. I'm Bob Anderson. Tom's been telling me all you've done for him and thinks I can be helped, too."

A few questions showed the priest he was talking with a fairly intelligent man, though the suavity in the soft voice and the ingratiating smile and gestures spoke both of superficiality and artificiality. He would do all he could for this man's soul, but from the outset he saw that the headlong co-operation with God's grace, the full surrender of self to the truth, that had marked Penney's capitulation, were not in Bob Anderson. Father George tried the same technique: told Bob to pray and read the books he had given to Tom, but felt the careful reserve in the core of the man even as he outwardly acquiesced not only graciously but even with a show of gratitude and enthusiasm. It was already late when Bob came in, so Father George had to excuse himself but promised to be back before the end of the week. Then he wished Anderson all the luck in the world.

"Looks as if I'll need it," was Bob's only reference to his plight.

Two weeks later, on December 8, the trial of Bob Anderson began. The day was consumed in challenges, but as night fell a jury was impaneled, and at 7:45 p.m. Tom Penney mounted the witness stand. It was 10:20 when he came down — very tired, but conscious of an inner feeling of triumph. He had not let God down. He had kept his promise to Father George.

In a clear, clipped voice he had told the hatching of the plot to rob; then the execution of that plot with its unplanned, unexpected, unwanted denouement. W. Clarke Otte, the defense attorney, questioned him for an hour and a half, and though he used every trick and tactic known to the skillful lawyer, he had been unable to shake Tom in his testimony. Slyly he attacked Tom's character in order to destroy his value as a witness.

"Why did you change the story you had told at Fort Worth when you were returned to Lexington? Why did you implicate Baxter only when you got back here?"

On reading the question, Father George saw all that it implied, and feared for Tom's reply. But then his eyes fell on the answer his neophyte had given. "This crime's bad enough. No use having a lie on your soul, too." And the priest thrilled.

The next attack was on Tom's motive. Insinuation was not enough here, so Otte came out boldly with: "Have you any hope for a life sentence?" The entire force of Detectives believed that Penney had confessed with that in the back of his head. Most people in Lexington thought the same. But Chief Price had told the boy down in Fort Worth that he would promise him nothing. He marveled now at Penney's resignation and full acceptance of his situation as he answered. "No, I have no hope." The brevity and finality in the reply shocked the courtroom to closer attention. What surprised all was that there was no hopelessness in the voice. Price caught the paradox and knew its explanation. Silently he blessed God and Father George Donnelly.

But Otte took the attention of all as he introduced notes which Penney admitted to be his. One read: "Bob Anderson was not in Lexington, September 27." Another told how he, Tom Penney, had stolen Anderson's two-toned Buick sedan. If the judge, jury, and audience were surprised at the nature of the evidence, they were more surprised at Tom Penney's reaction. He was laughing. Not derisively. Not sarcastically. Just amusedly.

"That's my writing," he said. "Those are my notes. But . . . that is not my composition. They are but copies of the notes of instruction thrown to me by the defendant while we were in jail together."

For another hour Otte went on with questions whose purpose was not to clear his client, but to discredit this witness. It was not a pleasant hour and a half for Tom Penney.

Henry Miller took him for re-examination. Another hour went by under a barrage of questions whose answers would condemn not only Bob Anderson but the very man who was making them. Tom Penney knew it. He became monosyllabic. But he kept on telling the truth.

It was after midnight when the prisoners were returned to their cells. Tom was thinking of a line he had written to his mother just two weeks before: "Life is beautiful — even in jail." He didn't feel that way about it right now. Bob had spoken but one word as he was led past to his cell. But it held volumes. It held, Tom felt, the verdict of the entire world. The word was "Rat!"

Tired as he was, Penney could not sleep. The faces of Otte, Nicholson, Park, and Miller swam before him. Their questions and his own answers echoed and re-echoed. But it was the face of Bob Anderson that puzzled him most. Bob had sat through it all, chewing gum and smiling confidently. What could his lawyers have concocted? After the testimony of the night it would have to be something most unusual to impress the jury.

The restless night passed. The morning brought the paper and Tom was relieved to find that the sneak attack of the Japs on Pearl Harbor had all but crowded him and the trial off the front page. As soon as he had eaten and shaved, he took pencil and paper and wrote:

Dear Mother:

Just a line to let you know I am O.K. Hoping you are too.

Well, Mother, I guess you've seen the papers. That was the hardest thing I ever did. But there was no alternative. I had to tell the truth. And I am not sorry.

Just try to bear it, whatever the outcome. I won't be tried until next Monday. And, Mother, if you only knew how this thing has changed me, you would not worry half so much. I know you are going to worry. That is natural to any mother. And anything I say

seems so small. . . . I just can't express my regret, Mother. All I
can say is, if I do go, I'll go to a better world. So try to look at
it that way.

Charlie came by Saturday and brought me some cigarettes. I
know how hard it is for anyone to come here. Sisters Mary Laurentia
and Robert Ann, from the hospital, were here Saturday afternoon.
They certainly have been good. They want to go to see you again.
Guess they will, too. Tell everyone hello and keep your chin up.

He was not tried on Monday; for Anderson's case consumed
a week. On Tuesday the jury learned that only one bullet came
from the .38 — the gun Penney used — yet both victims had
been shot more than once.

Tom saw that they were pointing the case toward Bob, but
also saw that his lawyers could use all this matter to point the
case away from him. He hoped they were on the alert.

On Wednesday the guns were traced to Anderson with unim-
peachable evidence. Thursday the case was closed, and when
Park, the prosecutor, climaxed his case with Tom's testimony
and closed with: "Penney has been promised nothing; this crime
is so terrible that everybody connected with it should pay with
their lives." Tom knew what he could expect when he came to
be tried.

The jury was out almost twenty-four hours. One of their number was holding out for a life sentence instead of death in the
electric chair. But finally, at 9:30 p.m. on Friday the twelfth,
the verdict was given. Bob Anderson was found guilty of the
Miley murders, and his sentence was: "Death in the electric
chair."

On Monday, the State prosecuted Raymond Baxter. Again Tom
Penney was the star witness. He told how Baxter had hatched
the plot, saying there would be between three and ten thousand
dollars at the Club; promising to cut the wires, open the doors,
and see to it that no one was around but "one old lady." Delmer
Howard cross-examined Tom for an hour and a half, but accomplished no more than W. Clarke Otte had the previous week.
Penney was telling the truth and no one could shake him.

When Harry Miller took him for the prosecution, Tom furnished one of the few laughs of the trials. Among the routine opening questions the attorney asked was the one, "Where do you live?"

Tom smiled and asked: "Now?"

The courtroom rippled with appreciation.

Miller colored and corrected himself: "Ah — er — before you were confined."

The case carried over until Tuesday. When Park, summing up, admitted that Baxter was not guilty of murder physically, but was guilty of it morally, Tom knew what his own trial would be like. The jury was out only two hours. Its verdict was "guilty," and the sentence: "Death in the electric chair."

Tom's trial began the next day. The courtroom was crowded as never before in the entire case. Tom scanned the crowd anxiously; then breathed with relief. He had espied his sister and knew that the family was loyal; but he saw that his mother was not there. She had heeded his plea not to come. A jury was impaneled and soon Penney found himself again on the stand.

There was no need for long questioning. Tom had confessed at Fort Worth, again at Lexington when returned there, and lately in each of the two trials. Park asked why he had testified against Anderson and Baxter.

"To satisfy my own conscience more than anything else."

"When did your conscience first bother you?"

"When it happened at the Country Club."

That was too favorable a bit of testimony. Tom Penney was appearing at his best. So Park shifted his ground. It would never do to allow the jury to grow sympathetic or entertain favorable opinions of the defendant. Park would inform the jury indirectly of the sentence they were to pass, so he asked Penney: "Do you think the death penalty justified in the cases of Baxter and Anderson?"

But Tom was not to be caught so easily. "I don't believe in the death penalty," he replied. "I never have."

Once again Park felt himself checkmated, but he knew the

sentiment of the town and felt reasonably sure that the jury
shared it, so he quickly concluded his case and turned the
defendant back to his attorneys.

Martin summed up his case in exactly twenty-six minutes.
In the circumstances he did about the only thing possible. He
showed Tom's worth as a witness. For this purpose he had called
Chief Price and Guy Maupin to the stand. From their testimony
it was patent that Tom Penney had broken the case not only for
the police but for the State. Next, two jurors from each of the
preceding trials were summoned and made to tell the court how
Tom Penney's evidence had enabled each jury to reach a decision.
Even Harry Miller was put on the stand and made to admit that,
practically speaking, Tom Penney had prosecuted the entire case
from beginning to end for the State of Kentucky.

It was a good case — as good as possible in face of the open
confessions Tom had made. Martin insisted that the penalty for
robbery was not death; but the jury knew Tom Penney was not
being tried for mere robbery. His was not only the shortest of the
three trials, but his jury was quickest in arriving at a verdict.
It was out just fifty-one minutes. At 11:18 that morning it filed
back to the courtroom and Tom Penney's fate was sealed: "Death
in the electric chair." That afternoon was still young when he
was writing:

> I am sorry, Mother, that I have brought all this sorrow, heart-
> ache, and suffering to you. I guess you know how I feel about it.
> I'm glad you didn't come to the trial for your own sake. Just
> rest easy now, Mother, and please don't worry. . . .
> The lawyers did everything possible, but it just wasn't enough.
> But have no fears, Mother; I'll never die for a crime I did not
> commit!

As the mother read the letter, she wondered how much of it
the boy believed. She thrilled to his line about not dying for
a crime he had not committed. From all she had read and all she
had heard, she knew it was unquestionably true that while Tom
was a robber, he was not a murderer. So even if he did go to

death for the murders of Marion and Mrs. Miley, she could hold in her heart the truth that the child to whom she had given life had sent neither of these women to their death.

Three days later she received a letter that had the spirit of Christmas in it — a spirit of exultant life, peace, and joy. It was dated December 21, and read:

> Dear Mother:
>
> I am about to tell you something that should please you very much.
>
> Father Donnelly just baptized me! So I've got a clean slate, Mother. I feel so much better, and I know that from now on, life will be very different.

Mrs. Penney's gray head came up. Tears sparkled in her eyes. "Oh God," she prayed, "how good to have Tom talking of life when he has just been sentenced to death!"

A mile away, three people were talking about the same man and had used almost the identical words. Father George Donnelly had just said to Sisters Mary Laurentia and Robert Ann: "I waited purposely until he had been sentenced to death, so that I could reverse the judge's sentence and sentence him to birth — and a far different life."

"We saw him yesterday," exclaimed Sister Robert Ann, "and never have we seen a happier man! He told us how Father Sullivan had given him his First Holy Communion."

"And," added Sister Mary Laurentia more calmly, "he showed us the Scapular Medal Father Sullivan had given him. No soldier could be prouder of his decoration."

Sister Robert Ann clasped her hands. "Think of it, Father! He said to me: 'Sister, I have been condemned to death, but never was I so happy in my life. . . . Last night I slept for the first time in a month!'"

"I met his sister this morning," said Sister Mary Laurentia, "and in all seriousness, she told me she feared that Tom was losing his mind. When I asked her why, she said, because he laughs and jokes and appears as happy as a schoolboy."

"Sisters," said Father George in a judgelike tone. "I think Tom Penney *has* lost his mind. I'm sure he has! In fact we can say in all truth that Tom Penney died last Sunday afternoon — that is, Tom Penney, the criminal — and a new Tom Penney was born. I've converted other people, Sisters. That is, God used me as His instrument in other cases. I've baptized adults. But I've never come across anything like this Penney affair in all my life. Grace has been palpable. That Visitors' Room in Fayette County Jail will always be the antechamber to heaven to me after my hours there with Tom Penney."

Father George looked away for a moment, then resumed with: "Ever since I left the jail Sunday afternoon, I have been meditating — I think you can call it that — meditating on the words of St. Paul. He writes grippingly of death and life when he writes of baptism. That is why I can say I have already executed the sentence of the court. I have put Tom Penney, the man adjudged guilty of murder, to death. I have even buried him. But since both death and burial were 'in Christ Jesus,' Tom Penney has 'risen to a newness of life!' "

The priest paused, then continued slowly, "Never, never did I understand that passage so clearly: 'If we have died with Christ,' says St. Paul, 'we believe that we shall also live together with Christ.' There, Sisters, is our prayer from now on for Tom Penney — that he live 'to God *in Christ Jesus.*' "

CHAPTER FIVE

Solitary Confinement

CHRISTMAS brought mixed emotions to Mrs. Leona Penney. Christian that she was, the Birthday of Christ gave her a peace, joy, and hope no other day can give; but mother that she was, the day brought an indescribable ache to her heart because a child of her own had been sentenced to death. It was true that he wrote brave letters and that his lawyers had appealed his case. But a mother's intuition is sharper than the cleverest legal mind; so her head told her what her heart did not want to believe: Tom's days were numbered.

Shortly after the holyday and holiday she began making plans for a visit to her son; for a long letter enumerating the many gifts and visitors he had received, told her that public sentiment had shifted. Now that the trials were over and the sentences passed, people seemed to remember that the prisoners were human beings. Mrs. Penney was happy about the sympathy shown her son, but she divined what it connoted: Tom was sure to die. To his letter he had appended a postscript which served to lift her heavy heart:

Father Donnelly came to me when no one else was interested. He was concerned about my soul. He brought me books, took great care and interest in teaching me truth, so that now I believe all that the Catholic Church teaches. That is one reason why I was baptized into the Catholic Church. It is not so unlike your Church, Mother.

49

And we both know that if we live right, we can get to heaven. So don't ever worry about my hereafter, Mother. I'll never go wrong again.

As she laid the letter on her lap, Mrs. Penney knew the greatest gift her boy had received this holiday season was from God. It was Faith.

The New Year was hardly out of the womb when Mrs. Penney was climbing the dozen stone steps which lead to Fayette County Jail, to see her son for the first time since his trouble. Roger McGuirk, the guard, who had become Tom's godfather, led her to the Visitors' Room, closed the door, quickly turned the key, and resolutely walked away.

Not a word was spoken, but a lifetime of love, a full and complete pardon, and a veritable world of sympathy were in the mother's embrace. Then came a sob that sounded the deeper abyss.

A second sob made Tom draw back. Then with a steady hand he lifted his mother's head and smiled: "Come, Mother, keep that chin up!"

An hour went by; then another. They chatted, almost feverishly; but that night neither could tell what the other had said. Lips had spoken, but only hearts had listened. Mrs. Penney knew that some new and strange strength had come to Tom. She found him utterly unafraid. There was no blind hope to which he clung; the serenity he radiated gave the mother a strange joy and sent her home with a new strength.

That visit changed life for Mrs. Leona Penney. Unconsciously she now went around with her "chin up." Not ten days passed before she was climbing those stone steps again, and this time there were words which each heard and understood. There was also a pie she had baked.

February came and Tom wrote that things were even better at the jail; for now they were not locked in their cells until eight o'clock at night, and lights didn't go out until nine. On the eleventh of the month, the ever more reconciled mother visited him again and had a long chat about the appeal his lawyers were making. When Tom spoke of a new trial, a slender streak of light broke on the horizon that had been black, and Mrs. Penney hugged hope to her heart.

Two days later, however, she received a letter in a familiar hand but with a most unfamiliar postmark — Eddyville, Kentucky. It was dated February 12, 1942. She opened it nervously and felt her heart leap as the cold blue heading KENTUCKY STATE PENITENTIARY stared at her from the large sheet. She read anxiously:

> I certainly am glad I saw you yesterday; for I had to leave this morning at 5:30. I knew nothing about it myself until I was on my way.
>
> It is much different here from up there. I am in a cell by myself — no one to talk to or play cards with. But, Honey, I'll bear it if you promise not to worry. I can't receive anything to eat or read, no cigarettes or tobacco of any kind. The only things I can receive are stamps and money.
>
> It certainly was a shock to me this morning when they called me and told me to get ready.
>
> I did not get to say good-by to anyone, much as I would have loved to. Please don't worry and keep your chin up!

Mrs. Penney had not dried the tears caused by this shock when Father Donnelly was opening a letter from the same inmate of Death Row.

> Dear Father:
>
> Well, the thing I dreaded most has finally come to pass. I was transferred this morning from Lexington to Eddyville State Prison. It all came as a surprise, just as I knew that it would. But I did get to see Mother, Wednesday afternoon. Thank God for that.
>
> I haven't been here long enough to know much about the place, but from what I've seen I don't like it, although the officials are splendid. I am going to miss the nuns, yourself, and Father Sullivan. I understand a priest comes here from Paducah twice a month. I am the only Catholic in Death Row at present; for Anderson is

still as stubborn as ever. . . . I know the trouble with him now.
　I know it is too far for you to come here, Father, but you must
write to me. You have no idea how it helps. My mailing list is very
limited, but I hope to write to Sister Mary Laurentia and Sister
Robert Ann. . . .

The priest pushed a litter of papers, letters, a magazine, and an
open theology book to one side of his ever untidy desk, laid Tom's
single sheet before him and studied it paragraph by paragraph.
He got down to the one telling of the Catholic priest coming but
twice a month. When he read the first sentence of the next
paragraph his fist struck the desk. "Oh, no, Tom. It's not
too far for me. It's too late today. I have confessions tomorrow.
Then comes Sunday. But Monday is another day."

It was a long, dreary drive in desolate mid-February weather.
The approach to the penitentiary seemed bleak and forbidding.
The great stone edifice itself appeared angrily scowling. The
formalities of winning entrance to visit one in the Death House
were depressing and irritated somewhat the tired priest. But
finally he was led across a yard into a building that was clearly
an annex. The guard took him along a row of cells the like of
which he had never seen before, and stopped before a door that
was not only heavily barred but thickly screened. The priest could
not see in. But when the guard cried: "Penney!" Father George
recognized the answering voice. He moved closer to the screen.
"Tom, I'm here. But this is worse than visiting a Carmelite. I've
got to see you, boy. Just a second — I'll be back. I'm going to
tell the Warden. I simply must violate your cloister."
　"Father George!" was all Tom could say to the retreating
footsteps.
　The giant Jess Buchanan knew men and recognized character
when he saw it. He smiled on Father George, told him he was
asking a lot, but ordered the guard to let him in. Back to Death
Row they went. The long, long bolt, that locks every cell at
once, was shot, and Father George's hands were on Tom Penney's
shoulders. A second later Tom had pulled down the bunk, which

folded back against the wall, being hung there from two chains.

"Will it hold the two of us?" asked Father George with a laugh, when Tom invited him to sit.

"If it doesn't, it will never be broken in a more worthy cause. Oh, Father, how did you ever make it? Will you stay overnight?"

"I'm only a little assistant curate, Tom. I must be back in Covington long before midnight."

"But that's impossible. We must be three hundred miles from there."

"Not bad reckoning, Tom. I drove 289 miles coming down. But I'll make it, never fear. Now tell me all about yourself."

As they talked Father George took in every detail of the tiny cell. It was narrow, windowless, solid concrete. The wall bunk was the biggest thing in it, almost the only thing in it. A commode in the corner completed the furnishings. No table. No chair. No stool. The priest smiled at the ingenious arrangement the prisoner had made for his books and letters. And laughed aloud when Tom caught him measuring the length of the cell with his eye.

"Don't tell the guard, Father," he whispered, "but when I want to change my mind, I turn a somersault."

The priest marveled at the high spirits of the man; for he saw that such a cell was an ideal contrivance to drive wildly insane anyone with the semblance of a claustrophobia. Tom had many questions to ask about religion; his duties to God in such circumstances, his prayers and private devotions, his trials and temptations, his difficulties with some of the books he had read. Before they knew it, an hour and a half had slipped by.

"Oh, Tom, I must say hello to Bob and Baxter."

"Go to it, Father. I think we ought to leave Baxter in what you called 'invincible ignorance.' That will be his way to heaven. But you must work on Bob. He is still stubborn. But if he will yield to any man, you're the man. Now how about Holy Communion for me?"

"I'll tell the Warden you desire to receive and that Father Libs should be informed. I don't think there'll be any difficulty."

They parted with that. Father George blessed him and promised to see him soon. The next day Tom wrote his mother:

Father Donnelly came yesterday. He sure has stuck with me, Mother. I almost worship that man. He always knows just what to say and how to say it. I feel at home with him, perfectly at ease. And don't you go having any doubts about me being ready, Mother. Here is one thing I want you to remember always: Regardless of my past, I am clean at last. And now Death holds no terror for me. A coward dies a thousand times; a brave man dies but once.

A week later, when Father Donnelly called on her, she showed him the latest letter from Eddyville. In it Tom told of the stay that had been granted and the appeals that had been filed. That was cheering news. But she asked the priest about a postscript which puzzled her: "Mother, if you should see anything in the papers you do not understand, please don't worry about it. You will understand in time. It will have its purpose. Promise me?"

Father George read it twice then shook his head. "It's beyond me. . . . But let's both trust Tom."

From South Spring Street the priest went to St. Joseph's Hospital.

"That Warden must be a very nice person," said Sister Mary Laurentia. "He let Tom have the three pound box of candy I sent; then had Tom tell me I must send no more. Tom hasn' much liberty now, has he?"

The priest shook his head, then described the cell in which he had found the boy.

"What can we do for him, Father?" Sister Robert Ann cried.

"Pray, write, send plenty of good reading matter."

Father George garnered no information from the nuns on th one thing that bothered him — that postscript to his mother' letter. He knew that almost anything can be conceived by a man in solitary confinement. A vague fear was growing in him, bu he was not telling the Sisters about it. He quietly resolved to b on the road to Eddyville soon again.

That resolution was reduced to action a few days later whe a letter came saying that Father Libs had been to the prison o

Wednesday but had talked with Tom only through the door of his cell, saying that he would not be able to bring Holy Communion until, as Tom put it, "the worst comes to the worst."

The visit to Eddyville was short, for Father George was anxious to talk to Father Tom Libs in the rectory at Paducah. It was a pleasant chat until the subject of communicating the prisoner was broached. Then was revealed to Father George Donnelly another of those bewilderingly strange ways of God — that drawing of a soul into closer union by first seeming to abandon it; that building of love's fires by first seeming to withdraw all love's glowing embers; that peculiar process whereby the Divinity seems to work on the human adage that "absence makes the heart grow fonder." Before leaving Paducah, Father George feared that Tom Penney would be without Holy Communion for many a day. Father Libs was a very busy curate — and Eddyville was visited only once a month. Furthermore, Father Tom Libs was not convinced of Tom Penney's sincerity. He had cited cases of fraud and told Father George of the skepticism a prison chaplain develops.

As he drove home the long, lonely two hundred and eighty miles, Father Donnelly realized he had failed with Father Tom Libs and failed even with Tom Penney; for while he had not persuaded the priest to communicate the prisoner, he had also forgotten to ask Tom Penney about that puzzling postscript in the last letter he had written his mother. But then a more harassing problem occupied his mind as he covered the bleak miles at a perilous speed: How was he to direct this lone man in a solitary cell without Sacrament or Sacrifice?

He got his answer before the month was out. Sister Robert Ann, without any knowledge that Tom was without Sacramental Communion, had the happy inspiration of instructing him how to make a Spiritual Communion. Sister Mary Laurentia, conscious of the Lenten Season, sent him a set of small stations with suggestions for their use.

On his next visit to Lexington the priest was presented with letters that not only filled him with happiness but with the determination to collect all Tom's letters and study God's ways with a human soul.

Sister Robert Ann wanted a line in her letter explained. Tom had written: "Thanks for the calendar, Sister! I had tried all over to get one and failed. But now I can settle all arguments: I have a calendar, a dictionary, and by far the best pair of lungs. The others haven't a chance."

Father George told her how prisoners in solitary confinement carry on conversation: they yell through the walls. When the nun asked what kind of arguments they had, the priest smiled and said: "You'll soon find out."

But with Sister Mary Laurentia the process was reversed; she had to explain to Father George a line in her letter. Tom was thanking her for a three-pound box of candy. "I thought he told you not to send any more."

"He did, Father. But a good nurse never obeys patients — and Tom is my patient. My first duty is to see that he is comfortable. Warden Buchanan knows that nuns will never send him anything that is not good for him. I sent cigars along with the candy. He got both."

Father George laughed and then read aloud the letter to Sister Mary Laurentia. It was dated Easter Sunday, April 5, 1942.

Dear Sister:

This certainly has been a beautiful day. Although I could only glimpse a wee bit of sunshine through a barred window, I rejoiced in the knowledge that others more fortunate than I were enjoying it.

I have spent the day very quietly, reading and thinking; and there seems to be so very many things I never thought of before.

Sister, I find the Stations a great comfort. I have them in a position that gives me constant view. My pains and sufferings are small in comparison. In fact, so small, I can't even think of my own. I complied with your request on Good Friday many times, Sister. I imagine I join you in your prayers in the wee hours of the morning. I have no way of knowing the hour at any time, but that is my intention. Sometimes I am retiring about the time you are rising. The days, you see, are noisy, so I sleep most of the day. We have the radio from 5 to 9:30 p.m. Then all is quiet. I may turn my light on and off as I please.

I imagine Father Donnelly will visit me soon. I haven't heard from him in two weeks. I have missed him terribly. He is so busy I hate to see him drive so far; but I know he will come anyhow.

Father Libs will be here the eighth — Wednesday. Mrs. Lewis sent me two prayer books and "The Faith of Our Fathers."

Words are so futile, my feeble efforts could never reveal to you my spiritual attitude, so let me just say: My future lies with God. In Him I place my love and faith. May His Will be done. I pray continuously for a better understanding and a deeper devotion to Him. . . .

Father George handed the letter back, saying, "Now I want you to know the kind of letters I receive." He drew a sheet from an inside pocket, unfolded it and read:

I have a pet roach — a large one too! He eats with me, and I have caught him on my bed several times. I just can't keep him out of my candy. But, Father, he won't learn anything at all. He won't even run the right way. He's as dumb as I am.

"How does he keep his cheerful spirits?" exclaimed Sister Robert Ann.

The priest put out his hands. "Sisters, I'm collecting letters. I want to see how cheerful Tom has been. . . . How about it?"

Late one night in May Father George packed his meerschaum, swept aside the usual litter on his desk and began with the first letter he had received from Tom Penney. He completed his little pile, then turned to the larger set addressed to the nuns. The tone was distinctly different, though the matter treated was frequently the same. The priest smiled. Was there chivalry in this man who had been condemned as a murderer?

It was nearing midnight when he laid the last letter down. His pipe needed repacking. As he tamped in the tobacco he marveled at the way Tom Penney's soul had grown and wondered if he had not detected a definite plan to the process. He lit up, took pencil and began jotting:

CONTRITION AND GRATITUDE

To me, Mar. 22: It is a great consolation to have the opportunity to see, recognize, and admit my mistakes. I cannot erase them before the eyes of men, but there is not a day or a night that I do not ask forgiveness from God.

To Sister Robert Ann, Feb. 22: I have buried my past, and think only of the future. Sister, there is nothing on earth that can shake my Faith now. I close with my very best wishes and sincere gratitude.

DESIRE TO DO GOD'S WILL AND COMPASSION FOR CHRIST

To Sister M. Laurentia, Feb. 22: This moving business was a great surprise to everyone. But it was God's will — as I firmly believe — and since that is my greatest desire, I have no complaint.

March 5: I received the medal, Sister, and I pray God, if it is His holy will, that I may wear it as long as you have, and do equally as many good deeds, loving and serving Him with my whole heart and soul every day, every hour, and every moment until my last heart beat.

To Sister Robert Ann, Apr. 5: Sister, I find the Stations a great comfort. I have them in a position that gives me constant view. My pains and suffering are small in comparison. In fact, so small, I can't even think of my own.

To Sister M. Laurentia, Apr. 5: I complied with your request on Good Friday many times, Sister. . . . In Him I place my love and trust. May His will be done. I pray continuously for a better understanding and deeper devotion to Him.

Father George was sure there was a plan to it all when he began the letters of May. For he saw that if Lent had been used by God to make Tom Penney conscious of Christ's Passion, the month of May was used almost exclusively to arouse devotion to Christ's Mother. So he jotted on another sheet —

MAY: DEVOTION TO OUR LADY — PRAYER

To me, May 6: Father, I'm devoting most of my time this month to our Blessed Mother. The rosary three times daily, the Litany of Our Lady, the 30-day prayer, and many others along with much meditation. If I fail in any way, surely it is my own fault; for the

Sisters have provided me with material enough to educate a nitwit.

To Sister M. Laurentia, May 1: I will start the month by writing to you. It is now somewhere near 2 a.m. Friday, and I have said my rosary once, the evening prayer to the Blessed Virgin, the Litany to Our Lady. I do that every day now. You'll laugh at the "evening prayer" at 2 a.m.; but I haven't slept yet, so this is evening to me. When I awake I say all the prayers I know by heart. You see, I have nothing else to do but pray and read, write and draw.

To Sister Robert Ann, May 14: Sister, devotion to our Blessed Mother came quite natural to me from the first. . . . I don't find it difficult to meditate on the mysteries while saying the rosary. I can even close my eyes and see them. I usually complete the fifteen mysteries, Sister, unless interrupted. My Beads are my favorites, Sister. I go to sleep with them. They avert my mind from many unpleasant things.

The picture of our Lady that I drew I placed on the wall at the head of my bed so that she may watch over me while I sleep. I used no model. It is 9 by 12, but only half view. I certainly will draw one for each of you two Sisters, but 9 by 12 would be too large for your prayer books, wouldn't it?

To Sister M. Laurentia, May 27: I shall be very happy to see you, Sister. I don't know how you conceived the idea that I might not be too anxious to see you, but you were not altogether wrong. It was not of myself I was thinking; it is the visiting regulations that prevent me from encouraging anyone to come and see me. . . . We will pray our Blessed Mother to obtain a special privilege for us on this occasion — shall we? Many requests she has granted me, Sister; and I do not fail to return thanks.

I am sending two drawings. . . . Someone asked why I did not draw her smiling. I cannot picture her smiling, Sister. She smiles in her heart. And to prove to you I am not an artist, let me tell you the poor fellow did not know who it was I was trying to portray. So praise me — only for my good intentions.

Father George shook his head knowingly. Indeed there was definite plan here. He saw now why Tom Penney had been hurried off to Eddyville. Solitude was unknown in Fayette County Jail. If Tom Penney was to find himself and God in that intimacy which alone means sanctity, he had to be taken from the environment of Lexington and placed where he could think not only with his mind, but with his heart. He needed solitude.

The priest sat back and pictured to himself the little cement hole-in-the-wall, which was now Tom Penney's world, and saw it as the one place in all creation God had chosen to hold rendezvous with the man the world called a murderer.

Again that silken-white head nodded knowingly. To his priestly discernment, these letters revealed the fact that Tom Penney was soon to die. They told him that God was preparing the man, as only a loving God can.

But now a frown gathered above Father George's staring blue eyes. Somewhat uneasily he bent forward and took up the letters again, to study Tom's attitude toward death.

In a letter addressed to himself on April 29, he read:

> Bob and Baxter have very strong hopes of getting out. They talk as if they wouldn't need God then! All I can say is that if it breaks a man's spirit to believe in God, then I do not believe; for my spirit certainly is not broken. But I have changed my point of view completely. I simply could not care for the things I once did. If the next to impossible should happen, and I am permitted to live, I know with absolute surety, I could never go back to the old life.
>
> Some people seem to think that I want to die. They are sadly mistaken. . . . But if I must die, then it is God's holy will. And I will try very hard to walk to my death with my chin up and my step unfaltering. What more can I do?

After reading that, Father George felt more relieved. Among the letters to the nuns, he found a few passages that increased this relief. He continued making notes:

> *To Sister Robert Ann, May 22:* I have had some people say to me: "Mr. Penney, how can you laugh and joke the way you do, knowing that this terrible thing is almost on you?" I did not tell them that the only people who fear death are those who do not understand the love of God, because they were supposed to be religious people, and I would not offend them; but that *is* the answer, Sister.
>
> *To Sister M. Laurentia, May 27:* My most earnest desire is to

die an honorable death. If that cannot be accomplished, then His holy will be done! I do not fear death, Sister; it is only the unworthy cause for which I die, that I detest.

As the priest was rearranging the letters in a neat pile, his eye was caught by a passage in one addressed to himself on May 27:

Why did I so willingly, so determinedly accept the true Faith? Ah, Father, it is easy for me to answer. From the very beginning I knew you were interested in my soul, not curious about a criminal. You explained to me the love of God and the joys of heaven, and not the fear of the devil and the torments of hell. You gave me all the warm marks of friendship until my knowledge of you deepened and developed and finally glowed into a high admiration. But, you were always working to give me one thing: a deep and ever increasing love for God and our beloved Lord, Jesus Christ.

Not so bad, thought Father George, but ruffled through the pages until he found a letter of April 16, addressed to both nuns simultaneously and read:

It is now 2 a.m. Soon you will begin a new day. You know, Sisters, I once thought that nuns were the saddest people on earth. (How could I ever dream they were the happiest?) But now I know — and what a wonderful revelation it has been.

I think I told you once that Mr. Price was responsible for my conversion. He did start me thinking seriously. But the climax came after one of your visits to the jail in which you told me of the circumstances under which Father Donnelly came to see me. That day I said to myself: "Here is Father Donnelly driving over a hundred miles to see me. Here are two Sisters who inconvenience themselves to come to this foul jail, just to see me. Surely, there is no earthly compensation in it for them. So there must be, yes there must be something about me worth saving. I'm going to save it!"

Father George was smiling as he put the cold meerschaum on the overfilled ash tray and gathered his notes. At one time he did harbor the notion that he had played an important role in the conversion of Tom Penney. Now at 2:15 a.m. he set the three closely written pages to one side, telling himself he could retire from the case without a qualm, so long as the two nuns stayed on the job. God had a definite plan.

As he slipped into his pajamas he said: "You've done a wonderful work, Lord."

Just as he was falling off to sleep the memory of the postscript in Tom's letter to his mother in late February or early March came back to the priest. All these weeks it had remained unexplained. Now it rose like a cloud to move across the tranquil beauty of a night sky and mar the pale loveliness of the moon. What could have been in the boy's mind? Father George shifted on his side. "Oh, God," he prayed, "let nothing go wrong!"

CHAPTER SIX

Birthdays in the Deathhouse

THE graduate nurse on the corridor wondered what could be on Sister Robert Ann's mind. No patient was desperately ill, the student nurses had done their work well; yet, the ever efficient Instructor of Nurses was fidgety and nervous.

What the Graduate Nurse did not know was that Mother Ann Sebastian, superior-general of the Sisters of Charity of Nazareth, had just arrived in Lexington for the graduation exercises at St. Joseph's Hospital, and Sister Mary Laurentia had decided to ask a very special permission which included Robert Ann.

The slender Instructor of Nurses went into the linen room with no definite purpose. She came out and wandered into the diet kitchen just as aimlessly. Dear Lord, she was thinking, how I'd love to be in Chapel. But I must be here when Doctor Rankin comes. She came out and rearranged the things on the supervisor's desk for the fifth or sixth time within the hour. "Why am I so anxious?" she asked herself. "If God wants us to have this permission, it will be granted. If not . . ." But then she reminded herself of the Gospel lines, "ask and you shall receive," and quite earnestly she pleaded: "Please, Lord, grant it. Dear Lord, put Mother Ann Sebastian in a most receptive mood. Have Sister Mary Laurentia ask in the right way. And please, dear Lord, hurry! I'm getting awfully nervous."

It all began three weeks ago when she had nursed Sister Mary Laurentia's cousin. The good woman was so taken by the nun's gracious ways that toward the end of her convalescence, she said to her cousin: "I'd love to do something for you and Sister Robert Ann. Why couldn't I give you a trip of some sort? I could easily finance your way down to her home in Fancy Farms." Sister Mary Laurentia seemed only half attentive, but that evening she asked her friend, "When were you to visit your folks last?"

"Three years ago — why?"

"It's time for another visit. My cousin will finance the trip if we get the permission."

"Oh, Sister, maybe we could even get permission to visit Tom Penney. . . ."

Sister Mary Laurentia made no reply, but a few minutes later was telling Sister Mary Benigna, the superior of the hospital, all about it. The kindly Superior joined in the plan, promising to solicit the necessary permission from Mother General. But before she had managed a letter to Nazareth, it was time for commencement at Lexington. With characteristic honesty she called Sister Mary Laurentia to her and confessed the oversight, urged her to seek the permission herself, assuring her it would be granted.

Sister Mary Laurentia was not so sure. She had not lived all these years in religion without learning that unexpected refusals are as common as unexpected concessions, if not more common. But since it was more for Sister Robert Ann than for herself, she decided to ask.

Sister Robert Ann saw her as soon as she turned the corner of the corridor. She strained her sparkling blue-gray eyes in an effort to read what was inscrutable — the expression on Sister Mary Laurentia's face. "Well?" she gasped as the elder nun reached her side.

"I haven't seen Mother yet."

"Oh!" There was both relief and disappointment in the exclamation.

"She was busy when I went there this morning. I'm going to try her right now. Come along."

"But I . . ."

"Come along!"

"But Doctor Rankin . . ."

"Bother Doctor Rankin. Your two graduate nurses are here. Come along."

They found the Mother General alone at her desk. Sister Mary Laurentia wasted no words.

"Reverend Mother, Sister Robert Ann has not been home in three years."

"To Nazareth?"

"Excuse me, Mother; I meant to Fancy Farms to visit her folks."

"Oh, her *old* home." And Mother Ann Sebastian smiled.

"My cousin was a patient here a few weeks ago. Sister nursed her. She wants to finance a trip for Sister to her old home."

"And you?" Mother Ann Sebastian was still smiling.

"Such a young child needs a chaperon, Mother. Despite my great repugnance to such a trip, I offer my services."

Mother Ann Sebastian smiled even more broadly. "Sister Mary Laurentia, you're incorrigible. You may go."

"Just one other thing, Mother."

"Yes?"

"We pass Eddyville on the way. May we stop there?"

"You may."

"Thank you so much, Mother," said Sister Mary Laurentia with a bow, then literally pushed Sister Robert Ann out of the room.

"Sh!" . . . she warned until they had turned the corner of the corridor.

"Do you think she knows what Eddyville is?" asked Sister Robert Ann anxiously. "You didn't tell . . ."

"You heard the permission, didn't you?"

"Yes, but . . ."

"There were no 'buts' about it. We're going to stop at Eddyville. We're going to see Tom Penney."

June 4 dawned and the two nuns, after seeing their large, carefully packed carton placed in the rear of the car, excitedly took their places in the back seat, and begged Sister Robert Ann's brother to cover the fifty miles that lay between them and Eddyville as quickly as safety would allow.

Were they bent on any other mission the marvel of the countryside would have awed them. But now, not even the blue fire of gentians burning in a field alive with bowing daisies, so much as caught their eye. The goldfinches dipping among the roadside bushes, the laughter of streams, or the stately firs swaying in the early morning breeze drew no comment from them.

This experience was stirring them both more than they cared to admit. Tom had so often expressed his desire to talk things out with someone who understood. Evidently, the monthly visits of the Catholic chaplain did not satisfy this boy's needs, and Father George had been so tied up of late that he had not made the long round trip in three weeks. They would have to make the most of their time with him.

The rigid paragraph of "Rules for the Guidance of Relatives to Inmates" which burst upon one from the top of every bit of stationery that came from Eddyville said the visiting hours were from 8:30 to 10:30 a.m. and from 1 to 3 p.m. They could never reach there now on time for the morning hours. But then Sister Mary Laurentia remembered the last line: "Persons desiring to see prisoners on business will have to secure permission from the Warden." She would tell the Warden they had important business and would transact it in business hours. Excitement, nervousness, or fret did not shorten the miles, yet the two nuns were surprised when Sister Robert Ann's brother said: "Well, there it is, and it is not 11:30 yet."

Before them, set on a high hill, looking like some medieval stone castle with formidable battlements, stood Kentucky's State Penitentiary, glaring in the blinding brilliance of June's sunshine. They looked all around, expecting they knew not what, but found only the empty countryside. The place seemed like a deserted village.

"Shall we eat now?" asked Sister Robert Ann, thinking no doubt of the 1 to 3 visiting hours.

"I want to see the Warden before noon," came back the somewhat stiff reply from the older nun. "We'll eat later."

They climbed half a hundred broad stone steps and arrived somewhat breathless before the great iron gates of the entrance. They rang a bell, and drew back a bit startled as the massive gates swung open and revealed two armed guards standing within.

They smiled at the nuns, and one said: "We were expecting you today, Sisters."

"We would like to see the Warden right away, if that is at all possible," said Sister Mary Laurentia, very conscious of the nearing noon hour.

One of the guards beckoned to the nuns to follow him. Up on the second floor he ushered them into the presence of W. Jess Buchanan. Sister Robert Ann considered him just a heavy set, middle-aged man with a kind face and a very friendly smile until he stood up. Then she saw he was a giant of six feet, seven inches, weighing over three hundred pounds. She felt positively fragile in the presence of such a man. But he invited them to be seated, assuring them he felt privileged to have nuns visiting the prison and felt sure it was the first time two Sisters of Charity of Nazareth had entered Kentucky's State Penitentiary.

Later, Sister Mary Laurentia confessed that while she is no diplomat, she felt the cause demanded the full play of all her powers of persuasion. "We have heard so much of your kindness, Mr. Buchanan," said Sister Mary Laurentia, "we were anxious to meet you." The Warden smiled warmly. Espying a picture of "Happy" Chandler on his desk, she went on: "I see you have the Governor's picture. He is a friend of ours. Has been a patient at our hospital in Lexington."

"He appointed me," came the cheerful reply. "A great man."

Then Sister Mary Laurentia plunged: "Mr. Buchanan, we've come to help Tom Penney spiritually. We feel sure his time on earth is short. Has he given any trouble?"

"No. No, Sisters. A model prisoner."

"We've read the prison rules on the letterhead often. We did not see where edibles could not be sent."

"That's true, Sisters. But you see, those regulations are for the ordinary prisoners. To men condemned to death, edibles may not be sent."

"Oh, now I understand. But look, Mr. Buchanan, Tom is a baptized Catholic, yet is not allowed to attend the chaplain's Mass."

"That's right, Sister. Men condemned to death are never allowed to be with the other prisoners. At no time — "

"Oh . . . Well, may the priest at least visit him in his cell?"

"I always allow Father Donnelly to do that. . . ."

"I was thinking of the prison chaplain, the one who comes from Paducah."

"Father Libs? Oh, sure, Sister, I can grant him the same favor. He can enter Tom's cell."

The more reserved Sister Robert Ann, who had been listening attentively, felt her heart leap; for now she knew Tom could and would receive Holy Communion. But her companion was still speaking. . . .

"Mr. Buchanan, Tom's birthday is just a week from today. You know, and I know, most likely it's his last on earth. Can't we send him a birthday box of food? Won't you allow us to bake him a birthday cake?"

Jess Buchanan's big eyes blinked behind his horn-rimmed glasses. What man could resist such an appeal? "Send him anything but cigarettes, Sister, and I'll let it through. But now before you get any more out of me, allow me to say that my wife and I will be highly honored if you two nuns will take lunch with us." And Jess Buchanan rose to escort the Sisters to his apartments.

"Oh, Mr. Buchanan, we are honored by, and very grateful for, the invitation. But we, Prisoners of Christ, have our rules and regulations too, regarding food. You will understand our inability to accept your very kind offer, won't you? Explain to your wife and tell her we hope we have not caused her inconvenience. . . . Could we see Tom Penney soon?"

"You can see him right away, Sisters. I'll have Tom Penney brought here to my office in order to visit with you. It will be more pleasant than the corridor outside his cell in 'the walk.' Of course a guard must be with him."

The two nuns could only catch their breaths and exchange knowing glances. This was the answer to the novena they had made with Tom to the Sorrowful Mother of Christ.

Not three minutes later they saw Tom following a guard across the yard. They recognized and understood why he raised his unshackled hands to shield his eyes. It was all of four months since he had really seen the sun.

Freshly shaven and neat as always, Tom entered the room and greeted the nuns warmly, shaking their hands with an intensity that made them wince even as it made them most welcome. Then graciously he thanked the Warden. Buchanan waved aside the thanks and retired. The guard moved in and took the Warden's chair while Tom Penney went to the only empty one at the left of Sister Robert Ann. Sister Mary Laurentia was just about to move her chair closer to the prisoner when she recalled a line from one of his letters saying: "It is not easy to carry on a conversation when you have an audience." She turned to the guard and engaged him in such a spirited conversation that neither of them heard a single word Tom Penney said.

More than an hour passed before Sister Mary Laurentia stood up saying: "We had better not impose on you or the Warden any longer."

Tom Penney arose and turned to the guard. "Do you think it at all possible for the Sisters to see Bob Anderson?" he asked.

"Possible? I'll take them there myself. It is just about visiting time. But I'll have to take you back first. . . ."

"Of course," said the prisoner and turned to the nuns.

This, they suddenly realized, would most likely be the last time they would see one another this side of eternity. The same thought seemed to grip three minds at once and rendered all speechless. It filled the office with a tension that swept the guard into its orbit. He sensed what was making these people so taut, and eased the situation by saying: "After you visit Anderson, Sisters, I'll take you up to Tom's place."

Tom smiled, bowed, then said, "See you later, Sisters," and went out with his guard.

The door had not fully closed before Sister Mary Laurentia was at the side of the younger nun. "You would get the seat next to Tom, wouldn't you? Well you're going to tell me every single word he said!"

Sister Robert Ann smiled. "It will be a rare happiness, Sister; and thanks a million for keeping that guard's attention. Oh, Sister, Tom talked today, as simply as a child. . . . You can imagine what he talked of first and most."

"What?"

"His mother. He's so grateful. You'd think we had done something wonderful in visiting the dear old soul."

"What else did he talk about?"

"When you got so polite that you had to end it all, we were talking about the sacraments and about the Mass. Oh, Sister, that boy is just burning with love and longing for God."

"Well, you heard what the Warden said. Tom may have Holy Communion in his cell; but for Mass . . . I'm afraid he'll have to wait and look down from heaven."

"Isn't he interested in Bob Anderson?"

"Has been from the beginning. Remember how he worked on him at Lexington, then got Father George — "

"He's been working on him here, but Bob doesn't respond. Isn't it strange how two men — "

"Sssh! Here comes the guard."

"I wonder who's in the stranger position: you nuns or myself," said the guard. "I never escorted Sisters of Charity to the Death House before."

It was a long walk and a strange one for the Sisters. They went down lengthy corridors flanked by cells; through peculiarly constructed doors; along more corridors of gray cement and iron bars. Finally the guard said: "You are now entering Death Row."

The nuns looked up sharply. They had been spoken to by many of the prisoners as they came along, and both Sister Robert Ann and her older companion were busy with deep thoughts.

"How young the vast majority of these prisoners are!" was the whispered comment from Sister Robert Ann.

"This boy is to die tonight," said the guard *sotto voce* as they neared a cell in which a colored boy sat reading a Bible. When he heard the rattle of the Sisters' beads he looked up.

"Pray for me tonight, won't you, Sisters?"

Sister Mary Laurentia began to feel eerie. Death was not new to her; not after her hospital experiences. But death for men so much alive; death at an appointed hour. . . .

Another colored boy lay motionless on his bunk.

"That man hasn't spoken a single word in three weeks," said the guard quietly. Then in a louder voice: "And here's Mr. Anderson's cell. . . . Bob, I have a surpise for you. Very special visitors."

The resident non-Catholic chaplain had now joined the party. To Sister Mary Laurentia he appeared too anxious to hear what the nuns had to say to Bob Anderson, so after a warm handshake and a few words of greeting and encouragement to Bob, the nun walked a little distance from the cell saying to the chaplain: "I hear you have quite a library here." The man had to follow her in order to carry on the conversation, and thus Sister Robert Ann was left at Bob's cell door well out of earshot of the chaplain.

Once again Sister Mary Laurentia had to use her ingenuity. She manifested an interest not only in the prison library but in the chaplain's work with the prisoners. She listened attentively as he sketched his aims and assured him that he was doing a great and noble work. Whereupon the man grew enthusiastic and elaborated for his listener his whole technique. When she praised him for his formation of a choir, he promised her she would hear it before she left the penitentiary. Out of the corner of her eye she saw Bob Anderson and Sister Robert Ann in animated conversation. She smiled to the chaplain and told him he was very kind and generous. He went off shortly afterward to prepare the little performance.

Bob Anderson then thanked the Sisters for their visit and for their prayers. It was now that Sister Mary Laurentia got a good look at the man and his cell. Bob was clearly visible through the open work of the door. She found him quite handsome, and his cell comparatively comfortable. He had a table, chair, plenty of sunlight, and every opportunity for fresh air because of his large window.

The guard seemed to read what was going on in the nun's mind and explained that men condemned to die were given better quarters than the rest. "It's the least we can do before they step across to this," he said, and led the Sisters directly across the corridor from Anderson's cell to the twenty-foot green and tan room which held as centerpiece — the electric chair.

With care and exactness the guard explained the mechanism of this instrument of death to the nuns. They had often looked with keen interest on machines devised to kill disease and thus save life, and upon the bright burnished steel of scalpel and other surgical instruments that were for the saving of life; but this chair of death. . . . Were they not sure that Tom Penney would one day sit in it, they would have thanked the guard for his good intentions, but stopped his explanations. They stood in awe in this brilliantly lighted room and stared at the chair from which souls would go immediately to God's Judgment Seat. At last the guard led them from Death Row to "the walk," as the prisoners called it, where Tom's cell was situated. Naturally the Sisters wondered why Tom was placed so far from Anderson. They did not know all that had gone on at Lexington: conversation and the exchanging of notes, chats with Bob's lawyers, all of which led officials to the determination to separate them for a time. Finally they halted before that barred and heavily screened door which had so shocked Father George at first. The nuns peered in.

What a difference from the room Bob Anderson occupied! The Sisters could not even see Tom through the thick screening on the door. He had to open the tiny slot through which food was passed. They then glimpsed the narrow interior of the cell. No window. No sunlight. No air. A bunk chained to the wall. And in the corner, Tom's store of religious books, stationery and drawing materials. But the prisoner, laughed joyfully as he told the Sisters the guards were kind enough to let him put on his light any hour of the day or night.

"I couldn't see my hand in front of me without it," he said. "But it's wonderful to snap it on about two in the morning, when everything is quiet. That's when I write most of my letters now. I draw at that time, too. You'll take some of my efforts as mementos of this wonderful day."

He went to his little pile and selected five pictures: one of the Sacred Heart, another of the Little Flower, a third of St. Vincent de Paul, and two others of Our Lady of Sorrows. He slipped them under the door to two nuns who were almost ready to weep for this man locked in such a tiny space of cold concrete. But his bubbling spirits would not allow for tears.

Soon, they had to say good-by. This was the moment the Sisters feared. But now Tom took over. "Sisters," he said cheerfully, "I don't know what it is, but something tells me this is not the last time we are to see one another on earth. So I'll say only *Au revoir* and thank you for having given me one of the happiest days of my life. The Sorrowful Mother of Christ has answered all our prayers."

On the way to Fancy Farms the Sisters stopped at Paducah; and while Sister Robert Ann visited with her old Pastor, Sister Mary Laurentia talked with young Father Tom Libs. She told him of the Warden's permission for him to enter Tom Penney's cell, and of the latter's gnawing hunger for the Eucharist. "You'll find Tom not only well instructed, Father, but most sincere."

Later that evening, when Sister Robert Ann had given her sister explicit instructions on what sort of a cake to make, when it was to be finished, where, how and to whom delivered, the nuns felt that they had done a day's work.

The following morning, June 5, Tom wrote to his mother:

I have had a most happy day! The Sisters visited me! But I will not tell you about it. I will leave that to them. They will be seeing you shortly.

Mother, "Tommie" sent me $5 for my birthday, and Father Donnelly also left me $5. The Sisters are going to bake me a cake and send me something they obtained special permission for. I tell you this so that you may know that on next Thursday I shall be having a birthday feast. May God bless them all! Another reason for telling you this, Mother, is that you may know that God is good to me; good to give me such friends, Mother, my only regret is that I cannot share it with those I love. . . .

Tom was moved that day. Prison officials felt reasonably safe now, so they took him from his little cement hole-in-the-wall to the comparative luxury of the cell next to Bob Anderson. These men had not seen one another in four months. The warmth in Bob's greeting told Tom that the Sisters had effected much in their brief visit. At 1 a.m. the following day he was writing to Sister Mary Laurentia:

I just awoke from a very pleasant slumber, and since my thoughts are of you, I shall try to give you an idea of what's going on inside me. In brief I can say that you gave me one of the happiest days of my life Thursday.

I am now in the next cell to Bob, in the Death House. Oh, it is so much better here: more room, good light, good bed, and right now it is cool; fresh air, too. I have an outside window, and there is no one to disturb me. It is much quieter here. God is good to me. Pray that I be worthy of His graces, Sister. I will do my best always.

I was too happy, or just maybe incapable of speech, to thank the Warden and Mr. Rankin for their kindness. I would have, Sister, if I could have swallowed the lump in my throat. I think that we all sometimes laugh just to keep from crying.

I am eternally grateful to you, Sister. If I did not know that saints are dead, I'd suspect you of being St. Jude!

Anderson was certainly glad to see you, Sister. I didn't know then, but now I wouldn't have had you miss seeing him for anything.

That made pleasant reading, but Sister was waiting for the following week. She knew the instructions Sister Robert Ann had given to her sister about the cake. And she was curious about Tom's reaction to the box she herself had sent. On June 12 she received her letter.

Dear Sister Mary Laurentia:

If parcel post handled freight, you probably would have just mailed the pharmacy itself! Everything came O.K., Sister, and I see that I am going to enjoy myself for many a day to come.

The cake came also, and, Sister, it was beautiful! They must have brought it here in person. Mr. Rankin brought it to me so that I might see it before it was cut. On it was "Happy Birthday — Tom Penney." There were roses in pink and white icing, and trimmed with little green "do-hickeys." This was Bob's birthday, too, you know. He was 37 and I am 33. We've shared your bounty and will continue to do it for weeks, I believe.

Well, Sister, Father Libs was here yesterday. I was prepared. I was fasting. But it was 11 a.m. before he was through his Mass. He didn't have time, but promised me next month. I shall wait patiently.

Before June was out, Father Donnelly had heard all about the birthdays in the Death House and that unforgettable visit. He got it from four different sources. Tom's letter was brief, but one line said as much as volumes. "If I loved any of you more than I do, it would be sacrilegious." That was speaking gratitude not only to his friends, but to God. Mrs. Penney, tearfully but gratefully, gave the priest a recount of what Tom had written and what the nuns had told. The nuns themselves reported; and one thing that impressed Father George was Tom's preoccupation with Anderson.

The priest suddenly realized that with the passage of time Bob had become something of a preoccupation to himself; for he was proving a dark puzzle. The few letters the man had sent him showed him careful of any commitment, cautious and even cold on the subject of religion. He did say he prayed and read and talked with Father Libs, but then coldly added that none of these things really gripped him.

For a few weeks after the visit by the nuns, Father George

had brighter hopes; for Anderson had written saying the "Sisters had made him see things plainer than anyone else," and Tom had told the priest that Bob had been making more inquiries about religion and seemed to be making more serious efforts at prayer. But the last week in June brought a letter that dimmed these hopes. Father George saw clearly where Anderson's real interest lay.

He sat back and mused. Here were two men with the same fate upon them, visited by God with the same graces, through the same instruments, at the same time and in the same circumstances. Their backgrounds were not so different, nor their educations and environments. What, then, was the explanation? Bob was a little older than Tom, as was learned from the recent birthday they celebrated in the adjoining cells in the Death House; but he was not showing himself nearly so wise. Penney was spending his time writing letters to the nuns and getting advice for his afterlife; Anderson was busy with lawyers and plans for freedom in this life. Bob was sincere enough, but if one were to put it in technical theological language, he had only "Imperfect Contrition." His fear was of hell; his sorrow was that he might go there. Tom had "Perfect Contrition"; he grieved for having offended his loving God and was making amends now by returning love for love as far as in him lay. The Death House held two conflicts: In one cell, the world was triumphing over a man who was made for heaven. In the next cell, a man was triumphing over an angel who had caused an all-merciful God to create a hell. And Father George felt that he was more than umpire in each battle. He was joined with each protagonist so closely that their letters tore his soul as he triumphed with one and lost with the other. As the month closed he was rejoicing over the happiness of the birthday in the Death House, and being racked with a doubt that was growing to a conviction. He feared that death in the same Death House would not mean birthdays for the two men.

CHAPTER SEVEN

Satan in the Cell Block

"Hey, Tom."

"Yeah?"

"Watcha doin'?"

"Writin'."

"Home?"

"No. To Sister Robert Ann."

"How the hell many hours a day do you spend writin' to those nuns?"

Penney's laugh floated out between the bars of his cell, struck the wall of the room holding the electric chair, and then went echoing up "the walk."

"Why the horselaugh?" asked Anderson.

"Either you're a mindreader, Bob, or you've been peeking over my shoulder by some strange instrument. Haven't any hidden mirrors, have you? The sentence to which I just put a period reads: 'The privilege of writing to you, Sister, gives me three or four hours of good sound thinking, which is something to be thankful for.' "

"Humph!" said Anderson.

"With what does he do that 'good sound thinking,' Bob?" came a thin voice from further down the cell block.

"Another country heard from," cried Tom. "I thought you were asleep, Skeeter."

"Fat chance anyone has to sleep with you guys bellowing the way you do."

Somewhat reluctantly Tom Penney placed his pencil on the half finished sheet and approached his cell door. This was almost routine business now. At every change of the guards the prisoners would gather at the doors of their respective cells and hold converse. It was in this position they discussed the news of the day as garnered from the Louisville *Courier-Journal* and the Lexington *Herald;* the first came to Anderson daily; the second to Tom Penney. Thus they spoke of the letters they had received and the letters they wrote; told one another their thoughts on life and death; exchanged views on their possibilities for a new trial; talked of the weather, the radio, war, and religion.

As the three lined up this evening in late June, footsteps on "the walk" made them turn their heads and shut their mouths. Captain Rankin came along with two guards and a very young looking prisoner. The cell next to Penney's was opened and closed. The guards and Rankin went off down the corridor.

"Who's the newcomer, Tom?"

"What's your name, kid?"

"Elliott. What's yours?"

"Oh, we're the Miley murderers. Bob is on my left. I'm Tom. Skeeter is two cells to the south of you. You going to decorate the hot seat?"

"A week from tonight, they tell me."

"Whew!" whistled Anderson. "That's the night before the fourth. What a way to celebrate the birth of liberty!"

"Don't know about that, Bob. It may mark the kid's birth to real liberty. . . ."

"For God's sake, Penney, will you shut that face of yours? You'll drive me nuts with your talk of religion, religion, religion. All I hear is, death is life and life is death. Damn it, lay off that twaddle, will you? I'm hoping to get out of this hell hole alive."

"Me too!" came from Baxter three cells down.

"Don't mind these two dreamers, kid. Bob's got a mouthpiece who's fighting like a fiend, spending dough like a drunken sailor, and getting nowhere fast. As for Baxter down there . . . well,

Skeeter always had pipe dreams. Now even without his pipe he goes on dreaming. But you face facts, youngster. Death *is* birth to real life."

"I know it. That's why I got myself baptized a while ago. . . ."

"Catholic?"

"No, Protestant. . . . Say, it's hot as hell in here."

"Hope you're wrong, kid. For my sake as well as for the sake of my two accomplices."

"What d'ya mean?"

"I hope this place is only as hot as Purgatory."

"Poof! He's off again. I'm going back to bed."

"Pleasant dreams, Skeeter. . . . How do you feel about death, kid?"

"Oh, I don't know. Kinda used to the idea by now. We all have to go some time, somehow. I'm just wonderin' how it'll be in the chair. Where's the confounded thing anyhow?"

"Right across the hall there. Just opposite Bob's cell."

"Hmmm. Won't be much of a walk for him, will it? or for any of us for that matter."

"I should say not," cut in Anderson. "It'll be a cinch to step across if we have to. But I'm still hopin' I won't have to. And, kid, it all depends on Penney. He got me in here. He can get me out of here."

"Powerful guy, ain't I, kid? More powerful than Governor Johnson. He can only pardon a man. But to hear Anderson talk, I can lock 'em up and spring 'em too. Cheer up, Bob, I may yet use that mighty influence of mine."

"You'd better or I'll damn you forever and ever."

"Ah, kid, did you hear that? There's a greater guy than I. There's a man who plays God."

"Say, Penney, you sound happy. Have you hopes of dodging the chair?"

"Not a glimmer. Our cases have been appealed, of course. But I know we're only prolonging the agony. Bob won't admit that, and Skeeter is just his echo."

"Why the hell *should* I admit it? Haven't I some of the

cleverest criminal lawyers in the country working for me?"

"Working for you? Huh! They're only taking your dough, Bob."

"What good will the dough be to me if I have to step across this hall to that hot seat?"

"But why don't you think of your wife, your mother, and your family. . . ."

"Why don't *you?*" came the piercing question.

For a moment Penney did not see the point. "Why don't I?" he queried.

"Yeah, why don't you? You cannot only save my dough for me — you can even save me for my wife, my mother, and my family."

"Whew! Penney, you're not only powerful; you're all-powerful! What's the story?"

"The old story of drowning men grasping at straws, kid. Bob thinks we can get new trials just because one of the jurymen came from across the tracks — just outside the county, and because a newspaper was found in the jury room after the jury had come to a decision. Mere trivialities."

"Trivialities nothing! Those are technicalities of the law; and many a man has been saved from the chair by just such technicalities. But even if they were mountainous, Tom, they would be nothing compared to what you can do. You can set the whole trial aside, make the judge, jury, prosecution and defense, news reporters and editors look foolish by a mere word. Penney, you can turn this whole State inside out and upside down."

"See what a miracle man I am, kid?"

"Why don't you work the miracle?"

"I'd rather send Bob to heaven."

"You'll be sending me to hell. . . ."

"Whoa, Robert! Whoa! — Purgatory's bad enough."

"What's this Purgatory you talk about, Penney? The lady preacher who comes here told me there ain't no such place. She says it's not in the Bible. So, I guess that settles it, doesn't it?"

Tom Penney's laugh was musical. "When I was up on 'the

walk,' kid, I had a dozen arguments an hour about God and religion. They all went the same way. Most of the boys up there take the Bible as the last word. . . . But I've learned it is not even the first word. How old is the Bible?"

"How should I know?"

"Where did we get the Bible?"

"King James, I guess. It's got his name on it."

"Who was he?"

"Ask me another."

"Was he God?"

"Of course not."

"Yet you just said the Bible is the word of God."

"The lady preacher told me it was."

"Who told her?"

"Hey, whacha tryin' to do, kid me?"

"Just trying to steer you straight. The Catholic Church can tell you where we got the Bible; how old it is; what are God's words and what are not; what they mean and what they don't. It was the Catholic Church who gave us the Bible, kid. Neither Peter, Paul, Matthew, Mark, Luke, or John were Protestants, you know."

"So what?"

"So I'd listen to the Catholic Church when she speaks about the Bible or about anything else. After listening to some of the boys up on the walk, I can only conclude that the Bible is too strong a book for weak minds. It should never be allowed in the hands of the ignorant. It does them more harm than good."

"Is that why you keep away from it, Penney?" put in Bob.

"That's unkind of you, Mr. Anderson. You know I have the Gospels right here in my cell; that I read them in preference to the pretty preaching of . . ."

"Say, I meant to ask you: What in the world did you tell that lady preacher last Sunday? She came to my cell looking like a torch singer whose flame had just been doused."

"She converted me, Penney," Elliott said. "Better be nice to her."

"I was, kid."

"Yes, you were! No kiddin', Tom, what did you do to her?"

The Penney chuckle was good to hear in the prison's gray gloom. "Well, she wanted me to give testimony, to make a profession of Faith. I did."

"Yes, you did!"

"Honestly, Bob. That's exactly what I did. I can't get up and yell like Skeeter does. I don't get that stuff at all. I suppose it's all right for them; but I'm a Catholic."

Bob's laugh was short and guttural.

"This good lady preacher," continued Tom, "has been after me ever since I've been down here. She always asks for a profession of Faith. Last Sunday I gave her the only one I know."

"Let's hear it."

"Sure. If you promise to be quiet and make no interruptions."

"O.K."

"Well, I came to the door just where I am now and said: 'Lady, here's my Profession of Faith: "I believe in God, the Father Almighty, Creator of heaven and earth; and in Jesus Christ, His only Son, our Lord, who was conceived by the Holy Ghost, born of the Virgin Mary, suffered under Pontius Pilate, was crucified, died and was buried; He descended into hell; the third day He arose again from the dead; ascended into heaven, sitteth at the right hand of God the Father Almighty; from thence He shall come to judge the living and the dead. I believe in the Holy Ghost; the Holy Catholic Church; the Communion of Saints; forgiveness of sins; the resurrection of the body and life everlasting. Amen."

There was a momentary pause before Bob said, "So that stopped her, eh?"

"Why wouldn't it?" cried the newcomer. "It's all she teaches and more. But, say Penney, I didn't hear you say anything about Purgatory or the Bible in there."

"Purgatory, kid, is an invention of Divine Mercy for rats like you and me. We may not be good enough to go straight to heaven, but now that we're baptized and trying to live and die right, we're not bad enough to go to hell. That's why I want Bob to join us."

"The only true word in that pretty speech was 'rat.' "

"Say, Anderson, I don't know your gripe, but perhaps a bit of religion would do you good. You're as sour as vinegar. Tell me more about the Catholic Church, Penney."

"If you're interested, kid, I'll get you a catechism. The Catholic religion changed the world for me. It's made the days in this Death House the happiest of my life. Now I'm not only not afraid of death, I'm even anxious to meet it; for I know it will lead me to God."

"That's the kind of talk I like to hear."

"Oh, horse feathers!" came Anderson's disgust. But then he caught himself. "Well, I suppose that is the right kind of talk for you to hear if you've got to go next week, kid. But you see, I don't have to go. Ever hear of Buford T. Stewart?"

"Who's he? My mouthpiece is named Stewart, but not Buford T."

"He's the guy who was with Penney in Lexington last September 27. He's the guy who bumped off Marion Miley and her mother. He's the guy — "

"Robert H. Anderson, do you swear to tell the truth, the whole truth, and nothing but the truth?" broke in Penney in mock judicial tones.

"So help me God," came Anderson's quick reply. "Penney got sore because I wouldn't go through with him on a rotten whisky deal. He nurses the grudge for a couple of years. Then, when he's picked up in my car, which he stole from in front of my Club, he names me as accomplice. Me, mind ya, who wasn't even near Lexington!"

"Bob, you're the coolest cucumber outside a deep freeze."

"Where's this guy, Stewart?"

"Six feet under. He died February 2."

"Hmmm," grunted the newcomer. "Dead men tell no tales. But then, Anderson, dead men can't take the witness stand either. How are you going to get this tale to the judge and jury?"

"Easy. This dead man's blonde girl friend saw him get into my car with Penney the night of the murders."

"Thought of all the angles, haven't you?"

"Oh, he's clever, kid. But if he's thought of all the angles, he's missed some of the curves. And he hasn't thought of all the angles at that."

"No?"

"No. He's forgotten the angle of truth and the angle of coincidence."

"Whaddya mean 'coincidence'?" asked Anderson anxiously.

"Bob didn't you ever think that all this will strike some people as strange, especially since you said nothing about any of it when I testified against you in Lexington. You didn't even take the stand. It will strike most people as quite a coincidence that Stewart's name never entered the case until after he was dead."

"Haw!" derided Anderson. "My mouthpiece takes care of that perfectly and in so doing makes something of a hero out of you, Penney."

"Yeah?"

"Yeah! You'll call it another technicality, I suppose. But I'll remind you again that many a man has been saved by just such a technicality."

"What's the new one?"

"You were convinced, Penney, that no one could be convicted on the testimony of an accomplice. So you saw a swell chance to get square with me over that liquor deal and at the same time cover up on Stewart, your real accomplice."

"Whew!" whistled Penney in appreciation. "That is new! Send your lawyer to me next time he comes down, Bob. Maybe I'll have something to say to him. But right now let's talk of more important things."

"More important?" howled Anderson.

"Sure. This kid has only a week to live. Kid, you're going to face God soon. When we're not talking about Anderson's plan to get out of here, we do a much more sensible thing. We pray in kind of a round robin. One prays aloud as long as he can. As soon as he stops another takes it up. When he's through, the third goes on. And so we eat up hours of our time. How does that sound to you? Want to try it?"

"Sounds O.K. But let me get a little used to this cell, will ya? I'll try the bed and fix the chair and table to my liking. But tell me; aren't we ever bothered by the guards here?"

"They don't hang around much. Here comes one now, though. See you later."

Tom Penney went back to his table and the unfinished letter on it. He picked up his pencil, but instead of writing, stared ahead. After some moments he stirred uneasily and asked himself why it was that he felt so much less peace down here in Death Row than he had felt up on "the walk"? He had much better quarters — more light and air; more room and more freedom. Bob and Baxter were practically at his elbow. He really had company although he was supposed to be in solitary confinement. Skeeter was from his home town and he had known Anderson since reform school days. But something was wrong. Definitely wrong.

He looked at the letter before him and wondered if his uneasiness came from any neglect of the practices the good nuns had taught him. But no, as he checked each one he saw that he had been scrupulously faithful to all. What was wrong? He did not feel the same fervor in his prayer that he had felt up on "the walk." God did not seem so near as He had seemed in that dark little hole-in-the-wall where he had spent his winter and spring. But Father George had warned him about that. The priest had told him all life is undulant; that if today we are buoyant and find life wonderful, tomorrow we may be as gloomy and as grouchy as an old shrew — and all for no apparent reason. Tom knew all that was true, but he was surprised to learn from the priest that the same things happened in prayer; that one day we felt as if we could put out our hands and touch God, the next, He was more distant than the most distant star and prayer then seemed like talking into a telephone whose wires had been cut. True, Tom had never found it as bad as that, but since coming down from "the walk" prayer had been different.

Suddenly he realized that nothing had been the same. He did not write his letters as easily and found less thrill in the ones he received. Books and magazines he read with effort. Even his drawing was forced. He had been happy up on "the walk." . . .

Then it came to him. Ever since arriving in the cell next to Bob Anderson, the one topic of conversation that had recurred and recurred was how he, Tom Penney, could free the man his testimony had convicted.

Drumming on the knuckles of his left hand with the pencil he held in his right, Penney went over the story Anderson had concocted for him. How diabolically clever it seemed. And yet, how stupid! Before they left Lexington Bob had sent him word that Buford Stewart was dead — killed in Louisville on February 1, in a street fight.

Suddenly Tom stopped drumming and stiffened to sharp attention as he remembered it was on February 2, just ten days before they were transferred from the Fayette County Jail that Bob had tossed him a magazine with the note inside about Stewart's death. How rapidly Anderson's mind had worked! But was it Anderson's? Tom tried to remember whether the Louisville lawyers had been there that day. He could not be sure. But he was very sure that they had been most busy ever since; for after every one of their visits, Bob had some new detail to add to his story.

Tom smiled sarcastically, got up and walked to the window. He was thinking of Bob's latest remark about Stewart's blonde girl friend having seen them drive off in Bob's Buick. Another plant, he thought. Another detail to perfect the plot. And what was that other thing about no one being convicted on the testimony of an accomplice? These lawyers were forging a chain with no weak links. Every item, even his motive for speaking, was covered. They would make him, Penney, true to the code of the underworld even as he vented his grudge on Anderson. That was what they meant by this thing about no one being convicted on the testimony of an accomplice. But where was he, Tom Penney, ever to learn such a technicality of the law?

He walked to the door of his cell and called softly. "Hey, Bob."

"Yeh?" came the equally soft reply.

"You said something a while ago that set me thinking. Is it true that a man cannot be convicted on the testimony of his accomplice?"

"So I hear."

"Where did you hear it?"

"Right here in Eddyville."

"But, Bob, how could I have ever known that before you told me?"

"Couldn't someone else have told you?"

"Who?"

"The cops at Lexington before the trial."

"How would they know?"

"Dicks know plenty of law. . . ."

"And some lawyers think they know quite a bit about some dicks, don't they? Did Nicholson tell you all this?"

"What difference does that make? The only question before us is: Are you going to use it?"

"What did he have to say about our chances for a re-trial?"

"We won't hear anything until the fall."

"Well, that gives me plenty of time to think over your question."

"Listen, Penney," Bob said after a pause. "You're anxious for me to become a Catholic, aren't you? Well, I'm in your hands. Set me free or get me a commutation to life, and I'll join the Catholic Church. How about it?"

Tom Penney walked to the opposite side of his cell and stared out the high open window. A lazy puff of cloud moved dreamily across the square of sky framed by the window. As the faint and fading end of it drifted beyond the frame's heavy edge Tom turned back to his table . . . "His soul and the souls of others . . ." With a shake of his head he picked up his unfinished letter and stared at it.

Dear Sister Robert Ann:

Just received your very interesting letter, and as usual, Sister, it inspired me. I know your stay in Chicago must have been interesting. . . . I am extremely grateful for your visit to the Shrine of St. Jude for me and also for the Novena to the Little Flower on my behalf.

Sister, you don't know what good you have done and do me. The privilege of writing to you gives me three or four hours of good, sound thinking, which is something to be thankful for.

"Yes," said Tom to himself, "and much more profitable than thinking of a way to get out of here and how to get others out." Thereupon he lifted his pencil and drew himself into the table. When Sister Robert Ann received the letter, it ran on:

I wrote to Mrs. Fenwick only yesterday and I'm afraid I told her more about the wonderful sister she has than the wonderful birthday cake she gave me and my appreciation of her kindness.

I've been reading *Little Canticles of Love* (a pamphlet). It must have belonged to Sister Eleanor Jean. It has her name in it. Its contents are very beautiful. It seems as though God is really present and you are talking directly to Him. Oh, Sister, if I could only be as good as I want to be.

The Chaplain came down tonight and was talking to the boy in the next cell to me. He is to be executed July 3. He is a Protestant and was baptized here. I gave him a book of devotions. He likes the prayers. There is no hope for him here, Sister; but there certainly is great hope for him hereafter.

Some people might think we have strange conversations. We often speak of death as if we loved it. There can't be much wrong with a soul that can face death so calmly. Do you think so?

Sister, I know this is a question for my confessor, but I want to ask you, too. Is it a very great sin to tell a little lie to save the soul of another and maybe the souls of several? Don't answer if you had rather not.

Sister, I started this at noon yesterday. It is now 1 a.m. Saturday, so if it doesn't make sense, don't blame me. We have talked, prayed, eaten, sung, etc. — and I slept while the radio was on from 4:30 to 8:30. It isn't easy to write sensibly when your mind is distracted every few minutes.

There are five of us in the Annex now. We are of three different Faiths. . . . We have an agreement: when one man offers a prayer, we all do, one at a time. Then when it makes the round, someone will feel ashamed of having said so little and will begin all over again. That keeps us going for over two hours sometimes. Of one thing I am absolutely sure: we couldn't spend the time in a better way. . . .

May God bless you, Sister, and give you strength and courage to go on encouraging others as you have.

Your unworthy but very devoted friend in Christ,
Tom Penney

Sister admitted to herself that it was a jumbled letter, but wrongly laid the blame for the jumble on the boy "in the next cell," William Elliott, who was to die the night before the Fourth. She could not know it was Bob Anderson who had upset Penney. But if Sister could have read between the lines whereon the question about the gravity of a lie "to save the soul of another and maybe the souls of several" appeared, she would immediately have sent a kind, but very forceful and eloquently clear exposition of the evil of *all* lying.

But the question bothered Penney very little the entire next week, for the boy in the next cell took all his attention. The 28th, 29th, and 30th of June flew by. July 1 and 2 had even swifter wings. Then came the 3rd. Tom was up early and watched with fascination and an ever mounting excitement the proceedings customary in a death house the day a man is to "go." He thought it was sympathy for young Elliott who was living his last day on earth that pitched him to such keen interest, but the letter he wrote his mother late that night told that all unconsciously he had been going through something like a dress rehearsal of his own last day.

He began the letter at 10 p.m. "He is to go at midnight," wrote Tom. "I am sure God is waiting for him." Then immediately he began to write of himself. "Of course we are praying for another chance, Mother; but if that should be denied, I want you to know that I am not afraid to die. . . . I feel sure that God will be good to me; for though I have failed Him miserably here on earth, He understands my heart and forgives."

Penney got up, walked to the window and stared at the stars. He was not writing easily tonight, though he felt full to over-flowing with truths that needed to be told to his mother. He looked at the lonely night sky and wondered. But hurried footsteps coming along "the walk" pulled him from the window to the door of his cell. He saw Buchanan gesture to the men in the Death Room. Their high pitched voices and excited exclamations set Tom's hands gripping the cold steel bars. Guards, electricians, newspapermen, preachers, and even the undertaker crowded in front of the next cell. All Tom could hear was: "A stay! A stay!"

Twenty minutes later he was back at his letter, and again it was only the first few lines that were about the boy next door. "He does not die after all! At least not yet. My prayers are answered. He had eaten his last meal; had only two hours to go. But then came an Act of God; nothing less. So try not to worry about me, Mother. God is still God — and everything will come out O.K."

With this excitement still upon him he wrote a letter to Sister Laurentia telling her the stirring details. She was rather elated to be able to hand such a letter to Father Donnelly on his next visit to the Hospital. She watched him as he read and thought she knew the source of the light that suffused his features as his eyes went down the page.

"Exciting, wasn't it?" she said as the priest folded the letter. "Think of it: the undertaker was standing there waiting for the body!"

"Yes," said Father George quietly. "But that's not what excites me, Sister. It's the fact that Father Libs has promised Tom Communion on the eighth of this month. What a relief that is! I've been worried lately, Sister. Tom has sent me three letters in quick succession. Each showed him more and more troubled."

"About what?"

"That's what has had me worried: he doesn't say. He mentioned Father Libs and Communion, but I'm sure there is something else. However, this letter gives me comfort." Then as he handed it back he added, "Pray that Tom receives the Sacraments soon, Sister. I feel he needs very special grace; and that's where he'll get it. To tell you the truth, if my dad was not so sick, I'd spend my vacation in Eddyville, instead of Pennsylvania. Write that boy every week, won't you, Sister; and save all his replies for my return."

What really troubled Penney was the effect Elliott's dramatic stay of execution was having on Bob Anderson. Louisville's *Courier-Journal* had carried a colorful story of how Zeb A. Stewart, Elliott's attorney, had made a dramatic dash from Frankfort, where the Court of Appeals had denied him a writ of *coram nobis,* to Louisville, where he was successful in obtaining from Federal Judge, Shackelford Miller, a writ of *habeas corpus.*

The excitement of the denial at the State's Capitol, the telegram to the Federal Court in Louisville, the arrival in town after that Court had closed, the taxis to the Clerk's house, then to the Judge's home, and finally that urgent telephone call to Jess Buchanan to stop the execution, interested the chunky Anderson little. What fascinated him, and what had him plaguing Penney with sly hints and heated arguments was the line-up of reasons Stewart had presented to obtain the writ, chief among them being: that Elliott had been convicted on perjured evidence (How that fitted into Bob's case!); that two jurors, Gus Wells and Gabe Thomas, had said before the trial that if they were chosen on the jury they would send Elliott to the chair; that one juror, Bob West, was related by marriage to Joe Tuggle, the Whitley County Jail turnkey, whom Elliott murdered in an attempt to escape while waiting to be taken to prison on a 21-year armed robbery sentence (Bob had some facts about his own jurors!); that there was a conspiracy to convict Elliott regardless of the law and the evidence (He could say the same about Lexington and his own case!); finally, the most important witness for the defense, Grant B. Walker, was unable to testify because he was now in the army and stationed in Iceland.

"Tom," whispered Anderson late one afternoon toward the end of July, "we have a much better case than Elliott. He didn't die. We won't if you will only talk."

If Father Donnelly could have heard these whispered conversations he might have gone to Eddyville even before he went to Pennsylvania and the bedside of his dying father. But he had no slightest inkling how Elliott's stay was affecting all in Eddyville's House of Death. The thing that was on his mind was Tom's lack of the Sacraments.

But Father George did not have to wait until his return for the news he most desired. He had just arrived in his old home at White Haven, Pennsylvania, when he was handed an envelope carrying a penmanship he now knew quite well. Even before he unpacked, he opened that envelope and read:

> . . . I received the Sacraments Wednesday. Oh what joy! Especially as I had almost given up hopes. I think I like Father Libs now. Don't misunderstand me, Father. You know I always liked him, but I felt there was a certain amount of authority he was not exercising. But then I realize, too, that you had spoiled me and perhaps I expected too much. But my soul needs attention. I am doing my best, Father, but that seems so little. . . .

As Father Donnelly was frowning over the difficulty Tom was experiencing in getting to know Father Libs, the prisoner was frowning over a new difficulty from another quarter. He felt completely out of sorts. At first he blamed the heat. July had been hot, but August made him claim they had gone "from the frying pan into the fire." His statement could almost be taken literally, for the great stone house held the heat of the sizzling days' sun and made the nights utterly miserable. Next he blamed his own sensitiveness and selfishness. He missed Father Donnelly's visits, and Sister Robert Ann had failed to write him the week she shifted from summer school in Louisville back to the Hospital in Lexington. Now his own mother seemed to be misunderstanding him completely.

It was this that capped the climax of a series that had begun when Captain Rankin refused him the water colors Sister Mary Laurentia had sent for him to use on his drawings. From that moment everything seemed to go wrong and everyone irritated him. Bob and Baxter — even Trent, a newcomer, in the next cell

— got on his nerves. His outgoing mail, held up for censoring, failed to reach his friends at the time he desired. The letters that came in seemed always from the wrong parties and held the wrong messages. The radio angered him, and he turned from the newspapers in disgust. But so long as he had been able to write to his mother and feel that she would understand all, he knew some measure of contentment. But now . . . Well, the morning's mail held a letter which showed that even she had completely misread his outpouring about the nuns. She took his compliment to the Sisters as a condemnation of herself. How could she do it?

Tom looked around his cell. Everything in it spoke to him of the sympathy and interest of these good religious. The tiny Stations on the wall, the stacks of books, magazines, and papers on the floor, the rosary beads lying on his pillow, the letters on his desk, the cardboard carton in the corner with its litter of candy bars, even the drawing paper on which he had put so many images of the Child and His Mother . . . all was from these two Sisters of Charity. How could he fail to speak of them when he was writing out his heart? They had visited him at the jail in Lexington. They had traveled the three hundred miles and more to see him in Eddyville. Never a week passed that one of them did not write. How could his own mother fail to realize all they meant to him? Had they not visited her at South Spring Street? Did she not see for herself that they were angels?

When Anderson broke in on his thoughts with a question, Penney snapped so sharp an answer that he immediately cried: " 'Scuse me, Bob. I'm not myself these days. Either the heat is driving me nuts or there's a devil in this cell."

A thundershower in the late afternoon brought temporary relief and Tom took advantage of the comparative coolness of the late night and early morning to write to his mother:

> Your letter came yesterday. I am glad you made your trip O.K. despite the heat. It is certainly warm here. I was just sitting around waiting to smother when a shower came along and cooled us off a bit. . . .

I get the blues at times and occasionally get terribly lonesome. If it wasn't for the Sisters, what would I do? They keep me well supplied with books to read, and I read them from cover to cover. . . . Mother, please understand, it is not that they have succeeded in something at which you have failed. Never! It is only that they have brought out the good you put there. So don't feel that you have failed. You haven't! And I know you will always love the Sisters for their kindness to me and the assistance they have given to my spiritual welfare. . . .

Once he had put that in the mail he felt better and for a few days knew some of his old peace and happiness. But just as the high fever of August broke, word came to him that almost broke his spirit: Father George was off to war as a chaplain.

Now what was he going to do? Father Libs came but once a month, and he was always in such a hurry that he could only stand at the door for a few moments and talk from there. How could anyone talk out soul problems with the entire cell block and a couple of guards as audience? But even if he could disregard all these, there was something about Father Libs that kept Tom silent. What was it? The man was kind enough but . . . Suddenly Tom's eye fell on one of his own drawings. It was that of the Sorrowful Mother. "Yes," he said softly, "you are here, Mother. So is Jesus. And I should be content. But, Mother, so is the devil, and I am miserable." To ease the tension he snatched up his pen and wrote:

Dear Father Donnelly:

I suppose you think I have forgotten my friends entirely. But that is not true. I am terribly down in the dumps and there's the whole story. Your letter came last Friday. I have written several answers to it in my mind, but just could not seem to get any of them on paper. I don't suppose you ever had anything like that happen to you, Father; but I can tell you it gives one a very unhappy feeling. I don't think there is anything seriously wrong. I am just more disgusted than anything else.

Lieutenant Merviss sent me your photos, enlarged from the snap you gave me. I think they are very good of you and appreciate them extremely. I wrote to him and thanked him for his kindness.

So you are going to be a Lieutenant, too. Well, Father, I know you are eager to do your bit, but war, war, war . . . It is all so unnecessary. So much horror and grief — and what is it all about? Does anyone know? My only contribution to the War Effort is a prayer that it will cease. . . .

. . . Father, I drew some sketches of the Blessed Mother and the Sacred Heart of Jesus, some with Him carrying His Cross; some of the Little Flower, St. Vincent de Paul, and St. Jude — and even one of myself. All of them are for you. They are not so good, Father, but maybe some children will enjoy them. You may use my picture for most any purpose: bugs, mice, moths, garden insects, and even snakes. You told me yours would keep mice away. I know mine will do better than that.

Next week is to be Mission Week here in the pen. So Father Libs told me. He and another priest will be here all week. I hope I may see a lot of them during that time. . . . Father Libs is as nice as can be to me, but I just can't seem to give him my confidence. I guess the trouble is with me. I don't feel right with myself, Father. I wish I could tell you just what it is. . . .

I hope you get to see Mother before you go. . . . Let me know when you are leaving and all about what lies ahead. I hope you don't forget me in your prayers.

When Tom broke the news to Bob that Father George was off to join the colors, the latter came back with so hearty a "Good luck to him!" that Penney secretly wondered if Anderson was glad to have the priest out of the way.

"Guess that ends my visitors," mused Tom somewhat dolefully. "The Sisters can't come again, and I know none of my family will ever make the trip."

"Cheer up!" came Bob's cry. "I'll share all mine with you. My lawyers ought to be here today or tomorrow."

Tom went back to his drawings wondering if he wanted to see those lawyers. When Bob's voice came a little later in evident effort to cheer him up and ended with an exhortation that Tom make the most of the companionship in the cell block saying that "birds of a feather always flock together," Tom replied: "Now I know why there are six of us."

"Six?"

Then Bob heard the testiest remark Penney made all this trying summer. "Yes, six!" he snapped. "For besides the five of us scheduled for the hot seat, there's a devil here from hottest hell — and has been here for months! Here's hopin' the Fathers drive him out during Mission Week."

CHAPTER EIGHT

God Gives Compensation

Tom's conviction that he was living not only in the omnipresence of God but in the very specific presence of the devil, showed itself in most of the letters he wrote during these weeks. But oddly enough not a word of it crept into his correspondence with Sister Robert Ann. That is why she could not understand Father Donnelly's uneasiness about Tom the day the priest came to say good-by before setting off for training.

Father George had hardly left the hospital precincts when the slim Director of Nurses was re-reading her late mail to see if she could detect the cause of the priest's grave concern. The first one she picked up was of July 5. It ran:

Dear Sister Robert Ann:

Your letter came yesterday. Your package, the day before. And Sister, I want to say you could have given me nothing that I would appreciate more. This little *Manual of Prayers* is truly beautiful! I became so absorbed in it that I did not know it had an index until I had read clean through. I like especially the Prayer for Perseverance. I shall read it daily until I know it by heart.

The Holy Face will melt the heart of the most wicked. I love it. I find it much more effective than any other illustration. To gaze on His Holy Face and think of the Agony He endured makes me realize how utterly unworthy I am of the least favor. My heart nearly bursts, Sister. I forget my own little troubles and only want to give and give until I give all . . . and that seems too little. I see now why my life has been so empty. But it shall never be empty again! I pray each day for wisdom and strength to resist temptation — and an ever increasing love for *Him*.

I had word from Father Libs that at last I will be able to receive the sacraments the 8th. Thank God with me and for me, Sister.

Bob asked me to thank you for the rosary and the book.

The boy next to me also wishes me to thank you, Sister. Poor kid, he was all ready to go, had eaten his last meal and even talked with the undertaker. But God extended His mercies.

Well, Sister, it is almost 5 a.m. I shall say Good Day and join you in prayer in just a moment — or do you arise at 5 down there at Louisville? I shall say my Beads — 15 Mysteries — for your intentions.

May God bless you and reward you eternally for your kindness to

Tom Penney.

Surely nothing was wrong with a boy who can write like that, thought Sister, and turned to July 12's letter and read:

All your letters are food for thought. That's why I cherish them so. I know I have advanced greatly in knowledge these past few months. I also know the greater our knowledge, the greater our responsibility. But isn't it also true; the greater our sacrifice the greater our reward? That is why I'm really working overtime.

I have read everything I could lay my hands on, Sister. I think I got most out of *Faith of Our Fathers*. All the things you send I read from cover to cover. I do not recall the article by Father LeBuffe in the June *Messenger*. Bob has the magazine at the moment, I shall get it and read it again. Father LeBuffe has another article in the July issue and it ends with a truly beautiful prayer.

Whenever I come across such a prayer I offer it, together with all my other prayers, works, and sufferings, in thanksgiving for God's glorious gift of Faith, and in reparation for the many sins of my past life. I continue this until I know the prayer by heart, then I select another.

I received the sacraments Wednesday, Sister. So ask the Little Flower to thank God and help me keep my resolutions. I have vowed (to myself) a penance almost beyond physical endurance if I break my resolution, so you see I need help.

The dignified angle at which Sister Robert Ann usually carried her head was lost as she bent over her desk and read the next letter quickly. She was becoming more and more puzzled about Father Donnelly's attitude with each succeeding paragraph. The letter of the following week, July 19, had given her more than one chuckle the day she received it. Even now, despite her preoccupation, it caused her to smile. Tom had written: "You ask when do I sleep. The answer is easy. I don't. At least not much lately. It is altogether too warm. I manage to doze for 3 or 4 hours in the 'wee morning.' "

But the smile faded and the frown returned as Sister now read: "Suppose Mass is said for me the 11th or 12th of August. You see, the second Wednesday, the 12th, is Father Libs's day here. Am I expecting too much in one day? You must thank Sister Rose William for me. I am so grateful!

"Sister, I do not allow myself to think of liberty; but if the miracle should happen, I have made up my mind — or should I say God has made it up for me? — I shall spend the remainder of my life doing good for Him. I would feel out of place in the world doing anything else now."

Before the frowning Director of Nurses could finish the letter a knock came on the door. When she saw who it was, she cried: "You're just the person I want to see. Will you tell me what Father Donnelly is fussing about? Just before he left today he told me Tom was having trouble, and that I was to pray extra hard for him. You know we never interrogate priests on such matters, but Father saw I wanted to, so he said I would detect the trouble if I studied the letters Tom wrote. I'm studying them. They show me a man growing more and more in love with God with a love that wants to express itself in love's best language — sacrifice. He seems to be in perfect condition."

"What's the date of that letter you are reading?"

"July 26."

"That's over a month ago, Sister. Have you studied your August mail?"

"You sound as if you believed Father George is right in his

worry. Let's look at them together. Here's August 1. What's in it? — Here, look at the very first page. We find Tom acting as an Apostle. He had asked me for a Catechism. I sent it. He tells me in this letter that it was for the boy in the next cell — that is either Elliott or Trent. Tom tells me he has taught him how to say the rosary, meant to have Father Libs talk to him, but since he failed, I was to ask the Little Flower to help. Then a few lines about my coming retreat and a promise to pray for me. Anything wrong there?"

"Not a thing," was Sister Mary Laurentia's quiet comment. "Let's have the next."

"I was on Retreat. So he missed a week. But here's the one for August 13. In it he speaks of the Mission. . . . "

Sister Robert Ann read aloud: "Father Libs came yesterday, but being in a rush as usual, I had only a word with him. But next month, the first week, he will be here all week with another priest — a Passionist. How I am looking forward to that! Sister, there are almost 1400 men here, only 86 of them are Catholics. Of course it is wonderful to have so few Catholics come here, but it would be even more wonderful to see a greater number than that leave here as Catholics. I think it is terrible that Father Libs comes here but once a month. I should be thankful to have him come at all, and I am — but I also know that a little more encouragement would be welcomed by all."

"Aha! Now we're getting to it," put in the older nun.

"Getting to what?"

"Go on."

Sister Robert Ann resumed her reading. "You see, you outside have work to do to take your time and attention. In here, we have nothing; and idleness is a root of evil. Of course God has given us a free will to resist evil; but, Sister, that will must be encouraged — especially when it is surrounded by so much evil. . . ."

"Stop there and tell me of whom that boy is speaking."

"Of himself, of course."

"Humph! You're not as keen as I thought."

"He says so. Here's his next sentence: 'I am speaking of the average man — myself as well as the next.' "

"He's speaking not so much of himself as of the next."

"Whom do you mean?"

"Bob Anderson."

"Oh, Sister, you must be mistaken. Tom has always spoken highly of Bob; has asked my prayers for him."

"We're bound to pray for our enemies."

"Now you're being funny. Look, Sister, Tom's next sentence tells you I am right. He says: 'I, not so much as others, because I have no associates to influence me.' There, now!"

Sister Mary Laurentia's face did not change. "Will you let me see the rest of that letter?" When the somewhat aroused Director of Nurses handed it over, the elder nun read: "The devil comes around. We have some pretty stiff battles, but I have wrestled so long with him that I am pretty well acquainted with all his holds and have prepared my defenses. When I learn to control my temper I'll be a happy man indeed. Must say Good Night now and God bless you. Your friend in Christ, Tom Penney."

"Well," she sighed handing back the letter, "I still say you ought to learn how to read between the lines. But I'm very happy to learn I'm not the only one to whom he gives the devil — "

"Sister!"

"Oh, don't be so shocked. I had begun to think Tom had me down as an Exorcist and you as a Porter. I know he doesn't realize we women can't receive Minor Orders."

"What in the world are you talking about?"

"About Tom Penney, my dear. His first letter to me from Eddyville began: 'Just a few lines to assure you that the devil hasn't taken full charge, although he has attempted to do that very thing on many occasions.' And from that day to this he talks to me about the devil and to you about 'the Pearly Gates.' "

"Oh go on, you!"

"I'm going, Sister. Read this while I'm gone."

Sister Robert Ann read rapidly. "Dear Sister: We've had a little shower tonight and, for a change, it is very pleasant here.

I'll catch up on my sleep if it will stay as cool as this for a day or two. I hope your eyes are better. How I wish I could lend you mine. I have just finished reading the book you sent — *The Little Secret* — I could add a chapter of my own, Sister. Shall I tell you my 'little secret'? My little secret is this: 'My Jesus, in my agony I love You more and more. Grant me the strength to endure it.' "

The nun slipped into her chair and continued reading: "It may not sound like much to others, but it holds a world of meaning for me. To some people it may sound crazy; and I know countless folk who would laugh to hear me say the most serious and the happiest hours of my life have been spent in a death cell."

Sister rested her forearms on her desk and was again conscious of the gnawing puzzle which had set her re-reading her own mail. Surely someone was mistaken, she thought. She could find nothing in the lines or between the lines except holiness and happiness.

Sister Robert Ann finished the last lines which ran: "It is now about 3 a.m. Good night. And may all heaven bless you." She shook her neatly white-capped head and said: "What can these people be fussing about?"

Just then Sister Mary Laurentia returned. "Did you read between the lines?"

"There's nothing there to be read."

"Good-by, Sister. I'm off. So are you! Pray harder for Tom."

Sister Robert Ann's forehead furrowed. She knew Sister Mary Laurentia. She knew that under all her wit and dry humor there was keen and sound judgment. With a new anxiety she sat down and took up her next letter, that of August 26, and read carefully.

Tonight is another of those dreadful nights: two men go just after midnight. I am back up on "the walk" where I was when you were here. Just for tonight I gave my cell to the men who are to die. It is more convenient for them — and more pleasant for me. We have been arguing the Bible up here. They are trying to tell me Jesus had three brothers and one sister. I can't convince them that they are wrong. . . . People should have a certain amount of intelligence before being allowed to read the Bible. . . . It is too strong a book for weak minds anyhow. Perhaps they rubbed me the wrong way, Sister, but you must remember I am rather touchy where our Blessed Mother is concerned — and am a proud and fiery defender. . . .

With something like impatience Sister Robert Ann closed the file and slipped it into her lower drawer. "What *can* they be talking about?" was her final remark.

A little light came the next morning when she found a note on her desk saying: "The envelope bears my name, but contains your letter. No second vision or ability to read between the lines needed.

Sr. M.L."

Quickly a slender hand extracted the letter. Blue-gray eyes flew across the page:

Really, Sister, I don't mean to complain. It is just that I am not at peace with myself. The dangers that beset my path are not so terrifying, but the problems are too difficult for me to solve alone. That is why I so crave advice and need someone to understand. . . .

Nothing has happened to me that would not please you. I am promised the sacraments this week. . . . I shall be sure to be as worthy as a human can be. Please do not think me ungrateful or discontented. It is just my ignorance and my inability to express myself clearly that may mislead you.

Yes, I received your letter since Retreat. I hope I do see Father Eugene this week. I did not know of your additional responsibilities, Sister. I shall pray the harder for you.

I am tangled up as to whom I am writing, but, as usual, it is for both.

Always your friend in Christ,
Tom Penney.

He did not see Father Eugene that week; for a Passionist from Chicago and not one from Louisville was assigned to give the Mission at Eddyville.

It was just about midmorning on Monday, Labor Day, that Tom looked through the vertical bars of his cell door and saw a bushy-haired, rather stocky man come along from "the walk."

"Are you Tom Penney?"

"I am."

"Well, I was assigned to give a mission at Eddyville, but judging from my late mail, the mission is all for you. Do you know Father Eugene of Louisville and Sister Robert Ann of Lexington?"

"I know the one through the other and now I know Father Brian of Chicago, don't I?" and the prisoner squeezed the hand the priest had thrust through the bars. "But tell me, Father, how much time have you got?"

"All the time in the world, Tom. Why?"

"Get Captain Rankin to let you in here. I have a thousand and one questions to ask."

It was done. Father Brian Mahedy, C.P., sat in that cell so near the Chair of Death and talked with Tom Penney until nearly noon. Then Tom insisted that he leave him before dinner and go to Bob Anderson.

Early that afternoon the two prisoners were at their doors.

"Well, what do you think of him, Bob?"

"Nice fellow. But he's not Father George."

"There's only one Father George. But this man is close to him, don't you think?"

"Guess so. Fact is, Tom, I didn't have too much time with him; and there's more on my mind just now than religion. Nicholson tells me we'll hear next month."

"Does he expect good news?"

"He says 'Yes,' but the way he says it I know he means 'No.' So it looks as if it all depends on you again, Tom."

"Oh, no! — not this week, Bob. Not this week! No I simply won't be bothered with that this week. I was to Confession today. I'll receive Holy Communion tomorrow. And Father Brian will be back up here Thursday or Friday. Why don't you join me, Bob, in thinking only of God and your soul this week?"

"Why in hell don't you think of me and my life?" came the angry reply.

"Ah, Bob, don't talk that way. You know I'll do all I can for you when the time comes. But let's not cross bridges till we reach

them. This Father Brian is a real guy. Why don't you have as
earnest a talk with him as you do with your lawyers? Open up.
Tell him everything. Let him know you as you really are so
that he can direct you. The afterlife is much longer and much
more important than this life, Bob. Why not be smart?"

"Honest to God, Penney, there are times when I think you're
half priest. You've tried to convert everyone in this Death House.
You've been after Trent ever since he arrived next to you. You
were after Elliott before that. Why don't you leave me alone the
way you do Skeeter?"

"Because you've got brains, Bob, and Skeeter is proof that
'ignorance is bliss.' You know better. You're responsible. God will
be just with you. He'll be merciful with Skeeter."

Anderson's laugh was gratingly harsh. "Penney, if you ever
get out, go on the stage. You're a riot. . . . Hey, Skeeter!"

"Yeah?"

"Next time you see Penney out exercising, look close and find
out if he's got wings and a halo."

"Why?"

"Haven't heard a cussword out of him since we came from
Lexington. He's more pious than a parson. Wants me to make
the mission with him here in prison. He's getting holier than hell."

"That wouldn't be very hard, Mr. Anderson," put in Tom with
a light chuckle. "Think over what I said about making the mission. It will be a lot better than making a mistake. Bye now. I have
work to do."

This last was most true. Tom Penney was busy every waking
moment: reading, writing, drawing, praying. It was with zest he
now sat down to his table, for the talk with Father Brian had fired
him with more enthusiasm than he had felt in months. He must
prepare himself for Communion in the morning. Not another
word was heard from him that day.

Toward the end of the week he was writing Sister M. Laurentia
and Sister Robert Ann:

Father Brian was the missionary from Chicago. I had only two
talks with him, but they were full of understanding and I learned

much from him. He is the type that seems to know just what is on your mind before you speak, so it was easy for me to talk to him. Father Eugene wrote to him before he came here, telling him all about me.

Father Libs brought me Communion Tuesday and I had a chance to become better acquainted with him and I like him. He is just hard to know that's all. I plied Father Brian with so many questions I know he thinks I never saw a priest before. He preached in the Chapel, therefore, I could not attend. But I would not have missed seeing him for the world.

I feel more confident, more sure of myself. I have learned that the soul that endures always feels the weight of its burden, whereas the soul that yields, hardly feels it at all. Happy the souls who live in the state of resignation and have learned to will what God wills.

I know I have often been tempted to say there were evil spirits in things that seemed to take pleasure in thwarting me and the more petulant I showed myself the more irritating they became. But now I know that gentleness will cause us to look upon such things kindly and touch them delicately. I pray now to be strong to bear, pliant to yield, and above all kind! And I pray the grace to forgive all who have ever given me pain.

Of course, Sisters, I am quite sure it is impossible for you to realize just how much you have done for me. My heart is so filled with gratitude this moment that I could sing to high heaven.

That grand feeling, generated in no slight degree by Father Brian's talks, grew as September lengthened. Now the days were too short and the nights not long enough for Tom to accomplish all he desired; for Sister Robert Ann had enlisted the aid of Father Eugene Creegan, C.P., then stationed in Louisville, and Father Eugene through Father Brian had got Sister Francesca, an Ursuline of Owensboro, to write to Tom. Then the good priest exhorted the Magdalens in the Good Shepherd Convent in Louisville to adopt Tom as their protégé. So Tom could only sing of harvest time as Captain Rankin handed him larger bundles of mail each day.

There were longer silences in Tom's section of the Death House and Anderson grew resentful of the repeated cry: "I'm busy, Bob. Got to get this letter out today." It became routine for Tom to write five or six letters in a morning. On September 11 he bent over his table and wrote to Father Eugene:

I have been praying for a plausible excuse to write you. Not that I am adept in this particular line, as you will straightway see, but I've heard so much concerning you and your work, also of your wonderful kindness and sympathetic understanding that I feel I know you personally. All this is thanks to our mutual friends, the Sisters and Father Brian.

Sister Robert Ann forwarded the little prayer book. It is a treasure: it has the answer to so many things I have wanted to know. . . .

It took a terrible jolt to make me realize just how displeasing I had been to God, Father; and it is a petty price to pay for the joy and consolation He has given me. It is so astounding at times that it frightens me. I feel so unworthy of His tender love and mercies. I have so little to offer in return.

I tremble to think of having died a year ago with my soul in the condition it was. No, death is the easy way out. Preferably, I had rather live, but my constant and most ardent desire now is to do His Holy Will. Doing my own will has brought me misery, heartache, suffering, humiliation, and disgrace to those dear to me . . . besides being very displeasing to God.

Regardless of how long I may live — weeks, months, or years — I firmly resolve to do my very best to live and die in His friendship and favor. And who, I ask you, Father, can help me more to succeed than the most admirable and amiable Mother of God?

Father, I really enjoyed every moment of my very limited talks with Father Brian. He helped me much. He visited the Magdalens in Detroit on his way home and got them to promise to pray for me and also to write to me. I think I should like that. You see, I don't have any Catholic correspondents but those wonderful Sisters. Father Brian sent me some books from Chicago.

Please accept my thanks for the *Book of the Passion*. It will do much for me. May I ask you also to remember me in your prayers and then sometime when you have nothing better to do, write to yours

Very sincerely in Christ,

Tom P.

Then without pausing Tom began his next letter.

Dear Sister Mary Laurentia:

Your letter and books came today. *The Masterful Monk* came the first of the week. It was wonderful. *Jesus of Nazareth* and *God's Jester* came today. Father Brian also sent me four books: *The King's Achievement, By What Authority,* and *Loneliness* all by Robert Hugh Benson; and *The Long Way Home* by John Moody. I'll tell you all about them as I read them.

So you thought you'd catch me napping, did you? You may catch me forgetful of some of the other feast days, but not of our Blessed Mother. I may have talked too fast at that. Let's see. The 8th was the Nativity of the Blessed Virgin; Most Holy Name of Mary, the 12th: I'm sure of those two. The Seven Sorrows is the 15th and Our Lady of Mercy the 24th. How about it? Yes, Sister, I shall invoke her aid. I am sorry your eyes are no better; but I am confident this all-powerful intercessor will soon put all things right again. I can truthfully say she has not failed me yet. . . .

I just finished your drawings, and I know even she is pleased with them. They are good even if I say so myself. So good, that I will not worry if you give them away. When I say good, Sister, I only mean good for me. I'll mail them tomorrow in the folder with Father Donnelly's picture. You will keep this picture until I write to Mother and have her stop by for it, won't you?

As I am writing to Sister Robert Ann, too, I'll say good-by and thanks for the books. May God bless you and in His tender mercy restore your sight. I'll write again the middle of the week. . . .

Without taking time to put the above letter in its envelope, Tom addressed himself to Sister Robert Ann. After telling her about Father Eugene and the book he had sent; after insisting that he owed everything to the Sisters, he went on:

I do not know of anyone on earth who has as much as I do to be thankful for. It just does not seem possible that God could be so good to me when I have done so much to displease Him. But I dare not doubt His wonderful love. . . .

I remember reading this somewhere: A little child once said: "Mother, since nothing is ever lost, where do our thoughts and desires go?" "Into the memory of God," replied the mother, "there

to remain forever." "Forever?" gasped the child, then drew close
to its mother murmuring: "Forever! . . . I'm afraid."

If we think of it seriously, who will not make the same cry?
Suppose, Sister, every minute of our life represented a coin stamped
with our intention, and only those with God's image would pass as
currency in eternity. What millions there would be in counterfeit
money! Yes, I'd be a millionaire. But, Sister, if sorrow and submis-
sion to His Holy Will, and an ardent desire to love Him will open
the gates of heaven, then I have high hopes of seeing you in heaven.

Is Euphrasia Hall your new address, or shall I keep on sending
the letters to St. Joseph's? Yes, I would like to see it. I was so afraid
they would cut the tree in front, but I see they didn't. I believe I
told you I worked on that building. Thirteen years ago St. Joseph's
burned. All night long I carried patients in my arms over to the
Nurses Home. It was Milward's Funeral Home then. The last one
I carried died before I got there with him. He wasn't burned; just
old and feeble. The excitement proved too much for him.

I have no doubt of your success in your duties both to God and
the pupils, Sister. Your prayers give me more courage to pray for
you.

Always your friend in Christ,
Tom.

The morning was now gone. But before that day was done
Tom had two other letters ready for the mail. To his mother he
wrote: "I know September has been my unlucky month all my
life. And for that very reason I know it has not afforded you
much pleasure. But if you will look at it in the right way, Mother,
it won't be so hard to bear. This September I tell you to realize
that I could have come to a much worse end. Not in the eyes of
the world, of course, but in other eyes. . . . Mother, for my own
soul I am not the least bit worried. . . . I am not going to give
up yet. I will fight death as long as possible and in every way
I know. But . . . it is God's Will I want, Mother, and I know
He will not give us more than we can bear."

That theme and that enthusiasm stayed with Tom most of the
month. It was mid-September before he located Father Donnelly
at Harvard University, where the priest was attending the

Chaplains' School. Tom wrote immediately, telling of his newly acquired friends — the Passionists — and of their mutual, long-standing acquaintances: Bob Anderson and Skeeter and, of course, much about their mutual friends, the Nazareth nuns.

As the month neared its end, memory brought a spell of sadness to the prisoner. On September 28, the anniversary of the day Marion Miley lost her life, Tom Penney wrote to Sister Robert Ann saying that he "would prefer more pleasant memories" of that day and mentioning a letter he had just written to Sister Mary Laurentia.

The Director of Nurses hurried to the pharmacy where she demanded the latest letter from Eddyville. Sister Mary Laurentia did not joke or tease as she handed the slit envelope over. The simplicity and seriousness of the gesture almost startled Sister Robert Ann. She hurried back to her office and eagerly read:

> Your letter came today. As usual it made me very happy, but I am terribly afraid you overestimate my spiritual worth. . . .
>
> It is certainly comforting to know that God takes a personal interest in our salvation. Does He not tell us in His own words: "There shall be more joy in Heaven over one sinner doing penance than ninety-nine just." I am sure God alone knows how truly sorry I am for my sinful past. A year ago tonight . . . if they could only know I am sure they would understand. . . . Will you join me [in praying for them] especially Thursday and Sunday? I like to think they would do the same for me. . . .
>
> I need your prayers now more than ever for both temporal and spiritual goods. I may know my fate by the next time I write you. I pray that His will be done. Whatever happens this week, I hope it is for the best. But I will refuse to accept it as man's decision — only God's will please. I still have hopes of seeing and talking to you again. . . . Until next week I'll be thinking and wishing many good things for you.

The "next week" came for both those in Eddyville and those in Lexington, but it brought no word from the Court of Appeals. Instead God brought something new into Tom Penney's life as He sent into the Death House a spirit which that locality never knew before and is not likely to know again — it was a spirit of childhood with all its confident trust in, and abandonment to, the love of its Father; the spirit of simplicity and uncalculating generosity; of true holiness unblemished by any self-seeking. This spirit came in a bundle of letters from the Magdalens in the Good Shepherd Convent in Detroit.

As Tom Penney read them he blinked. He could not believe that in this sordid, lust-filthy, greedy world of ours there could be such utterly unselfish love. Could such innocence, such God-consciousness, such beautifully simple souls live in a century as sin-sodden as ours? Before he finished that first bundle of letters he was weeping. As he laid the last letter down he was actually sobbing in sheer joy at such contact with a sanctity unfeigned and utterly unconscious of itself.

This was really the beginning of a schooling in spiritual child-hood of this man who had been born again of the waters and the Holy Ghost, and who now must grow. Sisters Mary Laurentia and Robert Ann had always appeared to Tom as angelic. But, while accepting their teachings and carrying out their precepts to the best of his abilities, he always held these two Sisters in such high esteem that he would never even dream of attaining the sanctity he deemed was theirs. But the forty-nine Magdalens of Detroit were an entirely different matter. Here were women varying in age from the late teens to the scriptural three score and ten; women who had imprisoned themselves with and for the Prisoner of Love; some of them had known the world in all its worldliness and another some had known it not at all. Here were women of a type and a mentality Tom had never known. Now they wrote to him as to a long-lost and dearly loved brother. Tom was literally bewildered by what was actually God's compensation for the prisoner's loss of Father George to the army.

The letter that first set Tom sobbing ran:

Dear Mr. Penney:

The other evening, as we all knelt down in our Community Room to listen to the points for meditation, Mother began: "My dear Sister

Magdalens . . ." As we listened we thought she must be reading us a letter from Father Eaten, S.J. — it sounded so like our recent retreat master. But as the letter came to its end, what was our surprise and joy to hear: "Your friend, Thomas Penney." I was so touched I searched the faces as we filed out to Chapel and found tears in more than my own eyes.

How good God has been to you. What wonderful graces He has given you. It is our dearest wish that He continue to bestow on you His choicest blessings. But how sad it made us to learn you cannot receive our Lord as often as you desire. Since the day I heard that, I have been taking you with me in spirit to Communion. Each morning as I go up to receive the Sacred Host I tell our Jesus that you, too, desire to receive Him into your heart and that I wish somehow to share my privilege with you. On my way back I say the Magnificat in thanksgiving for all the graces that have been bestowed on you since your baptism. . . .

When Penney cleared his eyes and his throat, he turned the page and read:

Mother permitted us to write to the Apostleship of Prayer and send them a subscription for *The Messenger of the Sacred Heart* for you for one year. You ought to get it every month. If you don't, please let us know.

The next paragraph set him chuckling. . . .

Here's a peep into our family life. Mother is very particular about our meals. So every day after breakfast, she goes to the kitchen to see about our dinner. First one Sister will say: "Mother, please look at my soup." The second will say: "Mother, please look at my meat." Then comes: "Mother, please look at my vegetables." The youngest, just out of the Novitiate, who is usually washing dishes, and had nothing to show, began feeling very sorry for herself and determined to get something to show. So the next day she waited as patiently as she could until all the others were through with their "Please, Mother . . ." then she eagerly came out with: "Please, Mother, look at all my dirty dishes. . . ."

Hours went by as Tom Penney laughed and cried over forty-nine letters, each of which began with: "Live Jesus and His Cross," and ended with "Blessed be God!"

He was at last aroused from his absorption by the cry of "Hey, Penney!" It was Trent in the next cell. "Have you finished with today's paper?"

"Sorry, Herb, haven't even opened it."

"What have you been doing all morning — sleeping? You've been as quiet as a mouse — more quiet. I can hear those fellows."

"I've been reading some mail from my sisters."

"All morning?"

"Uh-huh. You see I've got half a hundred of them. I've just been adopted by forty-nine Magdalens up in Detroit."

"What's a Magdalen?" asked Anderson, who had been listening.

"The sweetest women in the world, Bob!" cried Tom. "You've never met anything like them. . . ."

"No?"

"No! Sisters Robert Ann and Mary Laurentia showed you something new in womanhood, didn't they?"

"Gosh!" exclaimed Anderson in evident puzzlement, "do you know I never once thought of those nuns as women."

Tom laughed. "They're flesh and blood, Bob. But they are something more. . . ."

"Yeah," cut in Anderson, "that's it. They are something so much more you never think of them as women. What is it?"

"It's grace, Bob. It's the Holy Ghost. It's sanctity. Those women are right. They live with God. The women we've known . . ."

"Ugh! But what's a Magdalen?"

"I really don't know, Bob. All I can say now is that they are different even from Sisters Robert Ann and Mary Laurentia. I lost Father George, but it seems to me that God is making up for it through Father Brian. That man got me Sister Francesca, an Ursuline in Owensboro as correspondent. I'll show you some of her letters. Best little 'cheer-er upper' I've ever met. Then he goes to Detroit and gets me forty-nine Magdalens and their Mother. I've just finished reading the mail they sent. I've been out of this world. I'm in love. All I can say now is what they say at the end of each letter: 'Blessed be God!'"

"Penney, you're nuts!"

CHAPTER NINE

Deeper Depths and Broader Horizons

SINCE mid-February in each of the letters Mrs. Leona Penney had been receiving week after week from Eddyville, Tom exhorted her "not to worry." But it was only as God was turning summer's greens to red, gold, russet, and flame, that she received letters that were distinctive because so substantially spiritual. She marveled at the depths her boy was touching and the broader horizons he was opening to her view. It was months before she realized that it was the Magdalens of Detroit and Louisville who were exerting a subtle influence on her son's mind and heart. As they wrote him their ordinary thoughts and told of their daily experiences, they were deepening his soul and giving him broader vistas of the spiritual world. Tom Penney found nothing ordinary about their thoughts or their thinking, and the experiences they considered simple, were to him utterly sublime. The more he learned of their life, its object, principles and practices, the more he absorbed a spirit about which America and the world at large, in this anxious, hurried, and very confused twentieth century knows too little.

Some will call it Faith. And they will not be wrong. But that substantive needs an adjective. It needs to be called vital and vitalizing, real and realizing Faith. It needs to be described as energetic and energizing Faith. For these Magdalens believe what they profess to believe; they live what they have learned and preach by their practices. God to them is not a word, a phantom, figure, convenience, convention, or even a conviction; He is no distant, dim, depersonalized blind force. He is their Ultimate, their Absolute, their All. To them He is as familiar as a Father; more real than reality, the Great Obvious Invisible whom they discover at every turn and turning. To them He is their Continual Creator who holds them ever in the hollow of His hands. Divine Providence to them is no dead theologic concept. It is their morning's coffee, their day's work, their physical aches and mental distresses as well as their innumerable hourly joys. To them God *is* God, and they are His children.

In his prison cloister Penney was assimilating these truths and, with a fluency that astonishes, was pouring them out as his written thoughts. In one letter he had said to his mother: "Have courage and patience. . . . Our troubles are only furrows which God makes in our hearts in order to sow His graces there. If injustices are patiently borne they will give at the end of day a peace that is extraordinary and a joy that is rare; for the seed cast by God has taken root and is blossoming."

In another: "God has certainly given you courage and strength, Mother. My suffering is nothing, dear, in comparison to yours — and that is precisely what hurts me most. If dying would relieve the pain in your heart, I would pray God to take me today! But it is not so simple as all that. We must do God's will, confident that it is for our best. I wish I knew something more to say that would cheer you. It will not help your heartache for me to tell you over and over how sorry I am. If it did, I would write ten times a day, rebuking myself for the suffering I have brought upon you. But all I say now is: Ask God for guidance and trust Him, knowing well that all this will one day bring not only relief but reward."

The mother not only trusted God, she thanked Him for the miracle He had wrought in the soul of her first-born. Late in the fall she discovered the source of the change. It came in a letter in which he was detailing their possible supports. With surprising force he had written:

Mother, I know the Sisters cannot help financially. These women take a solemn vow to serve God without pay once they have given up all their earthly possessions and inheritance to charity. They have dedicated their lives to the spread of Christianity throughout this vain, cruel, treacherous, and transitory world. And to me, Mother, that is positive proof of the Divinity of the Catholic Church.

Many people have been misled and hold very false opinions about nuns. Some think they have been disappointed in love. How wrong they are! Such people cannot begin to realize the beautiful lives of sacrificial love these Sisters lead; nor can they appreciate all the good that has been accomplished by their many organizations and charitable works — works which shall continue till the end of time.

There is one Order within an Order, Mother, that I would like to tell you about. They are called the Sister Magdalens and are governed by the Sisters of the Good Shepherd. Girls or women with problems go to the Good Shepherd to have them straightened out. Many of them do not wish to leave, so attracted are they by the goodness of God. So they remain and devote their lives entirely to Him. Many of them write to me. I'll send you one of their letters. I cry like a baby when I read many of them, they are so filled with saintly simplicity and childlike Faith.

The very next day Mrs. Penney had opportunity to judge for herself for Tom had forwarded a letter from Sister Magdalen of St. Helena. Its second page ran:

I want you to know, Mr. Penney, how much we appreciate your offer to say a "Hail Mary" for each of us every day. When you say mine will you kindly remember this intention: A young girl is going wrong. She sees her sin but has no desire to change. Ask our Lady to change her heart. How pleased we were to learn you admire St. Francis de Sales. His writings can be depended upon; for he not only preached perfection, he practiced it. I came across two of his quotations today: "Do not be disturbed about your imperfections, but always rise up bravely after each fall. Make a new beginning *daily*. There is no better means of progress in the spiritual life than to be continually beginning afresh." Isn't that consoling? St. Thérèse of the Child Jesus tells that God gets great glory from our falls; for they make us practice humility and contrition.

Your thoughts on reparation are very beautiful, Mr. Penney. You know that is our *life*. Our Holy Rule tells us to make reparation not only for our own sins, but to expiate the sins of others. Retreat Masters have told us that our Rule is the Fourth Degree of Humility, meaning that it is pure love of God. It tells us we should love to live unknown and despised. That is not easy for human nature, but it *is* possible. St. Augustine has said: "If others can do it, so can I!"

You know St. Augustine's youth was very wild. But once he became converted, he just flew to perfection. Such saints prove to us that we do not have to crush our human natures, but simply turn those very same human natures *toward God*. Look at Dorothy Day. She was a Communist. She is now fighting for the Catholic Faith, not only with the same ardor, but with the selfsame methods she used as a Communist. But now she strives to save souls for God. You see all she did was change her object. We can do the same. . . .

The following week Mrs. Penney was surprised to receive a letter directly from Detroit; and she was more surprised when she read it:

Dear Mother:

Since your Tom has adopted us as his sisters, he has made us your daughters, and since we are forty-nine you see what a large heart you must have to hold so many children.

We want you to know, dear Mother, that we are praying for you, begging God to give you the grace to bear this cross He has laid upon your shoulders. You can gain a lot of merit for yourself and your loved ones if you accept this trial with a submissive and humble heart. Think, dear Mother, of what our Saviour had to suffer for us. Think also of what this war is doing to the hearts of millions of mothers. You, at least, can keep in touch with Tom and you know where he is.

Oh, I know it is futile to try to console the heart of a mother, but we want you to realize that we are very proud to know your son and are most grateful to the priest who introduced us. We feel that your Tom is a chosen soul and that he received a wonderful grace from God when He gave him his Faith.

If you are able to write during this time of trial, we would be so glad to hear from you. We know nothing of the trouble except that the supreme penalty is to be paid. After all, who are we to condemn

a fellow mortal? We are all under sentence of death and shall pass
on sooner or later.

>   May God keep you in His Holy Heart for Time and Eternity.
>
>   Lovingly and with deepest sympathy,
>
>   Mother and Sister Magdalens of Detroit

Blessed Be God!

After such words, Mrs. Penney nodded in perfect understanding
when she read in one of Tom's later letters: "The Magdalens
of Detroit have been my very own sisters in every way. I will
have Sisters Robert Ann and Mary Laurentia tell you about
them."

Judging from the next few letters Tom wrote to Lexington,
Sisters Robert Ann and Mary Laurentia did not tell Mrs. Penney
about the Magdalens; but all unwittingly Tom Penney was telling
the two Sisters what a grace from God the Magdalens were to
him.

To Sister Robert Ann he wrote on October 2, 1942:

> I was overjoyed to hear of Mother's visit with you. . . . When
> you love someone very much don't you want to share your joy with
> them? She has shared my sorrow and disgrace. God knows I would
> give my life to know that she had received a joy greater than her
> sorrow. My own experience proves to me what the true Faith
> really means, and I know she would feel the same way. Oh, yes, I
> have my dark days; but don't we all? And God wins all arguments! . . .
>
> It is very painful to learn that some people are ashamed of ever
> being acquainted with me. It is more painful to find out that those
> whom I have loved and favored and looked upon as friends, have
> talked against me. But the worst shock comes when I am told that
> those whom I have trusted have turned against me and violated my
> confidence just because others are against me. . . .
>
> I often wonder if all this is but a guilty conscience speaking? What
> is our conscience, Sister, but the very voice of God. When He is well
> pleased with us, does not our conscience tell us so? And when He
> is displeased . . . Oh, I can readily understand why so many saints
> have adopted as their own the prayer of the Psalmist: "Oh, my God,
> be Thou not silent to me; lest if Thou be silent, I become like them

that go down into the pit." No better prayer could be said to remind us of the danger of becoming deaf to the voice of God. . . . I know I haven't said anything you don't already know much better than I; but I feel very much better for having said what I have. . . .

The slim Director of Nurses was feeling quite superior because of this letter, but Sister Mary Laurentia, with a wisdom born of experience, bided her time. Two days later she walked nonchalantly into the office of the Director of Nurses and very dully said: "Here's something that might do good to your soul."

Before Sister Robert Ann could open the letter, the elder nun was gone. Gray-blue eyes danced a moment in merriment over Sister Mary Laurentia's humorous ways, but then clouded as a nimble mind wondered what specific antidote for soul sickness the letter held. It was dated October 4, 1942.

Dear Sister Mary Laurentia:

I would have written you when I wrote to Sister Robert Ann, but I had already written so much I feared Captain Rankin would be asking me to publish it in book form if I added another page, so I let it go. Then, too, I thought the Court would do something Friday.

I do hope you have fully recovered from your cold. I am enjoying the best of health and I am almost pleased with myself. What I mean is that I am very pleased that God has given me the necessary grace to acknowledge and respond to His love.

For a long time, Sister, yes, since Time began, people have been in search of happiness. Some have traveled very far and risked all kinds of danger in their efforts to find it. But it is only necessary to open our hearts and remove the obstacles which prevent God's grace from coming to us, and we have a happiness as perfect as one can have on earth.

I can hardly hope to know pleasure in my present position, but true peace is always within my reach. Sister, there are thousands of ponderous books which have been written by learned men on the means to attain happiness, but all together they do not say as much for the peace of the soul as those four little words in the Our Father, "Thy will be done."

I had a letter from Father Eugene yesterday in which he marveled at the progress I have made in grasping the Faith so quickly and with so little aid, lacking, as I do, he said, the assistance of an instructor. I did not fail to remind him that I had two living Guardian Angels to guide me. . . .

Later that morning, when Sister Mary Laurentia happened to pass the Director of Nurses in the corridor, she quietly said, "I hope our soul is deepening as rapidly as Mr. Penney's."

Sister Robert Ann stopped the elder nun with the question: "Did you send him De Caussade's little book?"

"De Caussade? Don't know the man or his little book."

"Oh, Sister! . . . Well, was it Lehodey's *Holy Abandonment?*"

"What are you talking about?"

"You and Tom Penney. He has learned the Doctrine of Abandonment to God's Will more quickly and practically than anyone I ever met. I want to know who taught him."

"I was never Tom Penney's spiritual directress. I was only allowed to act as portress both here in Lexington and down there at Eddyville. But I saw a rather dignified nun from Nazareth sitting beside him at both places. Perhaps she . . ."

"Will you stop teasing?"

"Will you stop fussing? If Tom Penney has really learned the doctrine, thank God and let it go at that."

"Is that a confession you're making?"

"Of what?"

"Of having sent him the books?"

"My charming child, believe me when I tell you I did not even know those books were in existence."

"Well, someone must have sent him something just like that. My last letter and your letter here . . ."

"Oh, so you've read my letter. What did you think of it? Did the incense he threw your way please you?"

"Oh, you! What pleases me is his ability to say 'Thy will be done!' What I'm puzzled about is who taught him to say it."

As Sister Mary Laurentia tucked the letter in a fold of her habit she reminded her friend that they were not the only ones who wrote to Tom Penney. She pointed out that Father George,

Father Eugene, Father Brian, or even Sister Francesca could have taught him. "But," she said as she started down the corridor again, "if you ask me, I'd say most likely it was the Magdalens of Detroit. Cloistered contemplatives are usually far ahead of us in such matters. Of course there's always the possibility that Tom could have learned it himself. That boy is no dumbbell, you know; and even if he were, I need not tell you, that God's grace can pierce the thickest of skulls. Look at me!"

For all her seeming indifference and offhandedness, Sister Mary Laurentia was as deeply impressed as her friend, and equally as curious about the wider horizons that were opening out before Tom Penney. The letter of the following week, dated October 9, deepened the impression and sharpened the curiosity, for Tom let himself go on a favorite theme — the Mother of God. He wrote:

Dear Sister Mary Laurentia:

Your precious letter came today. I was beginning to grow uneasy about you, Sister. I am glad you are so much better. I am still hanging on: reading, meditating, making resolutions and trying to live up to them. Sometimes I think a fellow is much better off ignorant! Yes, "Ignorance can be bliss!"

No, Sister, I am only kidding. I love every blessed grain of knowledge I possess. But I do have my dark days. I read a short time ago of some pious person who always kept a book on his table or desk called *The Glories of Mary*. He called it his spiritual thermometer. I thought so much of the idea, I adopted it myself. And it works! You see, when I am faithful to grace, a page or two of this little book fills my soul with a heavenly peace and joy. It enlightens and invigorates me. But if I am negligent or lukewarm . . . it wearies me. Do you see what has happened, Sister? It is not the splendor of the light which has diminished, it is the eye of the soul which no longer can stand its splendor. At such times, I pray and labor to restore to the eyes of my soul their purity of vision and strength, and soon the thermometer rises, or rather my soul mounts up and soon finds itself in unison with and praises the Blessed Virgin.

As long as we are pure, Sister, I feel there is an intimate relation between us and the Blessed Virgin which manifests itself in a thrill of joy each time our intellects are occupied with a thought of her or our lips murmur a prayer in her honor.

The prayers I prefer are those addressed to Mary. Books please me more if they speak of Mary. The rosary for me is a special source of real peace. It is more than that; it is my safeguard. I feel that so long as I recite it despite my weariness, distaste, or preoccupations, I will never go far wrong. Devotion to Mary is to me like a beacon light placed on the road which leads to God. . . .

Father Eugene could have enlightened the nun on the source of the book Tom now claimed as his *vade mecum,* but the aging Passionist had a puzzle of his own in the letter Tom had just written him. There was such an utter "otherworldliness" about it that the experienced priest could only marvel. The prisoner had written on October 14.

Was very happy to hear from you again. You must remember, dear Father, that I have no specific duties other than reading, writing, eating, and sometimes sleeping. That is why I may be able to answer letters more promptly than a Godly man like yourself who is actually doing something for God. . . . I find that the useful employment of time is one of the hardest virtues to acquire.

"To commence promptly, to work steadily, to continue with constancy, to interrupt one's work amiably, to resume it calmly, to finish it slowly! — is the mark of a strong and virtuous soul." And believe me, Father, I have plenty of experience trying to practice this virtue; for there is not an hour out of the 24 that does not have its interruption and distraction. You would hardly think that under the circumstances, would you? But is is true.

Yes, Father, I have read about everything I could get my hands on. I am afraid my one great failure has been impatience. You see, when I like something, I never quite get my fill of it. So let's hope my former weakness will prove to be my salvation. I like prayer. . . .

Prayer has been a source of great consolation to me, Father. But let us not forget that wonderful little Sister Robert Ann. You know she has been sister, brother, friend, and at times even my Father Confessor!

Father, at this hour particularly I feel that I am not alone on this earth and whatever the future may hold for me, I know that I have Someone to guard, protect, console, and love me. . . .

The good priest may have wondered where Tom got his idea about the proper use of time and that desire to fill his day with profitable occupations, but had he read the letter the condemned man sent to Sister Mary Laurentia on October 17 he would have seen that it was no idle thought or passing speculation with the prisoner. For on that day Tom had written:

. . . You ask me to make an order for reading, etc. . . . Sister I have a system, shall I call it? I wake at 5 a.m. I say the usual morning prayers. If by the time I have finished them I have not excited myself to the proper feeling, I make the Stations. And these have never failed, no matter how distracted I have been. Then I can really make my Acts of Faith, Hope, and Love, my Acts of Sorrow, Humility, Desire, and Perfect Contrition. Next comes Spiritual Communion. After that, if there is any time, I read the Legends of the Blessed Virgin until breakfast time — 8 a.m. After breakfast I either draw or read after I have finished the paper. This brings us up to lunch at 10:30. Then I read a novel or talk with the boys. They are all awake in the afternoon. At 1 p.m. I pretend I am asleep and say five decades of the rosary — sometimes more. Then I rest and read just whatever appeals to me. At 2:30 p.m. we eat again. Then I write whatever letters I have to write. At 5:30 p.m. I walk for an hour. Then I lie down, read more or write more, whatever the occasion demands. Tonight I shall write; for it is now 5 p.m. and I haven't written Sister Robert Ann yet. About 8 p.m. I say the 30 days' prayer to the Blessed Virgin, then go to bed and begin with the Our Father and say every prayer I can think of until I fall asleep, being mindful of my friends, those dear to me, the men in the Service, their mothers, also my enemies, even the bitterest ones. . . .

Now that's about the way I live each day with a few exceptions here and there. If you have any suggestions I will gladly follow them.

Had a letter from Father D. He is in Turner Field, Albany, Ga. He asks about both of you and says he may drop you a line. (Believe me that is about all he will drop!)

Mother Holy Name of the Good Shepherd in Detroit wrote me a very encouraging letter and the Magdalens added about 12 pages telling me of their monastery, their habits, etc. There are 49 of them and they all pray for me and ask me to join them in their Grand

Silence Hour from 1 to 2 p.m. So I offer that as Holy Hour to console our Lord, repair my own offenses and those others who displease him. I say my beads mentally. Isn't that all right? I'll tell the rest to Sister Robert Ann. May our Lady protect you and God bless you always.

But all he told Sister Robert Ann was:

I have just told Sister Mary Laurentia all I know, so prepare yourself for a very dull letter. I have gained quite a few correspondents — all Catholics. And, Sister it really makes a difference to correspond with people who think alike and live alike and love alike. Even as bad as I have been I see now what I might have been. I never knew there were so many kind people in the world. But how could I — I never went to the trouble to look for them. Oh, merciful God, how really ignorant I have been!

I have one great consolation, Sister: God gave me an opportunity to save my soul. I lost it. But He has given me a second chance. This time my job is to see that it stays in His keeping. Surely I can do that! . . .

Haven't heard from Father Eugene for two weeks. Father Libs was here Wednesday but brought me only disappointment. But I know God understands, so I do not worry.

Did you notice the Biblical Contest in the *Register?* I am following it. I would send in my replies if I thought it would do any good. I have answered all the questions so far. Generally there is a catch to them some place.

Write any time, Sister, and do forgive me my poor effort tonight. I'll make up for it next time or shall I not make up for it in prayer right now for you and your works. . . .

One week later Tom was at his table answering a letter from Sister Mary Laurentia. She had told him that Sister Robert Ann did not look so well to her. Tom replied:

I grasp your meaning about Sister Robert Ann's appearance, and I can tell you the cause for it. You both have the souls of spiritual giants and try to carry the loads of physical giants. Sometimes it works, but sometimes . . . Well, I suppose it is all very pleasing to God.

I will remember to say the prayer you suggest. Many times I go through my prayers when I do not feel a bit like it, and always feel better for having done so. Unquestionably, many things, if patiently borne, bring us at the end of day an extraordinary calm and joy. . . .

He had just put a period to that sentence when over the Penitentiary's Public Address System came the cry: "News Flash. Frankfort, Kentucky . . ." Tom looked up. "The Kentucky Court of Appeals today upheld electric chair death sentences meted out against a scar-faced carpenter, a café operator, and a drug-addicted greenskeeper for the robbery-murder of Marion Miley, attractive golf star, and her 52-year-old mother. Unless the three men, now in Eddyville Penitentiary, file a petition for a review of their cases within 30 days, or receive executive clemency, they will die shortly after midnight, New Year's Day, 1943. Recently described as in good spirits, the three — Tom Penney, 33, Lexington carpenter, Robert H. Anderson, 37, Louisville bar proprietor, and Raymond 'Skeeter' Baxter, 28, Lexington Country Club greenskeeper — were convicted of murder last December in the Fayette Circuit Court and sentenced to die in the chair. Then they appealed to Kentucky's highest court. The high tribunal, in separate opinions written by Court Commissioner Charles Morris agreed unanimously that the three men had been given 'fair and impartial trials' and that there was nothing in the records to justify reversals."

The commercial program on the air at the time was then resumed and as an electrical transcription of Bing Crosby's voice floated out over the corridor, Tom stared ahead blankly. Soon he heard Anderson calling.

"Hey, Penney!"

"Yeah?"

"Did you hear that news flash?"

"I did."

"Hey, Skeeter!" cried Bob a little louder. When a thin excited voice answered, Bob asked: "Did you hear that?"

"Yeah! What must we do now: appeal to the Governor?"

Anderson's laugh was mockery itself. "The Governor, hell! Do you think any politician gives a damn about any prisoner? No,

Skeeter, we've got to appeal to Penney."

"What do you say, Tom?" cried the excited Baxter.

"I say I'm greatly relieved. Not a bit disappointed. And can't think of a better way to begin the New Year than by dying right."

Before comment was forthcoming, Tom bent over and continued his letter to Sister Mary Laurentia: "They just announced a news flash. Our appeals were denied. Well, Sister, surely God knows best. If that is His will, I have no complaint." He sat back to consult the nun's letter before going on. But before he had located his next topic, Anderson was after him again.

"Penney, it's too damn bad you didn't go on the stage. The theater missed another Edwin Booth when it missed you. But cut the acting for five minutes will you, and talk turkey. There's nothing final about that lousy thing you just heard. There are other courts, other judges, other lawyers. We all can have new trials if you'll only produce new evidence." Then in a much more conciliatory and even an ingratiating tone, the ex-Nite Club owner went on: "Listen, Tom. I've always played pretty square with you. I was never tight with the geld. Now there's plenty of it out there waiting for you and yours. Get me out of here, boy, and I'll never let you down. Neither you nor anyone belonging to you will ever want for anything. How about telling the world about Buford Stewart?"

"What does Nicholson think of that story?"

"Let's leave him out of it. I can tell you absolutely, a statement from you to the effect that Stewart was the guy who bumped off the dames will make the news flash we just heard a lot of hooey. We'll all get new trials. And our mouthpieces will have to be pretty dumb not to get us new sentences. What do you say?"

When no answer was immediately forthcoming, Anderson added quite nonchalantly, "Just remember, Tom, the cow jumped over the moon."

"Meaning?"

"Meaning that 'The Cat and Fiddle' can be opened up again.

And that would mean Easy Street for you and your mother and all belonging to you. Don't be a fool, you fool."

"I won't," answered Tom so promptly and cheerfully that Anderson did not know whether he had been triumphant or was being taunted.

Penney went back to his letter. He continued with:

> You ask me about the parable of the laborers in the vineyard. I have always accepted it as a way of expressing God's unlimited love and mercy; a way of saying that each of us who responds with all he or she has, will share equally. It hardly seems fair though, Sister, that I should merit an equal share with you.

The next morning he added a postscript to his letter.

> P.S. I hardly know how I feel this morning, but I think: "Rather relieved," expresses it fully. I don't know what course I will take, if any; but if I do not take any I have until New Year's Day. I hate to give up without a struggle, and yet I see hardly any use in struggling. If you see the Chief, will you ask him about my chances? He should know better than anyone else. A lawyer will promise anything if he sees the possibility of a little money for himself, knowing all the time that nothing can be done. That is why I would like the opinion of someone disinterested professionally. If I am asking anything contrary to your Rules, disregard it, Sister.
>
> About the Court's decision I don't know anything to say except that I was not disappointed. Of course I am sorry — not for myself, but for the few who will suffer and grieve for me. I must keep busy now more than ever, so as to keep my mind off of it. So if I write often, don't be alarmed. If only I could say some comforting word to my poor mother at this moment. I know she has heard it. . . .
>
> I shall write to Sister Robert Ann tomorrow. You know I shall continue to pray for you. You shall be thought of and even mentioned by name in my last prayer, Sister; for any of my prayers would be incomplete if I omitted either one of you. . . . Oh, Sister, how I would like to be all you would have me be — I do try, and try hard.
>
> I may not have time to complete the "Quiz" in the *Register*. It goes on for 11 weeks. But I'll keep up with it until the end.
>
> May God bless you always. . . .

The next week was one of mental and emotional confusion for the "scar-faced carpenter," as the papers were so fond of calling him. He had written truth when he told Sister Mary Laurentia that the news flash had given him relief; for the long, hot summer and the early fall had been an anxious, trying time because of the suspense. Every morning he had scanned the paper for a report on the activities of the Court of Appeals. Now no longer need he look. It was also true that the decision arrived at held no disappointment. From the day he heard the flimsy grounds on which the petitions had been filed, he had no real hopes for a reversal or a new trial. But this technicality of the law had afforded him time; it had postponed what his deeper soul knew to be inevitable; and his shallower soul reveled in the postponement. Now that the technicality had been brushed aside, he had to face the naked fact that unless some new technicality was employed he would begin the New Year by dying. . . .

At times this prospect pleased him. Busy as he had kept himself while in confinement, it was still confinement — and it told on him. Secondly, he knew we all must die some day, somehow. He was one of the very few who knew the day, the hour, and the manner. He considered himself fortunate in many ways; for after all, death in the chair would be almost painless; it most certainly would be swift — and he was not afraid! No. The nuns and priests had told him what the waters of baptism do to a soul. Yes, he was ready to die — even anxious.

But then he would think of his mother. The longer he lived, the longer he spared her the heart-splitting experience of final separation. True, he had disgraced her. But he could never forget that embrace at Fayette County Jail. She loved him still. Seemingly she loved him more now than ever. His letters were life to her. If he fought his case he could give her that much more happiness. And she was old. Could not God, in His great mercy, take her before He took him?

Then there was Anderson. . . . Tom knew his lawyers were clever. They would find some loophole in the law if there was any existing. And Bob needed time. He was not ready to die yet.

His mind was not right. His heart was not right. His soul . . . Whenever Penney thought of the eternity awaiting his chunky companion, he shuddered and prayed.

He did not have the same worries about Baxter. Somehow or other he felt God would be merciful to the young hop-head. There was no hope of converting him, as far as Tom could see; but he felt the ex-greenskeeper was living up to the little light his thin mind perceived — and this gave him peace.

When his mother's letter arrived five days after the Court's decision, Tom studied the lines she had written and finally decided to utilize every technicality the Law provided in order to prolong his life on earth to the utmost. Once the decision was made, he sat into his table and wrote to his mother asking her to call his lawyers for advice, adding:

> — When you call will you ask them to send me the exact grounds on which they petitioned for a new trial? You see, dear, it is new evidence we will need this time; so if I knew what they filed the last time I may be able to think of something new.
>
> Try not to worry too much. It will not help. I would not ask you to do this little were I not sure God expects me to make some effort. But, dear, let me make this plain: If nothing can be done, please tell me! This is no time for secrets. Let me have the plain truth. Then I can govern myself accordingly. Don't worry about it hurting me, Mother. It can't. I've passed that stage. . . .

After he had folded the letter he sat back and began to think of what he should say to Father Donnelly. Only two days before the news flash he had sent his first letter to Turner Field. In it he had said: "I am still waiting to hear my fate, Father. But should hear soon. I have no fear whatever of the results; for with so many people praying for me whatever comes must be the holy will of God."

The prisoner now wondered if his letter to his mother was contradiction to or corroboration of that statement. Surely he had accepted the Court's decision as God's will. Now he felt that God wanted him to make every legitimate effort to prolong his life for his mother's sake, if for no other. Suddenly the realization that he had not actually killed either of the women rose to the surface of his consciousness. He had not thought on this fact for months. He took its sudden resurgence as sign that heaven wanted him to fight.

Of course he should have talked the matter over with Father Libs, but that good priest was always in such a hurry on the one day in the month he appeared that Tom did not feel justified in detaining him for any long conference. He had had to tell Father George just as he had had to tell the two Nazareth nuns that although he had been fasting and all prepared for the Eucharist, month after month he received only disappointment. "However," he would always add in such letters, "I make Spiritual Communions daily, and must be contented." He made one now, and after a short thanksgiving, drew a sheet of paper to him and wrote:

October 27, 1942

Dear Father George:

I don't suppose you heard the news flash Friday, so I'll just send the clipping and thus save space. . . .

You have been very close to me this past year, Father, and I hope it will be some comfort to you to know that you and those wonderful Sisters have been my inspiration during all these dark days. . . . God knows the sorrow that is in my aching heart. My hopes are fixed on Him alone. I pray that in His infinite goodness He will not turn away but let His merciful eyes rest on me in pity. . . .

Mother has been doing very well, Father. I have been trying to prepare her for the worst. I don't know exactly how she stood the news; for I have no one to tell me but herself. No one else in the family has written since I have been here. . . .

Father, could you come if I called for you? Do not feel bad about telling me if you cannot come.

His mother wrote, as all mothers would write, that she would spend her last cent, move heaven and earth, for the sake of her son. But, as yet, she had been unable to get in touch with the lawyers. It was not an encouraging letter. But that same day —

November 1 — God did send something that cheered the prisoner to such an extent that he could write to Sister Robert Ann:

> Thanks for your encouragement. . . . I think I should go completely mad at times if someone like you did not reassure me. You know, Sister, even though we are certain of our destiny so long as we comply with our Lord's wishes and resign ourselves to His holy will, nevertheless it is a great comfort to be reassured. But, Sister, let me tell you the resignation to His holy will is not always as easy as just saying it. Often as soon as I have said: "May His holy will be done!" I hurry to do something else lest my heart should cry out otherwise. . . .
>
> Mother informs me that we will not give up until we have to. So maybe I won't go January 1 after all. Sister, it is hard for me to talk to Mother about death. Of course I don't want to give up if there is any chance for life. I don't think God would want me to. But I certainly don't want them spending money if there is no chance for me. Believe me, Sister, it is not for myself that I suffer. It is my mother who is carrying the load. You know, Sister, she would appreciate seeing you almost as much as I would! . . .
>
> P.S. It certainly must have been your own and the prayers of others that have helped me through this past year. Only God knows how grateful I am. . . .

A week went by. Then came a group of letters that made the prisoner look again into the depths of his soul. For months now he had been reading letters that told of Abandonment, Spiritual Childhood, Complete Trust in God, and Pure Love for God; letters that spoke of reparation, expiation, the art of love shown in making little sacrifices. A new world had been opened up to him through contact with the Magdalens of Detroit. On this morning in early November he had to ask himself if he could say in all honesty that he did believe; that he did have blind trust and unbounded confidence; that he was a little child.

After a good half hour of searching his soul to its final fathom he took his pen and devoted the rest of the morning to answering his mail. His first was to the Magdalens:

> I have just finished your most beautiful letters and honestly, Sis-

ters, I do not know when, if ever, I enjoyed anything so much. May God bless Mother Holy Name for giving you permission to write to this penitent sinner.

Sister Magdalen of St. Gertrude, I am not ashamed to confess that your beautiful letter brought a flood of tears from me. It was so very much like my dear old Mother! I had a letter from her today. Part of it runs as follows — "only God knows how it pains me to tell you this, but the lawyers inform me there is no hope for clemency."— Can you think of anything more heart-rending for a mother to tell a son? I have tried to prepare her for the inevitable. Oh, please God, grant her the necessary courage and strength to endure. May I ask you to join me in that prayer, Sisters? All I ever ask for myself is the privilege to love Him.

Thank you, Sister Magdalen of St. Leo. Be assured that I shall not retreat. My life is a small sacrifice in comparison to the sacrifice of our Lord. My only regret being that I have not two lives to give him.

Now Sister Magdalen of St. Felix, you must not think I am such a miser with my prayers that I could not spare more than one Ave for each of you. I remember you many, many times a day; and often at night when I am reading, I find myself thinking of you and murmur a fervent: "God bless them!" And don't forget, Sister, we have a date.

Sister Magdalen of St. Teresa, thank you indeed for your Order of the Day. Henceforth you are one stronger in everything you do. Please continue my Spiritual Communion. That is a wonderful thing. I will convey your message of thanks to Father Brian.

Sister Magdalen of St. Helena, I certainly enjoyed your letter and I will remember your special intention. Continue to take me with you to Holy Communion and may heaven bless you always.

Sisters, I would like to write to each of you separately, but I cannot. So I extend to all my Sisters my kindest regards and will now tell you some news. . . .

The date for my execution is set for New Year's just after midnight. Now Sisters pray at that moment, pray that . . . He reject me not.

Thank you, dear Mother — thank you for allowing the Magdalens to write; thank you also for the *Messenger*, and may I hear from you soon again? Please, Mother!

May the most just, most high, most adorable will of God be in all things done, praised and magnified forever,

> Your most grateful adoptee in Christ
> at the right of the Cross
> Thomas Penney

P.S. Sisters, cannot I offer my life for the conversion of sinners? or should I petition for the release of the most abandoned soul in Purgatory?

There were other letters Penney wanted to answer that day, but he was so plagued with interruptions that he found he could not concentrate sufficiently well, so he decided to wait until the morrow.

Next day, without so much as unfolding the morning paper he sat at his table and wrote his mother:

Your letter came yesterday. I know it was hard for you to give me the news, but it is better to face facts. I don't know what to tell you to do. In my letter to the lawyer I told him some things that could be done. But I suppose he'll tell me they already have been done. And how am I to know whether they have or not? So all I can say, dear Mother, is do your best and leave God do the rest.

I heard from the Sisters today. They told me about the visit. I am so glad you feel you can talk to them, Mother. I know it helps lots. You know Sister Mary Laurentia is Austin Price's sister-in-law. She has asked him three times, and he has said he can do nothing — and I believe him. . . .

Tommie said she was coming to see you. I am surprised she has not already done so. I told her to call the lawyers. Let her do what she can, Mother; she'd never feel right if you didn't.

Just remember, Mother, that whatever happens, I'm ready for it. Let that fact, dear, be a consolation to you.

When he had folded that he felt easier and hurried on to write two other letters which set two Nazareth nuns marveling. To Sister Robert Ann he said:

The "cross" in some form or other is the gilt-edged guarantee of God's special love. A seeming contradiction, yet absolutely true.

For proof we have only to look at the lives of our Lord, our Lady, St. Joseph, and the other saints. I seldom see God's reasons for things, but my trust in His love must remain firm. I will not make a sour face, Sister; for as St. Leo says: "Not to thank God for everything is to reprove Him for something." I don't want to do that.

To Sister Mary Laurentia he wrote:

Do not worry, Sister, I am resolved to meet just whatever God wills. If I can think of anything to help me within God's law, I will use it; if not, I will remain as a little child who has no worries, no possessions, no anxieties, no preoccupations about the past or future. Many times His ways in my regard have appeared mysterious, and right now certain of His dealings seem strange and contrary, not only to all human prudence, but even to justice. Yet I shall never waver for a single instant; never doubt that His love and wisdom are directing all.

Joseph was sold by his brethren out of envy, then falsely accused of a shameful crime and cast into prison unjustly; but all these were steppingstones to the throne of Egypt. So too, shall I hope against hope and abandon myself to the boundless love of my heavenly Father with the complete abandon of a little child who amid the fury of the greatest storm, rests fearlessly in the arms of his mother.

Write when you feel like it, Sister. I will continue to keep you in my prayers. Thanks for everything.

Your friend in Christ — at the right of the Cross. . . .

P.S. . . . Father Libs brought me Holy Communion this morning so remember to thank God for His goodness in granting me this divine privilege.

Those lines lighted the usually expressionless face of Sister Mary Laurentia with a grateful smile and made her lift her head heavenward: "Thank you, God, for all You have done and are doing for this boy."

CHAPTER TEN

Christmas Gifts

THE surest sign that a man has found his God and knows Him to be his Father is an honest and full confession made not only with contrition for sins but with a vibrant confidence of pardon. Time and again Tom Penney has made such a confession, but perhaps the best example of his contrition and confidence is contained in the confession he addressed to one of the Magdalens of Detroit, on November 12.

Sister Magdalen of St. Gertrude: In your last letter you asked me if I had ever made up one of those cut-up puzzles. Said I to myself: "What in the world does she want to know that for?" Yes, Sister, I did. I had bought one of two lovely dogs, and I thought it would delight two little children whom I greatly love. But as I was making it up, I found there were three or four pieces missing. Oh, Sister, what a sight it was when I had finished! One dog's eye was gone; the other had no mouth. I was so disgusted, I burned the thing.

Now you ask me if I have ever looked upon life as one of those puzzles. I must confess you have set me thinking.

I have made a great mess of my "puzzle" from my youth up to the time I became a Catholic. And, Sister, I am afraid that I may have lost many precious pieces even since then. But now, with your kind help, I am going to make it right. I am starting today. You tell me the only sure way to make the puzzle right is to let our Lord hand me the pieces one by one, day by day; and to take them from Him bravely and trustfully.

Thanks a million for the suggestion. If you have any more like it, please send them on to

Your grateful brother at the right of the Cross.

P.S. Sister, will you kindly make this point clear to me: You say that now and then we see a few pieces that fit into one another perfectly, and marvel to see how the most unlikely pieces have worked in beautifully. Then you add: "But as a general rule, we must be content to understand only in part." I'll be looking for the explanation in your next letter.

This signature "At the right of the Cross" began to appear now in all his letters and was puzzling most of the recipients. Down on Turner Field, Georgia, Father Donnelly's white face wrinkled into a smile and his white head nodded knowingly as he read: "Sincerely yours at the right of Holy Cross."

"The modern Dismas," the chaplain said aloud. Then he thought of the Magdalens. It would be normal for those cloistered contemplatives to associate Tom with the man who died at the right of Jesus Christ and who not only won heaven by a single act of Faith, but, while yet alive, won canonization from Christ Himself, as it would be for robins to fly north as snows melt or for ducks to fly south when trees grow bare.

The letter heartened the weary Chaplain. On the second page, Tom had written "how a Missionary, working among the Indians in Oklahoma, once asked a little Indian lad: 'Where is Jesus?' — 'Here!' came the prompt reply as the boy placed his hand over his heart. Puzzled for a moment, the Missionary repeated his question. But without the slightest hesitation the boy gave the same reply. Then the Father realized how excellently the good Sisters had done their work. This little Indian lad had grasped a truth of which so many supposedly good Christian people are ignorant. One that is among the most consoling, fascinating, and fruitful truths of our holy Faith."

The Chaplain laughed at himself when he found himself wishing that some Magdalens were writing to his army lads. No, that was not God's technique. Letters from cloistered contemplatives would never take with his rowdy rookies.

Father George would have had a heartier laugh at himself for trying to parallel his army boys with the man in prison if he could have seen the letter Tom had written Sister Mary Laurentia: "The Magdalens sent me *The Following of Christ* by Thomas à Kempis. In his last days he said: 'I have sought rest everywhere, but found it only in a corner of my cell with a little book.' His little book has been a source of great peace to me. I read it to the others at night, when all is quiet."

What a picture for the religious skeptic of 1942! Five men seated in separate cells in Eddyville's House of Death; four of them listening intently to the fifth as he read from Thomas à Kempis!

One night a veritable pleading crept into Tom's voice as he began the twenty-third chapter of the First Book. Penney addressed himself so directly to Anderson that Baxter, Elliott, and Trent felt themselves spectators at something in the nature of a deadly duel between two souls.

"What good is it to live a long life," read Tom earnestly, "when we amend that life so little? Indeed a long life does not always benefit us, but on the contrary, adds to our guilt." He paused purposefully. He felt that Bob needed to grasp that truth, but he dared not repeat it. That would be too obvious a bit of preaching. He skipped the next two sentences, then went on: "If it is so terrifying to die, it is nevertheless possible that to live longer is more dangerous. Blessed is he who keeps the moment of death ever before his eyes and prepares for it every day."

Baxter coughed nervously. Penney's clear baritone went on: "How happy and prudent is he who tries, now in life, to be what he wants to be found at death." If anyone else tried to read such stuff to Baxter, he'd pick up a funny paper or busy himself rolling a cigarette. Yet he listened to Penney and liked it. The same seemed true of Elliott and Trent, who listened to Penney as snakes listen to their charmer. But Anderson . . .

Tom's voice took on a new vibrancy as he read: "Who will remember you when you are dead? Who will pray for you? Do now what you can. . . . Gather for yourself the riches of im-

mortality while you have time. Think of nothing but your salvation. Care only for the things of God. . . . To Him direct your
daily prayers, your sighs and tears, that your soul may merit
after death to pass into the happiness of the Lord."

"Isn't that beautiful, Bob?"

"Eh-yah," came the slow but definite acquiescence. "Great
stuff all right. But that's enough for tonight, Tom. I'm now going
to pray on the rosary Sister Robert Ann sent me. Next time you
write to her tell her I'm making good use of it."

"Why don't *you* tell her?"

"I haven't your gift of gab. Which saves me a lot of time . . .
how many letters did you get today?"

"Only eight."

"*Only* eight!" exclaimed Trent. "That's more than I get in a
month. Where did you get the book you were just readin'?"

"The Magdalens of Detroit had someone send it from New
York."

"Cripes! These nuns send you everything, don't they?"

Tom was stopped by the question; for he caught the overtones
of envy and indignation; heard the accusation and something of
a condemnation in the voice of his fellow prisoner. He finally
managed to say: "Herb, no one knows better than I how little I
deserve their attention. . . ."

"But how in hell do you manage to get it?"

"That's a deep question, Herb. I'm going to give it a deep
answer. *I* don't manage to get it. *I* couldn't. As I see it, God took
over up in Lexington and has been running the show ever since.
Of course I've got to play ball with Him. But He furnishes everything from the ball, bat, and glove to the grandstands, the
grounds, and the groundskeeper."

"Meaning what?" put in Elliott.

"Bill, the day I arrived in my home town a confessed criminal,
two Nazareth nuns and a peach of a priest walked into my life
all unasked. They changed everything about me — even my
way of thinking and talking. The priest goes off to war, and God
sends another swell sky pilot in on me. He gets about eighty

different Magdalens to adopt me as their brother, write me stuff you can't find in books, the real McCoy, stuff that goes right to your guts, grips you, holds you, makes you new. Then they pray prayers for me that pierce the very clouds."

"But how do *you* rate all that from them — or from God?" asked Elliott.

"I don't. It's all pure gift from God."

"I don't get it," said Trent with a trace of a snarl. "But I will say you're a lucky guy. You're different, Penney. I sensed it the second I arrived in this hellhole. And I'll go further and say you haven't done any of us any harm."

What Trent could have added was that Penney had changed that hellhole and made it less of a hole and much less like hell for all of them. The source and the secret of his power Penney now put in a letter to Sister Robert Ann:

> I have understood things much more thoroughly these past few months. And what a difference that clearer understanding makes! God will keep us ignorant, Sister, so long as we put Him in second place; for He is a jealous Lover!
>
> Oh, I have learned so many things this past year. It really makes me feel sorry for myself when I think of all the real happiness I have missed. I know now how people can jest while dying. Why not? Nothing else matters when we love God.

It was just under a fortnight later that Sister Mary Laurentia sought out the ever busy Director of Nurses and with a trace of a worry in her tone asked her to check her last five or six letters from Eddyville to see if there was anything in them indicative of a crisis coming in Tom Penney's life.

It was a strange request, but in answer to all her urgent questions the only answer she received from the elder nun was: "Look closely — I'm concerned."

It was quite late that night when Sister Robert Ann got to reading her mail. The first letter she re-read was that of Thanksgiving Day. It showed Tom in anything but a tense mood. He had written of the nice dinner that had been served; told how he had spent most of the day reading, "but did not fail to thank God for the thousand and one things for which he had to be thankful"; assured Sister he would not die New Year's Day, as he had just read in the paper how his lawyer had filed a petition for a rehearing.

No, there was nothing in this letter to warrant alarm. He also told how one of the Magdalens had sent him *A Guide for Victim Souls* about which he promised to write in his next letter.

He never did. The next two letters showed him in a light-hearted, slightly excited mood because of the Biblical Contest he had entered. He felt that he was doing well in it. His only worry was about being on earth when the contest ended.

He had spoken about Holy Communion in each of the letters and had ended with a request that brought tears to blue-gray eyes. "Take me to Holy Communion with you," he had written; "that will be Christmas present enough for me."

The last letter she had received just that morning. She read it again. When she finished the little white bonneted head shook with a rare finality. "Crisis!" she whispered very incisively and quite disdainfully. She had reason for the disdain; for Tom's latest letter ran:

> I shall be awake until midnight Christmas Eve, then I shall say "Dear Infant Jesus, come into my heart, which Thine own sweet Mother has prepared and made warm for Thee. Come, and I will love Thee forever and ever!"
>
> That sounds very like my favorite Spiritual Communion. I don't think I ever told you about that. It goes: "Dear Jesus, abandoned by so many cruel hearts today, come into my heart, which Thy Most Pure Virgin Mother has prepared for Thee, and I will love Thee."

But the indignation and incisiveness vanished the next morning when Sister Mary Laurentia after listening patiently to her companion's report on her findings, somewhat crisply asked, "Does he mention Bob Anderson in any of your letters?"

"N-o-o-o."

"Well, he does in mine, and I'm worried. I didn't see anything in the papers about Anderson re-appealing. He has sharper law-yers than poor Tom or Baxter can afford. I grew curious about that strange silence; so I asked Tom. His answers frighten me."

"What are they?"

"Read this one," and the elder nun pointed to a few lines in her latest letter.

Sister Robert Ann took the sheet with mounting curiosity and read: "You ask about Mr. Anderson. No, Sister, he did not re-appeal. However, he will not go the first of the year, and maybe not at all. Ask God to give me wisdom, Sister."

"What in the world can he mean?"

"That is something I wish I really knew," answered a very serious-faced Sister Mary Laurentia. "He's too positive to suit me. He's got something up his sleeve; something that will aid Anderson. But I know Tom Penney well enough by now to know that he is about to do something that will do himself no good. He knows it, too. Keep your eyes open, Sister. See what the papers have to say about Anderson. Frankly, I'm nervous. I'm afraid those lawyers might be too smart for Tom."

"What do you mean?"

"Anderson should die January 1 if no appeal is made by his lawyers. There's no possibility of executive clemency. I know — I've inquired. Yet Tom states positively that Anderson will not die that day. That's bad enough, but then he adds that he may not die at all. Sister, that's too strong a statement to come from one like Tom. Believe me, something's afoot."

This wise old nun would have been more nervous if she could have glimpsed the letters the prisoner was penning to Father Donnelly.

It is elected that I do not die just yet, Father. My lawyers have filed a petition for a rehearing. I don't know whether to laugh or cry. I can see no advantage in prolonging agony. But rest assured I shall make the most of the time allowed me. It may well be that God is not satisfied with me and wishes to put me through a more severe test. At any rate, give me a special intention in your Mass and prayers. I am going to try to do something, Father. I don't know how successful I'll be. But nothing beats a trial except a failure. So don't let the delay of my execution hinder your visit. I really need to see you.

Bob has had a beautiful letter from your friend, Sister Adelaide. He is trying, Father, but has some terrible difficulties in the interpretation of Scripture. I tell him if reading Scripture causes so much doubt, then stop reading it. I may be wrong, but it seems to me we must know God first, or at least desire to know, love, and obey His adorable will, and not doubt. Then we will understand the sacred text better.

The busy Chaplain never even wondered what it was that Tom was going to try. He himself had made an unsuccessful attempt to get time enough off to fly to Paducah and spend a few hours with the prisoner. Had he any idea of what Tom was planning, higher officers would have heard more insistent pleas and even importunate demands for a leave of absence.

In a letter dated December 16, the prisoner wrote an entire page on his religious experiences, admitting that he had walked in dark places, had known black days and nights, then added:

But, Father, I can truthfully say I have had one great advantage in as much as I have never doubted for a single moment. I know only too well how unworthy I am, but I can say every moment of my Catholic life has been beautiful. I had, and still have, much to learn. I used to envy you and others like you who had been nurtured from childhood in the Catholic Church, but I wonder now if such favored souls ever experience the rapture that comes to a convert who suddenly awakes to the splendor of our Father's House. I no longer envy you, Father.

I suppose you never get the Kentucky news. Bob is due to leave this world January 1. However, I do not believe it will happen. My date and Baxter's is set for January 22. They lost no time in acting on our cases this second time.

There are many things I want to tell you. . . . My whole soul has been transformed, Father. I have written a thumbnail biography for our good friends, the Sisters. They will be only too glad to give

you a copy if I do not get to see you before I go. But I am hoping
to see you. . . .

Bob is doing fine. Sister Adelaide has been writing to him. God
bless her. She has accomplished more in two letters than I with all
my poor efforts. But that is logical enough! Bye for now, Father.
God bless you.

Had the young Army Chaplain adhered to his earlier plan of
exchanging the prisoner's letters with the nuns, wise old Sister
Mary Laurentia would have seen that her fears for Tom Penney
were exceptionally well grounded. His fertile brain was bringing
to birth something that had known a long gestation.

Could the nun have peered over Tom's shoulder as he read
the little book Sister Magdalen of St. Elizabeth had sent him
she would have seen Satan in one of his subtlest works. He was
appearing as an Angel of Light to this man condemned to die
and deluding him with a wiliness that makes the cunning of
Eden's original temptation seem crude.

Tom Penney was bent over *A Guide for Victim Souls*. He was
devouring the doctrine contained therein with the avidity of one
famished. With a pencil stroke that told of thrill and determination he checked the sentence: "A few rare souls consecrate themselves to God as Victims for others; that is, they offer themselves
to suffer for the guilty." He looked through the bars to where
Bob Anderson lolled in his bunk, and his eyes narrowed as he
stared and thought. With a sudden, almost imperceptible nod of
his head, he clenched his pencil and checked sentence after sentence. He bent closer to re-read all he had checked. They made
rare reading for a man in Penney's position:

"As the host lends its exterior form to Jesus, so do these souls
long to lend their entire selves to Christ. Our Lord can suffer no
longer, so they offer their hearts, their souls, their bodies, so that
Jesus may find in them those sufferings which He is so desirous of
offering to His Heavenly Father to the greater glory of the
Trinity and the fulfillment of the Divine purposes, especially the
salvation of sinners." Tom put an extra check beside the last
clause and read on:

"Thus these special Victims realize in themselves what St. Paul says: 'Who now rejoice in my sufferings for you, and fill up those things that are wanting to the sufferings of Christ in my flesh, for His Body, which is the Church' (Col. 1:24).

"These souls could exclaim with the same Apostle: 'I wished myself to be an anathema from Christ, for my brethren, who are my kinsmen' (Rom. 9:3)." Another extra check went against that final phrase.

A smile spread slowly over the scarred face of the prisoner as he read on. "In a spirit of self-oblation, these Victim Souls strive after a perfect conformity to Our Blessed Redeemer, who was immolated as a Victim of Atonement, not for His own sins, but for the sins of others." His fist clenched as he read the next lines "Very often these souls offer themselves for the conversion of a particular soul." A triumphant "Ah!" escaped his lips as he read: "The beauty and sublimity of self-oblation for others is thus described by a noted author: 'A voluptuous and sensual generation beholds the rare spectacle of saintly souls, whose one desire and purpose in life, whose sole happiness consists in offering themselves for their fellow creatures.'"

"What's eating you, Penney. You're beginning to act as if you had ants in your pants."

"Better than that, Bob. Much better than that!"

"What's up? Did you get a reprieve from the Governor?"

"No, but I got . . . Well, I won't say exactly what I got; but I'll give you a hint. Maybe . . . Now note that I say 'Maybe' . . . Maybe I'll be able to play Santa Claus this year."

"Whew!" whistled Anderson as he settled back in his bunk. "I knew you'd go nuts before you got out of here. How many shopping days to Christmas?"

"Not enough according to my calendar. Don't bother me for the next twenty minutes. I'm going to do some of that shopping you just mentioned."

For months now Penney's almost imperturbable cheerfulness had puzzled Anderson. In some hazy manner he knew that religion was its source, but since God had never been the Supreme

Reality in Bob Anderson's life that He now was in Tom Penney's, the older man could not understand his fellow inmate of Death Row.

Anderson knew the tall, thin, Lexington man had a very warm spot in his heart for him. He knew that Tom had been burning with a desire all these months to communicate in some way the peace of soul he had received at baptism. Week after week in the beginning, and now day after day he argued, pleaded, and even prayed aloud that the gift of unquestioning Faith might be given to Anderson. Bob knew the anxiety of the ex-carpenter was more than that of a younger brother; and he could not understand. What was eating Penney? Was it remorse? Was the fellow sorry he had squealed? Was he trying to make up for the condemning testimony he had given at Lexington? If it was, Anderson might be able to use that remorse to good advantage. He suddenly wondered if that could be what Tom had meant when he spoke of playing Santa Claus.

"Hey, Tom!" he called loudly.

"Line's busy. Call back in twenty minutes."

"Aw, go to hell!"

"Never! And I am praying you won't either."

With a muffled curse Anderson turned on his bunk; but he was moved by the sparkle in Penney's voice and the warm friendliness in the overtone. A secret hope grew in the depths of Anderson's being. Something in Penney's double talk spoke to Anderson's subconscious and hope grew. He smiled conceitedly as he turned his face to the wall and closed his eyes.

Had he been able to read the letter Penney was so engrossed in composing he would have found much to foster the growth of his hope, for Tom was telling Father Eugene how the Magdalens of Detroit had sent him *A Guide for Victim Souls* and was saying:

> I should like very much to become a Victim Soul; but is one in my present position privileged to do so? I know I should ask my confessor Father Libs that; but I won't see him for two more weeks and won't get to talk to him even then if he brings me Holy Communion — and I pray that he does that!

Father, I do not wish to offend anyone — Father Libs is a good priest and a splendid fellow, but he just doesn't have time to give the proper attention here.

That remark sent Father Eugene to his files for the first letter he had received telling of Eddyville and its men. It was from Father Brian and read in part:

I was in the Death House yesterday morning (September 1) and had a chat with Tom Penney. He is a very fine lad. That, incidentally is Father Libs's opinion of him, too. And let me tell you parenthetically that it would be difficult, if not morally impossible, for Libs to get to the Penitentiary much more often than he does. They are in charge of two parishes here in Paducah where the work is real and insistent. And there are only about seventy Catholics — of all descriptions — in Eddyville.

With that before him, Father Eugene wrote Tom explaining the Chaplain's situation as clearly and completely as possible. It was a happy thought. But a happier one would have been to inquire into the prisoner's object in becoming a Victim Soul; for that was the lure the devil was using at the moment — a lure that had Tom Penney with furrowed brow.

A letter in mid-December from Sister Magdalen of St. Gertrude smoothed those wrinkles and set the ex-carpenter writing:

Thanks a lot for the answer to the P.S. of my last letter. I see now what you mean about life's puzzle. Of course a picture would not be beautiful if only bright colors were used. Dark colors and shadows are a necessity. I have plenty of dark shades just now, Sister, but am taking them as from His loving hand, and trying to fit them in their right place. For I want the picture of my life's puzzle to be perfect when the divine Artist turns to look at it when the last piece has been put in — which will most likely be, Sister, just after midnight January 22. So please remember my date and keep me in your prayers. Thank Mother for me for allowing you to reply so soon. Hope I will get another letter from you before I go.

Until we meet in Heaven, may God bless you for all your kindness and encouragement to me.

Your brother at the right of the Holy Cross. . . .

As he signed his name, he knew his mind was made up: he

would offer himself as a Victim Soul; and he well knew for whom he would be offering himself! It was with a new-found assurance that he wrote a long letter addressed to the 49 Magdalens in Detroit and their Mother, who had just been notified that she was to go to Louisville. After four pages of personal messages the letter ends with:

> Now my dear Sister Magdalen of Compassion, God is here in Kentucky, too. And if things do not go well with our dear Mother Mary of the Holy Name the echo of our grief will disturb the peace in the Holy Land. Let me know when she is to arrive. I have a very dear friend who goes to the Good Shepherd Convent sometimes — a Father Eugene, C.P., of the Sacred Heart Retreat, Newburg Road, Louisville. I shall no doubt hear of her through him, too. He is a very holy priest. I love him as my own father. He has just obtained permission to visit me, also the permission to administer the sacraments. Let's hope other developments follow soon. . . .

"There you are!" cried Tom as he handed the letter to Captain Rankin. "That will make many people happy this coming Christmas."

"Good boy, Tom." The officer had come to respect this tall, scar-faced prisoner whose one ambition seemed to be to make other people happy.

As the officer slipped out of Death Row with the mail, Trent turned on Penney with, "Where the hell did you get all the Christmas joy?"

"Yeah, Penney," chimed in Anderson, "all you need are white whiskers and a red suit."

"How about the reindeer and the sleigh?"

"Cripes! You don't even need the suit and the whiskers," sneered Trent. "You're Santa Claus even without the fat belly."

Baxter, who had been awakened by the chatter, began, in his thin, off-key soprano, to sing: "Jingle bells, jingle bells . . ."

"For God's sake shut up, Skeeter," growled Anderson who had been deeply stirred by this talk of Christmas. "Tap dance, play the harmonica, fill your face with the Jew's harp if you want to; but don't try to sing."

"You don't appreciate my lyric tenor . . ."

"No, I don't. That's why I'm tellin' ya to pipe down."

"Aw, let the kid alone, Bob," put in Elliott. "He's only a month to live and Christmas is only a week away."

"What does that mean to me?"

Penney crossed to the bars which separated the two cells and very softly said, "It may mean more than any other Christmas in your whole life, Bob."

"Whaddya mean?" The cunning eyes of the chunky Anderson narrowed.

"You once said you'd become a Catholic if I got you life or freedom."

"So what?"

"So I'm playing Santa Claus."

"You mean . . . "

"You know what I mean."

"You mean . . . you'll . . . "

"I mean you won't go New Year's Day — and maybe you won't go at all." As Anderson's mouth worked soundlessly and his tongue flashed over his dry lips, Tom added, "Tell your smart mouthpieces that Santa Claus came to Eddyville early this year."

"Tom!" gasped Anderson. "Tom, do you mean you're gonna go through?"

"Don't stare a gift horse out of countenance," said the taller prisoner with a light laugh.

"My God, Tom!" gasped Anderson again, and passed a shaking hand over a brow that had broken out in beads of perspiration. "Can I . . . Do you . . . Can I really tell Nicholson that you . . . "

"Yes, and you'd better hurry; for His Excellency, the Governor, may be out of town for the holidays.

"Christ! . . . " gasped the chunky Anderson and actually staggered to his chair.

Penney watched him a moment, then lifting his voice from the little more than whisper he had been using, said, "Merry Christmas, Bob. And a very, very Happy New Year!"

Tom Penney at the time of the murders.

Few Clues Are Found As Officers Seek Solution To Murder Of Marion Miley

Mother, Also Wounded, Is In Critical Condition

Women Shot By Assailant In Their Apartment At Lexington Country Club

Police early this morning were pushing their watch for the slayer or slayers of Miss Marion Miley, 27, nationally prominent Lexington golfer, who was shot to death before dawn Sunday at the Lexington Country Club as the condition of her mother, Mrs Elsa Ego Miley, 54, who was shot three times in the abdomen, was pronounced critical at St. Joseph hospital.

After reconstructing the crime, police were turning over in the story that only one or two would-be robbers were in the brutal attack upon the two women who were shot in the rambling two-story club house when their second-floor apartment was entered by the assailant.

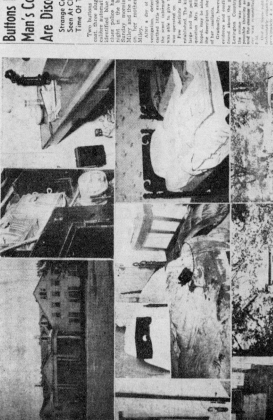

Buttons From Man's Coat Are Discovered

Strange Car Also Was Seen At Club Near Time Of Tragedy

Two buttons from a man's coat, three slugs from a .38-calibre automatic pistol, and an unidentified blue sedan were clues police had found last night in the brutal murder Sunday morning of Marion Miley, the golfing queen, and the wounding of her mother, Mrs Fred Miley.

After a day of painstaking investigation, detectives had unearthed little more than they could tell.

The most information Mrs Miley was able to give them before she was operated on.

Gradually, however, from bits of evidence and conflicting half-clues...

Anderson, Penney And Baxter Are Electrocuted At Eddyville Penitentiary For Miley Murders

Executions Started At 1:01 A. M.; Anderson Denies Guilt To Last

EDDYVILLE, Ky., Feb. 26 (Friday)—(AP)—Three men convicted for the slaying of Marion Miley, 27-year-old Lexington, Ky., golf star, died in the electric chair at the state penitentiary here early today.

The executions were started at 1:01 o'clock with Robert H. Anderson, 37, former Louisville cafe operator; Tom C. Penney, 33, former Lexington carpenter, and Raymond S. Baxter, 28, of Lexington, dying in that order. Baxter was pronounced dead at 1:33 a. m.

They were followed to the chair by Ernest Trent, 27, convicted of killing Hiram Smith, a Breathitt county constable.

Trent entered the chamber at 1:36 and was pronounced dead at 1:42. Anderson, who ate late yesterday was denied a stay of execution by the Kentucky Court of Appeals and Gov. Keen Johnson, maintained his innocence to the last.

"Gentlemen, the only thing I can say is that I'm innocent of what I've been charged with," he declared as three attendants strapped him in the chair. He was chewing gum and smoking a cigarette as he entered the room, and shook hands with Warden W. Jesse Buchanan.

He kicked off his tan prison shoes just before the current was turned on at 1:08. He was pronounced dead five minutes later.

Penney entered the death chamber at 1:14 and when asked by Warden Buchanan if he had anything to say, he replied, "I want you to publish my closing statement."

Penney's Statement

In his office after the execution,

Robert Anderson

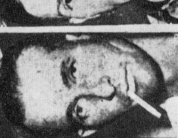
Thomas Penney

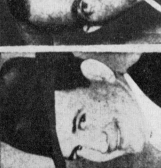
Raymond Baxter

Appellate Court, Governor Refused To Halt Electrocution Of Anderson

KENTUCKY STATE PENITENTIARY

EDDYVILLE, KY _Feb 9th_ 19_43_

NAME _Tom Penny_ ..... CELL NUMBER ....

TO WHOM .... STREET ....

RELATION .... CITY AND STATE ....

RULES FOR GUIDANCE OF RELATIVES TO INMATES

Inmates may write one letter each week to persons on their mailing list. In writing to inmates put cell number and name written plainly in English on the envelope.

Letters written to prisoners must not exceed four 4 pages in length. Prisoners may receive small boxes of edibles once each month, not more than enough for two 2 meals. It is strictly against the rules to send bananas grapes, raisins and cigarettes to the prisoners and they will not be allowed to receive the above mentioned.

Prisoners may receive visits from members of their family once each week between the hours of 8:30 to 10:30 A.M. and 1 to 3 P.M. Sundays and Holiday hours will be from 8:30 to 10:30 A.M. only. Persons desiring to see prisoners on business will have to secure permission from the Warden. IMPORTANT. We solicit your co-operation in carrying out the above.

W. JESS BUCHANAN, Warden

Dear Sisters. M. L. and R. A.

It's now 11.20 P.M. dear Sisters and I won't say much, — but the joy in my heart is unspeak as I calmly await the approaching end. Only Then dear Sisters will my life regain.

Fr. Lebs will write you, later and fr. you all. I am assured of heaven Sisters, I won't forget you in my happiness, be assured of that. Thank you for all you have done I will in a very short time be repaying some of those favors

So until we meet up there I'll be watching and waiting. Thank mrs. Camph and God bless her charitable heart.

I have great hopes of many accomplishment

May God Bless and keep you under the protection of Our Bl. Mother.

In loving Gratitude

Tom P.

Penney's last letter to Sisters Mary Laurentia and Robert Ann, written one hour before his execution (see p. 200).

KENTUCKY STATE PENITENTIARY

EDDYVILLE, KY _Feb. 25_ 19 _43_

NAME _Thomas Penney_ CELL NUMBER _Annex_

TO WHOM _Rev. Geo T. Donnelly_ STREET _Turner Field_

RELATION _Chaplain_ CITY AND STATE _Albany Fla._

RULES FOR GUIDANCE OF RELATIVES TO INMATES

Inmates may write one letter each week to persons on their mailing list. In writing to inmates put cell number and name written plainly in English on the envelope.

Letters written to prisoners must not exceed four 4 pages in length. Prisoners may receive small boxes of edibles once each month, not more than enough for two 2 meals. It is strictly against the rules to send bananas grapes, raisins and cigarettes to the prisoners and they will not be allowed to receive the above mentioned.

Prisoners may receive visits from members of their family once each week between the hours of 8:30 to 10:30 A. M. and 1 to 3 P.M. Sundays and Holiday hours will be fron 8:30 to 10:30 A. M. only. Persons desiring to see prisoners on business will have to secure permission from the Warden. IMPORTANT. We solicit your co-operation in carrying out the above.

W. JESS BUCHANAN, Warden

Dear Father.

I have neglected you terrebly Fr. but I so counted, on your being here tonight, and thought I could tell you my appreciation personally, but it seems that Our Lord has ordained otherwise, so now I am out on a limb, how can I write all the things I want to say. I have no secrets from you Fr. unless it is that I have kept you in ignorance of the meracle that God has wrought in my soul.

It looks like I am going to have to cut this short. Fr. I have been interrupted several times already and I see that I am not going to able to concentrate. I will ask the Libe to finish for me. and God will have to thank you for me: mere words may prove meaningless but God will give the credit where it belongs. Fr. he assured it in this case. yours will be great. I will not forget you in my happiness. Keep up the good work and we know God will make all right some sweet day. Say Hello to

Photostat of Penney's letter to Father George T. Donnelly. The first of the four last letters he wrote (see p. 198).

Sr Adelaide & won't be able to answer
(her beautiful letter. Give more hours
Dear Fr. & we'll meet our Lord and Lady
with all the Holy Saints and Angels. Get
your socks you'll get talked about too.
Until we meet
My Love & fondest regards
Sincerely in Our
Lord and Lady
Jesus,

Am enclosing a copy of my
last will.

Fr. Letz will write you.

"Mizpah" is the watch word

KENTUCKY STATE PENITENTIARY

EDDYVILLE, KY _Feb 25_ 19_43_

NAME _Thomas Penney_ CELL NUMBER _Cond_

TO WHOM _Sister Magdalen_ STREET _2650 W. Fort St_

RELATION _____ CITY AND STATE _Detroit Mich_

RULES FOR GUIDANCE OF RELATIVES TO INMATES

Inmates may write one letter each week to persons on their mailing list. In writing to inmates put cell number and name written plainly in English on the envelope.

Letters written to prisoners must not exceed four 4 pages in length. Prisoners may receive small boxes of edibles once each month, not more than enough for two 2 meals. It is strictly against the rules to send bananas grapes, raisins and cigarettes to the prisoners and they will not be allowed to receive the above mentioned. Prisoners may receive visits from members of their family once each week between the hours of 8;30 to 10:30 A. M. and 1 to 3 P.M. Sundays and Holiday hours will be fro n 8;30 to 10;30 A. M. only. Persons desiring to see prisoners on business will have to secure permission from the Warden. IMPORTANT. We solicit your co-operation in carrying out the above.

W. JESS BUCHANAN, Warden

Dear Mother and Sisters

Thank you for your beautiful letter of Yesterday.

I only have time for a note but feel that I must have the last word. So that I am almost "feminine" eh?

I can not say that I shall miss you. dear mother and Sisters, because where I am going I'll be so happy and busy I wont have time to miss any one, but you can bet your boots I won't be too happy and forget you. depend on me to deliver every message you have given me.

I have felt the effects of your prayers these last months, you know, or else how could I sit here with the courage to face this thing so calmly. I feel fine, and have no fear & will continue to the very end. I must stop now dear Sisters and Mother Gr. will be here any moment now. So until God Brings you home. I'll be watching for you. and Oh, the Joy to see you.

Penney's last letter to the Magdalens of Detroit (see pp. 198–199).

arms.

May our Suffering Savior and Sorrowful
Mother Bless and guard you Night and
day Remember J.X.C. be watching and Waiting
and begging our Lord to give you the necessary
graces to attain the highest perfection.

I am always in Our Lord & Lady
Your Loving Son & Bro:
T Thomas King.
At the right of the Holy
Cross
God Bless you)

We can never do enough for
the good God who loves us.

"Penney, Penney," cried Anderson hoarsely, "don't fool me! For God's sake don't fool me! Do you mean you'll pin it on Stewart?"

"I said 'Happy New Year,' didn't I? Use your head. I'm going to use my hand. Warden Jess will soon have a statement that will set the wheels of Justice turning backward."

"Oh, God!" gasped Anderson and let his head fall on his hands.

Before addressing himself to a task he knew would take days, Penney decided to finish his Christmas mail. To his mother he wrote:

> I will have a very happy Christmas if I can feel that you are happy. I have a big job ahead of me. I have prayed for wisdom that I may act wisely and without any personal motive. If I can distribute a little happiness amongst a few grief-stricken hearts, I know you will understand. I offer all my sufferings, labors, and prayers to God daily. . . . I accept whatever it pleases Him to send me. . . .

When she read the letter, Mrs. Penney did not know exactly to whom the boy was referring when he spoke of "grief-stricken hearts" amongst whom he would "distribute a little happiness"; but on December 29, when her eyes fell on the scare headlines of the morning paper she read all he had left unsaid in his letter. Black, bold-faced print told that Tom Penney had completely exonerated Bob Anderson — and by a new statement had won a temporary lease of life for the man who had been scheduled to die January 1.

CHAPTER ELEVEN

Out of the Devil's Clutches

THAT headline was no surprise to Anderson's hard-working attorneys: S. Rush Nicholson and Frank Cahill, Jr.; for a few days after Penney had decided to play Santa Claus, the latter had visited Eddyville. The story he had to tell on his return to Louisville plunged himself and his co-worker into a search for something that would cover their case. On a plea of "new evidence discovered" they had won a stay of execution for their client from Governor Keen Johnson; but they knew the legal minds of the Commonwealth would be far less pliable. Having already denied them a new trial, the Court of Appeals might well question its competency to overrule its own decision. In that case they would be forced to the federal courts. A writ of *habeas corpus* would help; but to obtain such they would have to post a big bond — and Anderson's resources were running low.

As they searched their books for some precedent, the relief they had felt on learning of Penney's determination, and the elation which followed when they found his fertile mind considering angles even they had overlooked, turned to something tinged with desperation. The matter-of-fact tone adopted by the newspapers spurred them on to greater activity; for while space had been given on the front page of all Lexington and Louisville papers, the articles under the headlines were redolent with skepticism and mistrust.

Cahill had told Nicholson that from the questions Penney had asked him during his recent visit, he knew that Tom was going to account for everything that had happened since September, 1941. He would exonerate Anderson completely by incriminating the dead Buford Steward; then explain away his testimony at the Lexington trials by admitting vengeance and vindictiveness had led him to implicate Bob. The climax would come when he would fix the blame for his bold-faced accusation of the Louisville Night Club owner on the Lexington Police, who, he would claim, had deceived him.

When Nicholson learned that before Cahill had left, the prisoner had written over a hundred pages without using a single new name save that of Stewart, he openly spoke his admiration for the cleverness of the criminal, but wondered what his motive could be; for such a deposition, he said, would hurt no one except Tom Penney. Cahill, in trying to enlighten him, only confused him the more, for he told the almost unbelievable truth that Tom Penney was writing not so much to save Bob Anderson's life as to save Bob Anderson's soul.

But all puzzlement, both as to Penney and their own position, vanished when, between them, these two lawyers discovered that they could enter a plea for a writ *coram nobis*. Kentucky practice offered them no precedent, but they knew they could prove that this writ was as old as the better known *habeas corpus* — if not older — and that it fitted their case perfectly. As the old year was dying, they knew they had fallen on something that would make Judges Adams, Thomas, and Lorraine Mix, wrinkle their legal foreheads. It was with verve that they wished one another a "Happy New Year."

Just as they made this discovery, the man who had set them on this search drew his pen with a flourish across the last page of his deposition. Penney had not blotted the signature before Bob Anderson broke into a chuckle and cried: "Congratulations! Tom. You've made the front page in the *Courier-Journal* again."

As Penney arose he caught up a double-column cut from a newspaper. "Here's the only front page stuff that counts, Bob."

Anderson's hand stretched between the bars. He took the tiny clipping and read:

NEVER TOO LATE, TOM

Tom Penney has high hopes of winning a prize in this paper's Biblical Contest. His only fear is that the prizes may not be distributed soon enough.

On December 21, Tom, one of the most enthusiastic competitors in the Contest, will celebrate the first anniversary of his reception into the Church by Father George T. Donnelly, now a chaplain in the army.

"I only hope I am not too late, as I could certainly use some money," writes Tom from his death cell in the Kentucky State Penitentiary, Eddyville, where he is awaiting death in the electric chair.

Tom is not too late to win a prize. His execution, originally set for January 1, will be postponed for at least two months because of an appeal filed by his attorneys. By then, the big cash awards will all be distributed.

"What are you doing in a Biblical Contest — you who tell us all to lay off the Bible? What paper is this from?"

"The Denver *Register.*"

"What are your chances?"

"None. I finished the questions, but Rankin was busy. He couldn't censor my mail on time. But I won just the same."

"Won what?"

"Friends all over the country. Catholic friends. Have you noticed my mail lately?"

"Yeah. It's been piling in."

"Twenty to thirty letters a day — and every one of them filled with good wishes."

"Where will they get you?"

"To heaven, Bob; for they are prayer-filled wishes. These people are praying for me. They are having Masses said for me. One kind soul gave Father Brian — remember him? — "

"Yeah."

" . . . Well, one kind soul gave him an offering for a high Mass to be sung for me on the 22nd. Another had me enrolled in 600 Masses. Why, Bob, over 200 Masses were said for me Christmas Day. That's a lot better than money to me."

"O.K., Penney, if that's the way you feel about it. But have you finished my contest yet?"

"Your contest?"

"Yeah. Have you finished writing that thing that's going to save me?"

Penney's big hands gripped the bars which separated the cells. "Bob," he said tensely and in a hoarse whisper, "I've done my part. You've seen the papers. You've got everything to win; nothing to lose. I've got nothing to win. I've done it for your soul. Now what are you going to do for yourself? Father Libs is not like Father George or Father Brian; but he can baptize you. Come on now, be good to yourself. . . . Be wise. . . . Don't be a fool. . . . "

"O.K., O.K.!, Parson. Let me run my own wagon. I told you under what conditions — "

"Bob, time is running out. I'm scheduled to go the 22nd. That's less than a month away. You won't go then just because of what I've written. But for God's sake — "

"Now, Preacher, let Mr. Anderson take care of Mr. Anderson. If your stuff really springs him, he'll take exceptionally good care of him I assure you."

The long scar on the left side of Penney's face shone livid as his teeth set. His knuckles went white under his grip on the bars. How he would like to reach through, seize his chunky companion by the shoulders and shake some of that complacency out of him. He knew his eyes were blazing as he stared at this sneering man. But even as his blood surged he felt a wave of pity sweep over him. His grip on the bars loosened. Better to pray. Heaven alone could now move Bob Anderson.

"O.K., Bob," he said quietly. "I've done all I can. I hope — and I'll pray — that Mr. Anderson does take exceptionally good care of Mr. Anderson."

For the next few days Tom Penney was extraordinarily quiet. The decision he had made troubled him because of the consequent newspaper publicity and the possible reaction of his friends. He felt he owed them an explanation, and yet did not see how he could give it. He would ask them to trust him and promise them ultimate clarification. With this determination made, he sat down and addressed Sister Mary Laurentia:

> . . . Of course you have seen the papers. Their insinuations and intimations have left me somewhat disturbed. Please do not think too ill of me, and believe only half of what they publish. You may be assured that no one will suffer by any action taken by me other than myself. It is too complicated, Sister, to try to explain now. So I would like you to trust me and ask our Father in heaven to guide me so that I shall do no wrong. . . .
>
> Sister, Mother wants to know what I want done with my body. She was not so blunt as all that, but that is what she meant. I cannot tell her. I do not know how badly a person electrocuted is burned. I would not want her to see me disfigured, but I would like to lie as near her as possible. Perhaps you could find some way to tell her. I told her to ask you. Oh, Sister, I do not know what I would do without you.
>
> Yes, Sister, I am going to ask for Father Donnelly. I have told him so.
>
> You may tell my friends — that is, the ones who care to know — that they are not to censure me yet. They should know enough about newspapers to realize how much truth is in one.
>
> Keep me in your good prayers and write soon. . . .

On January 4 he wrote Sister Robert Ann, and to her perhaps more than to anyone else, he manifested his uneasiness:

> I am mighty glad to hear that the newspapers have not disturbed your trust in me. Sister, it is so wonderful to have friends who will believe there is some good in every bad boy! And let me assure you now and forever nothing will disturb my Faith or lessen my love for God. Some things may be hard to understand, Sister, and will naturally cause publicity, but our merciful Father in heaven will certainly not condemn where no evil is intended — it is only of God I am thinking.

After telling how much he regretted his lack of opportunity

to receive Holy Communion on Christmas Day, the letter continued:

It would mean so much if we could have a priest here with us! I have been forced to make decisions in many matters too deep for my own spiritual understanding. But I believe it is not what I do, or the way I do it, that God regards; but *why* I do it.

What I do, what the whole human race, what all creation does, or how it does it, is nothing to God. Plainly He could dispense with His creatures' aid entirely, if He so wished; for their very power of aiding comes from, and is supported by, Him alone. He could do by Himself perfectly, what we do so imperfectly under His hand — but no! He wishes otherwise.

He was conscious that he was in deep matter, but because of recent reading, felt sure of himself, so wrote on:

The work we do and the manner of doing it He could supply. What He yearns for is the consecration of that work to Him. He never forces the human will. It is always in the power of the creature to choose what is right or wrong. Grace helps, enlightens, quickens our endeavors. God is working with us in everything we do. He begins, accompanies, perfects every act. And yet all the while the act remains our own free offering to Him. Our heart always remains our own, and that is why He longs for it and even stoops to beg for it. St. Augustine beautifully says: "God crowns us in His own gifts." They are His own, yet ours, too, in a very true sense. They express what we wish to do for Him.

When we stand, sooner or later, at His Judgment Seat, the question put to us will not be: "*What* have you done?" or "*How* have you done it?" but only "*Why* did you do it?" Did you mean well for all your blundering? Did you rise to your feet again after all your falls? Was it for *Me* that you did it? — Ah, Sister, that will be the moment!

There is no storm so furious, no darkness so thick in human life, that we cannot be sure of pleasing God during it, if we wish; for the sincere wish to please Him is the pleasing itself. I write you this, Sister, to tell you that I have done nothing blindly, but only for the purpose of doing good and without the slightest intent of doing any evil. If God will only judge me according to my intentions — and I firmly believe He will — then I have no fears. . . .

Sister Robert Ann passed this letter, as she had passed every other letter, to Sister Mary Laurentia, who read it thoughtfully. When she finished she simply said: "That boy is not at peace." More quietly and reflectively she added: "I'm sure, that he has the best of intentions in what he is doing for Anderson. But, Sister, this letter tells me he is not at all sure of himself — and death is only two weeks away. Oh, if Father Donnelly could only get to him!"

But sighs and exclamations were never Sister Mary Laurentia's forte. She hurried off a letter that, to judge from Tom's reply of January 7, showed her wise in the ways of the human heart and mind. Tom wrote in reply:

> Your letter came today and you don't know what a relief it was to learn what I should always have known — that the papers cannot poison your mind.
>
> I am glad you received the books. I miss having something to read, but I'll make out. It isn't long now and I am kept pretty busy. But it is just as you so often told me, Sister; the devil never sleeps. He is always on hand, but I think I shall be able to identify him in any form. . . .
>
> Sister, I have been receiving so many letters that it is impossible to answer them all. Some lady in Minnesota is sending me a Crucifix — a Pardon Crucifix from Father Purcell in Alabama. I shall hold it in my hands at the last moment. . . .
>
> Yes, Sister, I shall offer my all to our blessed Saviour in perfect love and in reparation for the many sins of the world that are hourly committed against Him. And in my last moment I shall give you and all my friends a very special intention. Surely God will not refuse my petition at such a time. As for myself I only ask that He judge me according to intentions and grant me mercy. . . .
>
> I am writing to Father D. tomorrow. I am sure that he will come.
>
> I must stop now and sleep a while. Until next time Good Night. I am awaiting the consent of Father Libs to be enrolled as a Victim Soul. Please remember my intention, Sister. . . .
>
> P.S. Sister, I have all of your letters except two. Do you mind if

I send them to Mother? I don't want to destroy them. It would be like destroying the Testament. . . .

It was that postscript which changed his mind about going to bed. While still in the high mood induced by Sister's letter, he wrote his mother:

> I know how hard it is for you, and I ask God in union with many, many good Christian people, to give you strength. And He will, I know; because if He had not already helped you, you could never have stood it this long. . . .
>
> All my friends — and they are many — tell me to assure you that you will not be forgotten even after I am gone. . . . The prayers of these good people are priceless. I know; for they have already obtained things for me that were seemingly impossible.
>
> The next time you go to the Hospital, ask Sister to take you to the chapel. When you come to our blessed Mother's station, ask her to obtain for you the courage and strength to endure these days of grief. And she will. For no one can understand better than she what you are suffering. . . . Then thank her for all the sweet and loving care she has accorded me.
>
> We are all her children, Mother, just as surely as our all-loving God in heaven is our Father. She is the Mother of our Crucified Saviour, and likewise our own dear Mother. She is always eager to help us love her Son. And it pleases Him to have us love His Mother, just as it pleases me to have people love you. . . .
>
> Mother, with regard to the question you asked me — I cannot lie to you. So please just trust me, dear, and remember I have no evil intention and no thought of self. . . .

Though it was already very late, he felt he should not sleep until he had answered one particular letter out of the batch of twenty-six he told of receiving that day — it was the letter from the Magdalens. He opened with a confession that turned into a very neat compliment. "When I feel myself slipping," he wrote, "I get me a handful of my sisters' letters and start reading them. Pretty soon I have thwarted the devil and am feeling fine again. Yes, your letters are more helpful than some spiritual reading. . . . I allow myself to envy you at times being so close to God.

But then I console myself with the thought that perhaps I will see Him soon and will be able to tell Him all about you. And, Sisters, that will be the 22nd of January. I am pretty sure this time."

Without lifting his head he went on to treat of the topic as constantly on the surface of his consciousness as the thought of death: "I hope you do not see the newspapers," he wrote, "for I have been getting some very unpleasant publicity these last few days and know it will grow worse before long. But it matters not what the public think of me. God is my Judge now."

That truth lifted his heart, and a happier note crept into his lines. "I will be very busy the next few days," he told them, "but I will write a long letter before I go. In the meantime keep me in your good prayers. Tell all my Sisters I remember each daily. And, Mother, I want to thank you for permitting the Sisters to continue writing to me. May God love you for your kindness. Mother Mary of the Holy Name has allowed the Magdalens of Louisville to adopt me, too. All I'll have to do when I get to heaven is seek out Our Big Sister, St. Mary Magdalen, and beg a brown habit. I know the good Dismas will be in sympathy with me. He robbed heaven, too."

He closed in his usual fashion: "Thank you, dear Mother, and remember your devoted adoptee at the right of the Holy Cross. . . . "

Tom was right about the publicity. It did grow much worse. On January 5 the morning paper told how time sheets cleared Buford Stewart by showing he was at work at the hour the murders were committed. That bit of news set plenty of tongues wagging. But the legal minds of the community saw that the law would have to be given its full consideration. On January 11 Judge Lorrain Mix gave a court order for a "testimony perpetuation." This empowered Anderson's attorneys not only to take the depositions from Baxter and Tom, but enabled them to initiate steps for a *habeas corpus* or *coram nobis* writ, or even to enter a plea that Bob's conviction be set aside on the grounds of "perjured evidence." Only Tom and Bob saw how similar all this was to the plea submitted by Elliott's lawyer six months earlier. It had all worked for him. Perhaps . . .

Not a few in Lexington and Louisville thought the wedge had been entered which would ultimately split the solid sentence handed down by Judge Adams thirteen months earlier. They could envision a mass of technicalities and evasions that would effectively block the course of justice and finally set Bob Anderson free. What they could not envision was Tom Penney's motive in this latest move.

On January 11 the depositions were taken in the Warden's office at Eddyville. But Jess Buchanan surrounded the affair with such strict secrecy that the morning papers were able to announce only that the testimony would be given in Louisville on the thirteenth of the month. Many waited with mounting curiosity for Thursday morning's paper. When they got it, some were disappointed; for Tom Penney's deposition proved to be little more than what they had been able to piece together for themselves from statements Anderson had made before the trial, things reporters had shrewdly guessed, and a few facts given out by the Police. But others who read more closely saw that Anderson's attorneys had a story which was so closely knit that only the highest skill and most persistent patience could unravel it. Tom Penney had motivated his every major thought, word, and deed since September 27, 1941, up to and including this latest deposition. The tantalizing part of it all was that the one man who could gainsay it was dead. If under cross examination, Penney could stick to this written story the way he had to his original story, some legal heads were in for a severe straining.

The following day's paper showed how determined Anderson's attorneys were. For Herbert Monsky, who was now assisting Frank Cahill, Jr. (S. Rush Nicholson having gone to the army), told reporters that since the law demanded that new evidence must be submitted during the same court term, the Circuit Court had a technicality on which it could deny both a new trial and the release of Anderson. But if that was used, his attorneys were ready to go to the Court of Appeals or even to the Governor for a thirty-day stay of execution so that "innocence could be established through the regular courts." Monsky then added that the Governor, following precedent and the policy of the State of Kentucky, would most likely deny the stay. Then he and Cahill would seek federal court aid.

That these two men were not talking for the sake of impressing people was evident over the week end. For, as Cahill had expected, Judge Chester D. Adams denied Anderson a stay of execution, basing his decision on the fact that "it was not within the competency of the Circuit Court to grant such a favor." Adams also denied the attorneys a writ of *habeas corpus* when they were unable to post a bond of $25,000 and entered a plea naming Anderson a "pauper."

Cahill let it be known immediately that he would appeal both decisions before Kentucky's Court of Appeals on January 19. He then entered his plea for a writ *coram nobis*. It was a new title, so Judge Adams very prudently took it under consideration. That closed the Court's session, but Cahill hit back at the State by telling reporters that the new evidence was such "that regardless of all precedent and codified practice, any Court would be required to give a new trial." This was a direct attack on Park, the prosecuting attorney, who had labeled this latest development a "hoax, pure and simple," and had stated that "there was no great precedent for *coram nobis* or for *habeas corpus* of a pauper."

The next move of Anderson's aroused attorneys was an attempt to obtain all the finger prints the Lexington Police Department had found at the Country Club at the time of the murder. They claimed they wanted to compare them with Stewart's prints and see if they could not establish incontestable proof that the dead man was in the Club the night Marion Miley and her mother were shot.

Guy Maupin quietly quashed this move by announcing that no prints of the Miley slayers had been discovered, consequently he had nothing to offer for comparison with Stewart's.

On Monday morning Judge Adams denied Cahill his plea for

the writ *coram nobis*, saying that the Supreme Court of the United States had one time decided that, before such a plea as his could be admitted, the perjured evidence would have to be known as perjured when it was used as evidence.

On Tuesday morning Cahill was before Kentucky's Court of Appeals arguing for a writ of *error coram nobis*, appealing every decision Adams had given, and insisting that Bob Anderson was now "unjustly and unlawfully imprisoned, restrained in the exercise of his liberty under color of authority of the State of Kentucky"; for the evidence discovered at the last minute — Penney's deposition — completely exonerated him.

The Bench listened carefully. The judges questioned, discussed, then handed down the Court's decision. Cahill could hardly credit his senses as he heard this Bench overrule every one of Judge Adam's decisions, grant a stay of execution to Robert H. Anderson from January 22 to February 26, and send the case back to Lexington for another hearing.

It was not all the aggressive attorney desired; but it was more than he had expected. He was informed most clearly that the Court was not reversing its former decision; it was not granting Robert H. Anderson a new trial; it was merely insisting that he be given another hearing so that it could be decided legally whether or not he was entitled to a new trial.

The judges explained that the Common Law of England allowed a man, by a writ of *error coram nobis* to take his case to the King's Bench, and that this Common Law applied in states which had no statute to cover similar cases. They then added that this ancient writ applied in such cases as that of Anderson, where a last minute claim was made that new evidence exonerated him.

Down in Eddyville the news sent joy and hope geysering up in the being of Bob Anderson. He laughed. He cheered in his own restrained way and congratulated Penney on being smarter than all the mouthpieces in the State.

But Tom was hardly interested. For weeks he had been torn between concern for his friends and concern for himself. He was

looking Death straight in the face. The number of days separating
him from a full and final embrace with this creature dwindled
with disturbing rapidity as he endeavored to write reassuring
words to all who had shown interest in him and confidence in
his conversion. He was at his table constantly, yet was not accom-
plishing half of what he desired. When he allowed himself a few
moments for a quiet study of what lay ahead of him, he found
he was impatient with Time's unvarying pace. It was altogether
too slow to suit him. The paradox caused him a rare smile. It
also gave him insight into the affectionate heart God had granted
him. He was anxious to be on his way. Yet he was loath to leave
so long as any of his friends were apprehensive. The three who
first came into his life after he knew it was almost ended gave
him especial concern. On January 13 he wrote to Sister Mary
Laurentia:

> I am really distressed regarding the mystery that now shrouds
> everything. All the more so since I cannot enlighten you on the
> subject. For anything I might say would increase your fears. So
> perhaps it is best, as you say, to keep silence.
>
> Sister, if you find it hard to trust me, just trust the Infinite Good,
> which is God, to guide me and keep me on the path to which you
> have so patiently directed me. . . . In time you will understand
> everything. And it won't be long now. And honestly, Sister, if it
> were left to my choice it would be tonight. I am weary of a world
> in which there is no peace to be found anywhere.
>
> Father Libs will be here this morning, and I am very glad. For
> this past month has seemed like a year.
>
> I am sorry I have not had the pleasure of talking personally with
> Father Eugene. I know it is my loss — and a great one!
>
> I don't know whether I am going to have Father Donnelly with
> me at the end or not. Haven't heard from him yet.
>
> Now, Sister, please don't ever think for a moment that you have
> failed in helping me save my soul. I do not know what the papers
> have been saying about me, because I never read them now. I
> cannot help what they print. I can only hope that they will be as
> eager to print the full truth when it eventually comes out, as it

certainly will in the end. So just be patient and remember that I know my soul is at stake; my life doesn't matter. . . .

Just a few days before receiving this reassurance, the deeply concerned nun had read the letter Tom had hurried off to Sister Robert Ann on January 11. . . . It had several passages that told her the prisoner was striving to please God; but a line in the first paragraph made her think he was still unsure of himself. Tom had written:

Thank you for the assurance that all is well. I say again, Sister, you must trust me *not* to hurt my soul. That is one reason why I am so anxious for Father Donnelly to be with me; namely, that you will have the assurance that I have not abused your good teachings. But I am doubtful now that I will have him. As you will see by the enclosed clipping he is having troubles of his own.

Such anxiety was incompatible with full conviction, the old nun thought.

Sister knew that Father Donnelly had been called to the deathbed of his father. She didn't know that on his return to Georgia he had eagerly slit the first of two letters from Eddyville. After expressing sympathy for the priest's loss, Tom wrote:

Now I must tell you that I will go also on the 22nd of January. Father, I had intended asking for you to be with me during my last few hours on earth, and I still want you. But now I haven't the heart to ask it. So I will put it this way: if it isn't asking too much and if it can be arranged, will you come? Now Father, feel perfectly free to do as you wish, and I will understand. . . . But do let me know as soon as possible.

The way things stand at present, I see nothing to prevent my going, and I am glad to get it over, Father. But oh, how I have longed for you or the sight of any friendly face. It has been plenty hard lately. You know how the devil keeps knocking. I suppose he'll keep at it until I draw my last breath.

Father Libs will be here shortly. . . . So until later I will say a very fervent God bless you. May our Suffering Saviour and His

Sorrowful Mother comfort you and protect you always. You know
I do keep you in my poor prayers.

Sincerely in our Lord

The priest looked at the calendar. He had but two days in
which to make arrangements. While still making rapid calcula-
tions he opened the second letter and noted that Tom's handwriting indicated a hurried and nervous state. It was dated
January 16:

Dear Father:
Just a line. Thinking about my last letter I see that I have kinda
put you on the spot, by leaving it all up to you. But I did not want
to add to your grief — this following so close on the sorrow already
yours. But Father Libs assures me that he would be glad to have
you and will make room for you, and if you can come to come on
Wednesday. I told him you might have someone fly you down.
Probably assuming too much, but there is an airport at Paducah.

Now again let me assure you, dear Father, that if you cannot
come, or do not wish to witness the ordeal — for which I would not
blame you — I will understand perfectly. I do know that you will
be with me in spirit if you are a thousand miles away or even at
the end of the earth.

You could perhaps do more to save the soul of another — if he
should happen to go that night — than anyone else. He has great
confidence in you, Father, and that means something! Father Libs is
a wonderful little priest, and I think the world of him myself, but
he has not inspired and won the confidence of Bob.

Father George gasped, "Bob!" and allowed his eyes to run
down to the postscript: "Do not write after Tuesday, Father,
and if you should wire, send it to Father Libs, St. Francis de
Sales Parish, Paducah." With a start he looked up.

"Tuesday, Tuesday," he gasped. "Tuesday is already dead!
But, boy, I'll get to your side or die in the attempt!"

It was just at that moment that Sister Mary Laurentia was
reading what she thought would be her last letter from Tom
Penney. It came just after the exciting news that Kentucky's

Court of Appeals had overruled Judge Adams' decisions. But it read as if that action would not affect Tom's position:

> Father Libs was here Wednesday. I went to Confession and received Holy Communion. That blessed privilege is to be mine again Thursday afternoon at 3. I'll be anointed after it is all over. Father Libs and Father Thompson will be here for sure. You see Father Thompson is Pastor of St. Francis de Sales Church in Paducah. Father Libs is his assistant. Haven't heard from Father Donnelly as yet or from Father Eugene.

Sister lifted her eyes from the letter to offer a swift prayer that Father Donnelly would get there. The next paragraph made her catch her breath, then whisper, "Aha, I thought so!" It ran:

> I have an idea that Anderson will be baptized Thursday. Sister, I have nearly gambled with my own soul to win this soul for God. Help me by praying that all will be well.

She shook her head and read on:

> I cannot begin to thank you, dear Sister, for all your kindness and generosity. So we will let saving my soul be your merit. As I am sure you and Sister Robert Ann share largely in this accomplishment. As you see, Sister, I am very confident of going to heaven — all unworthy as I am. Nothing can harm me now. The devil is still lurking in the shadows, but he's had all he will ever get of me.
>
> I will write again, Sister, before I go, and I will ask Father to write you a line, too. So until later be assured of my prayers and every good wish imaginable. Keep me in your good prayers. Don't write after Tuesday. I will be in heaven before it gets here.

A thousand miles to the west of Lexington, Father Brian was reading from a letter Tom had written the same day as the one to Father Donnelly, January 17. One passage gave the young Passionist a twinge of regret. It was:

> Father, you may say that Mass for me on the 21st. I am allowed to have three visitors with me my last night. . . . I am sending for Father Donnelly, the priest who instructed me; and of course, Father Libs will be here. I wish you were closer to me, Father. No one has

given me more courage than yourself. But whoever I will have, I will ask to write to you and give it to you in detail. By that you will be able to determine just where I shall spend my eternity.

"I'm pretty sure, Tom," said the priest to himself.

I have not the slightest doubt myself, for God only knows how sorry I am for my misdeeds. Oh, I know I am stealing heaven, the same as the good St. Dismas. You see, Father, I still have larceny in my heart! But I will use it from now on to snatch souls from hell. Surely, God will love that, will He not?

"Indeed! Indeed!" said the priest and silently thanked God for the wonder He had wrought in the soul of this man.

Almost at the same moment, his brother Passionist, Father Eugene, was offering the same silent gratitude, for he had read in a letter penned January 16:

I grow more weary of this world every day. . . . I would like to have seen you before I go, but I will not ask you to come; because I have an idea it will not be pleasant, Father. So let me thank you for your good prayers and those you have enlisted for me. . . .

Father Libs, Father Thompson, and Father Donnelly will be with me as far as I know. I will ask one of them to write you, Father, after it is all over.

Dear old St. Jerome over there in a Bethlehem Cave told Baby Jesus when He appeared to him: "I have nothing but my sins to give Thee." And Jesus said: "Jerome, give Me thy sins." I, too, have only my sins and my love to offer. But, oh, Father, how I love Him and His Blessed Mother and poor old St. Dismas — outcast and hoodlum he may be, up there playing the outfield of eternity, making shoestring catches of souls, and so seldom getting to bat. But when he hits, it's a home run, Father. Many people have told me I was robbing heaven even as did St. Dismas, so perhaps he will allow me to help him snatch a few souls from hell.

I won't say good-by, Father, but until we meet continue to give me a thought now and then. I won't forget you ever.

Sincerely in our Lord and our Lady. . . .

P.S. Don't mail anything after Tuesday, Father. I will go Friday morning at 1 a.m.

He wrote his mother almost every day now, and practically the same theme is found in each letter: sorrow for shaking the faith of his friends; deeper sorrow for not being able to relieve them by a full explanation; a plea to be trusted; and an assurance of his own salvation. On January 12 he had written:

> The only thing that gives me a moment's chagrin is that I shall never hear your sweet lips say: "I understand." . . . Now, Darling, just remember that your Tom has not gone crazy, and that I never have had, and never will have, the slightest intention of damning my own soul for the sake of another. . . .

On the eighteenth he opened more cheerfully:

"Your letter came today, Honey, and I am so glad and grateful to God for the courage and strength He is giving you. I myself am feeling fine." . . . Then quite bravely he added: "Yes, Mother dear, I understand your not coming here. It would only make it harder for both of us. Furthermore, I want you to remember me as I used to look." He closed with: "Well, Dear, until tomorrow, good night."

But Tom did not write Tuesday night. He could not. Early Wednesday morning he was telling his mother all about it!

> I guess you will see the news before I can get it to you; so there is no need to go into details. The Warden, Mr. Buchanan, came to my cell last night and told me to make no further preparation for the 22nd, because the Commonwealth was asking a stay for me and Baxter so that we can testify. He said we would be in Lexington for at least one day next week, so keep your eyes on the paper. I don't know what day it will be, but I don't think it will be more than one.

> I have been up all night trying to figure out how I am going to let the people know who won't see the paper. Father Donnelly is flying down here from deep in Georgia. Oh, well, a good visit will do us both good.

> I must cut this short so that I can mail it this morning. It is now 5 a.m.

> The good Sisters told me about their invitation to you. The longer I know them, Mother, the more I love them and the more convinced

I become that angels are right here in this cruel old world.

Honey, I am sending you a letter from one of my adopted Sisters. Note what she says about keeping your head high. Every one of these Magdalens is with you in spirit, Mother, and is praying hard for both of us. And you know the prayers of penitents pierce the clouds! . . ."

It was some time before Mrs. Penney turned to the enclosure, for the thought of seeing her boy again had set tears running down her cheeks. Finally she unfolded the tiny sheet and read:

Dear Brother:

Your letter, filled with such deep, spiritual thoughts, edified us very much and made us feel that you are very close to God. To hear that you had been pardoned would not give me near the joy that the news that you had gone Home would give me. For I dare say you will never be so well prepared again.

After all, we must all meet death some day. The death agony can be hours long. But yours, thank God, will be over quickly. And as you are so resigned and glad to offer your life to God, I feel that there will be no purgatory for your soul.

Your Faith is truly wonderful! Your dear mother can hold her head high; for not many mothers have such sons who have thoughts of God as beautiful as your thoughts and who face death as fearlessly as you, looking on it as a going Home to the One you love. . . .

Mrs. Penney dried her eyes, then slowly looked up and silently thanked God for all the blessings He had given to her boy — especially for the friendship of so many nuns and priests.

It was at that very hour a guard told her son that he had a visitor. Tom looked up with a trace of irritation showing on his scarred face. He had many, many letters to write and he was growing weary and a trifle impatient with lawyers, reporters, and preachers — even with some of the prison officials. They had shifted him from the cell in Death Row back to the little hole-in-the-wall he had first occupied on coming to Eddyville, saying that it was by special order of the State Welfare Commissioner, W. A. Frost, who had demanded the separation of Penney and Anderson.

"Who is it now?" inquired Tom a bit testily.

"A friend of yours."

"I haven't any who can come all the way down here."

"Are you sure?" asked the guard with a light laugh. "Look down the walk."

Tom was at the door of his cell now and could squint down the long cement corridor. He saw a tall, khaki-clad figure coming toward him. His vision was so obstructed by the edge of the tiny square that he could not recognize the immaculately groomed officer who strode toward his cell. It was not until the overseas cap came off and the white face had broken into its friendly smile that Tom gasped: "Father George!"

A key turned. A bolt shot back. The door swung open and Father Donnelly grasped Tom Penney by the shoulders saying, "Well, boy, it looks as if I risked my neck for nothing. A cadet, who just got his wings, flew me into Paducah. What a flight! What a flight! But now they tell me you're going to Lexington instead of to heaven."

"That's the sad news the Warden gave me the night before last."

"Sad?"

"Certainly, Father. I was all set. My hands were out almost touching the stars. But now . . . Well, might as well look at the bright side. I may see my mother and the good Sisters after the trial."

The priest slumped into the chair and crossed his knees. "Yeah, Tom. What's this trial all about?"

"Aw, Father, I thought you'd guess. Look, I might as well do some good with my useless old life. I'm ready to go, Father. Bob's not. I thought I might as well save him and perhaps save many another through him."

"But, Tom, when you get on the stand you'll have to swear that this story is true."

"Sure . . ." Then the prisoner stopped. "Swear, eh? You used that word purposely, didn't you, Father. I know you and your ways. There'll be something wrong in swearing. . . . Come on, Father George, time's short. You know the whole story. . . . "

The priest pushed a carton of cigarettes toward his protégé, then lit a cigar for himself. As he blew out a cloud of fragrant smoke he said, "Yes, Tom, I believe I do. I know it down to its last detail. I even know now what's going on and what has gone on in that mind and heart of yours. You want to save Bob, don't you?"

"His soul, Father; his soul."

"That would be a very good thing, Tom. But you know . . . Well, you know two wrongs will never make one right." Ever since he saw the papers telling of Tom's deposition, the priest had suspected some quixotic motive lay behind the event and wondered how he would approach the matter. Feeling sure that Penney's heart, not his head, had prompted the deed, the priest had planned some appeal to that heart. But here he was appealing directly to the head! He watched the earnest-eyed prisoner and saw little reflective light in those eyes.

"Of course not," replied Tom rather hastily, "but there are so many wrongs in this whole case that nothing seems right."

This would never do, thought Father George. He must get into no argument over technicalities. He knew Tom held fast to the fact that it had been proved he had killed neither woman. He had won his assent to the fact of moral guilt over a year ago, but he knew how prone the human mind is to quibble over physical facts. He shifted his grounds. "God has been good to you, Tom."

"Oh, Father! Good is no word for it."

"You wouldn't want to hurt Him?"

"Never!"

"Perjury is a serious sin, Tom."

"But I've committed no perjury, Father."

"Not yet, Tom. But when you get to Lexington . . . "

The prisoner jumped from the table on which he had seated himself, thrust back a lock of blonde hair, rubbed the long scar on the side of his face and in a vibrant whisper said, "Oh, Father! How lucky for me that you came! I never thought . . . I never knew . . . I see, Father. I see now. Now I know why I have felt so uneasy about the whole thing from the very beginning." He threw out both hands in a gesture of appeal. "I thought it was only a little lie. I thought it would be O.K. to save Bob that way. But now . . . now . . . " Then straightening up he faced the priest fully and asked. "What shall I do? Shall I call the Warden right away and tell him the whole truth? I intended to do that before I went anyhow. . . . "

"Not so fast, Tom. We've got to think this thing out. Too many people are involved for a hasty judgment. Bob is banking on you. . . . "

"More than once he said he'd be baptized if I got him life or a new trial."

"Don't you see, Tom, that if you call the Warden now and stop the trial at Lexington, and Bob learns that I have just been here, he'll hate you, me, and the entire Catholic Church?"

"Let him, Father. I'm not going to offend God for Bob Anderson or for anyone else on earth."

"Now you're talking, boy. But let's see if we can't save the situation entirely. When is this hearing scheduled in Lexington?"

"I don't know exactly, Father. Some day next week."

"Umm. Well . . . why not wait until Monday morning or late Sunday night before telling the Warden? That ought to be long enough to keep people from connecting your confession with my visit. Tell him the truth, Tom. Tell him just why you concocted the whole story. Then let him do what he wants."

"I've got something better than that, Father!" cried the aroused prisoner. "Listen. We can let this thing go through. I'll tell the Warden the whole truth but put him under oath not to release it until after I am dead."

"What's the idea, Tom? How is that any better."

"Don't you see, Father? Bob can have the benefit of the hearing. His lawyers may be able to get something for him out of the mess. If they do, so much the better for Bob. If they don't well . . . I'll have done all I could."

"Ummm," was the priest's only comment as he puffed and

chewed at his cigar. "We're in a nice mess. You're going to recant the story, Tom?"

"Absolutely."

"You're not going to perjure yourself."

"Under no circumstances."

"Can we do both without arousing Bob's suspicions and rendering him antagonistic?"

"I think so. I'll give the Warden the truth and then refuse to go to Lexington."

"Ummm," said the priest again as he puffed and chewed. "I doubt that you could refuse to go, Tom. But here, boy, suppose you go and say nothing."

"What do you mean, Father?"

"Tom, if you refuse to answer, you'll avoid telling lies."

"Of course."

"Do you think you could do that? Do you think you could allow them to put you on the stand, then, no matter who questioned you, or what they asked, just refuse to answer?"

"How about contempt of court, Father?"

"Don't worry about that, Tom. It's recognized law that no one ever has to incriminate himself. You'll be standing on your legal rights and on no mere technicality. Can you do it?"

"You mean just shut up? That's easy."

"Good. A few days after I get away from here, you go to Buchanan and tell him the true story. Give him permission to release it only after your death. Better have Rankin there, and Lady, too. Make it really legal, official, and impressive. Then take the trip to Lexington, but say nothing. In that way you'll not offend — not God, for you'll tell the truth; not man, for you'll be standing on your rights. Bob will be getting every break you can give him. And you . . . well, you'll get to see your mother and the nuns. Price will take care of that, Tom."

The prisoner came over to the priest's chair, laid a hand on his shoulder and very affectionately said, "Oh, Father, God is so good to have sent you. I was actually in the devil's clutches and didn't know it!"

CHAPTER TWELVE

Into the Hands of God

FATHER DONNELLY's plane was hardly off the ground when Tom was writing to Sister Mary Laurentia:

Just had a most delightful visitor — Father Donnelly! And I have his promise that he will write to you and tell you all. So now I feel very, very much better!

Sister, I am really sorry about the stay, because I don't think any good can come from it. Everything was prepared. Now I must go through all that again. Oh well, I will not complain. I am thankful for everything. I can smile and thank God for suffering as well as joy. It is only a matter of time anyhow. Just a month. That will give me four weeks in which to pile up more merit for myself and for those I love.

Sister, I know that despite what you say, you are still just a little bit worried. I confess now that you had reason to be. But it was only through ignorance on my part. That is why I have wanted to see Father Donnelly so badly. He understands the whole case thoroughly, and can advise me in two minutes. . . .

Now everything is put right and I am much wiser than I was this morning. And I love God and you and Father Donnelly more than ever. Ah, Sister, there will never be another just like him. He leaves for foreign service soon.

Just remember, Sister, I only slipped; I did not fall.

He had just put his signature to this letter when the giant Warden of the Prison came along "the walk." "I've got good news for you, Tom," he said cheerfully. "We'll be heading for your home town early next Monday morning."

"I thought I'd be heading for my permanent home — heaven — tonight. I wish they had stuck to their schedule."

"Cheer up, Tom. You may get to see your mother."

"Before we take that trip I must see you in private, Mr. Buchanan. I have something very important to tell you."

The Warden was struck by the prisoner's serious tone and earnest gaze.

"Want to come over to the office now?" he asked kindly.

"No. Let's make it Saturday or Sunday. You'd better have Captain Rankin there, too."

"Sounds important."

"It is — very."

"All right, Tom. I'll see the Captain and fix the time. Just thought you'd like to know about the trip to Lexington."

Penney looked down "the walk" to be sure they were alone, then in what was little more than a whisper said, "It'll be useless to take me to Lexington, Mr. Buchanan; I'll have nothing to say." When Tom saw surprise mount in those large eyes behind the heavy glasses, he added: "I've said all I'm ever going to say on this case in public. But I have a lot to say to you in private. That's why it'll be useless to take me to Lexington. If they put me on the stand it'll do them no good."

"Oh well," said the Warden heartily, "we'll have a nice ride together anyhow. You won't object to that, I hope. I'll let you know later about the time for that meeting you desire."

Now that he had made the first move in the plan Father George had outlined, Tom felt better. He turned to his table with zest and wrote many telegrams telling people he would not die that night. Very few human beings would understand why there were tears in the pale blue eyes of the prisoner or why his wide upper lip was quivering as he hurried those telegrams off. But the letter he sent that day to Sister Robert Ann gives us insight:

Do you think you can put up with me for another month? . . .

I have told Sister Mary Laurentia all about Father Donnelly being here, so I'll tell you all about the beautiful letters I received from Waterflow, New Mexico. Four of them wrote with your good Sister Ann Rita — and all the Sisters are making the midnight watch for me tonight. Oh Sister, I feel so wretched about it! They will all be so disappointed. I hate to write and tell them. So the best I can do is get on my knees and watch with them, isn't it? Their prayers will not be wasted, I know.

Dear old Mother did not get to come, as you know by now. Perhaps I may get to see you all next week when they bring us back to Lexington.

Well, it is nearing midnight, so I'll say good night. Hard as I try, Sister, I still feel a tinge of regret that I am not now nearing my eternal home. Continue to pray for me, Sister, and be assured of my own prayers. I doubled my efforts the last two weeks, and I'll try to keep it up.

That "tinge of regret" was still with him in the morning. But this is what it produced:

January 22, 1943

Dear Mother St. Clare and my Sisters Magdalens:

It seems almost impossible for me to get on my way, but here's hoping that I have better luck next time! Surely, Mother and Sisters, you have been all ready, at some time in your lives, to go some place, then have it turn into disappointment. You know how it hurts in just a small disappointment, imagine what it must be then when the place in question has been described in the beautiful words of St. Paul: "Eye hath not seen, nor ear heard, nor hath it entered into the heart of man to conceive what things God has prepared for those who love Him."

Not many men have had the opportunity to just sit down in a chair, reach out and touch the stars, dear Mother and Sisters. Of course some have — and they are the miracles of God's mercy. Whatever my past has been, God has said: "Though your sins be as scarlet, I shall make them white as snow." Charity covers a multitude of sins, and charity means love of God and the God of love. And I know with that love in my heart, I have the essence of sanctity.

A sneering question was once asked: "Can any good come out of Nazareth?" And perhaps some or many will ask the same question about the room next to eternity here at Eddyville. The answer proportionately is the same! Oh Mother and Sisters, I know only too well how unworthy I am. I have no earthly wealth of good deeds as merit. I have only my sins and my *love* to offer; but dear old St. Jerome said he didn't have anything but his sins, yet Jesus said: "Jerome, give Me thy sins."

My plight is like the story of the raindrop that fell a liquid jewel from the heavens. It fell in the gutter and mingled with the mud and lost its radiant sparkle. But then a sunbeam sought it out, kissed it, and carried it into the heavens where in the cold brightness of the sky it became a pure white snowflake. God's love has been that sunbeam to me, Mother and Sisters, and if you'll allow me to change and modernize the figure, I'll say I know I'm coming in "on the beam!" So that, my saintly Mother and Sisters, is why I feel quite disappointed.

However, I am not discouraged. My date is set again for February 26. Perhaps I can perform a few little acts of kindness or do something pleasing to God these next few weeks. . . .

I hope the telegram reached you on time, Mother. Oh there are many thousands whom I could not let know on time, and who will think I am gone. But I have spent quite some time asking our good God to accept their prayers and the Masses that are being said for me and apply them to my earthly store that I may be more worthy. . . .

The telegram of the 21st had caused both excitement and disappointment within the quiet Detroit cloister, and the long letter of the 22nd had not as yet been read to the assembled community when Tom was calling to Porter B. Lady, Deputy Warden of Eddyville's great stone house. It was Saturday, the 23rd.

"Did Mr. Buchanan say anything about seeing me today?" asked the prisoner.

"Not to me, Tom. Why?"

"I've got something important to tell him. He said he'd fix the time. I wish he'd do it today."

"I'm on my way to his office. I'll remind him."

Five minutes later the Deputy was back, unlocking the door. "The Warden's ready, Tom. Let's go."

For the next hour and a half three men listened to an earnest, humbled prisoner whose honesty was evident in everything from the light in his eyes and the insistence in his voice to the gestures of his large hands.

The Warden asked a few questions and got replies that were unhesitating and direct. Finally he said, "O.K., Tom. So I am not to publish any of this until after you are dead?"

"That's right. When I'm in the Chair you'll ask the usual question about having anything to say. . . . I don't want to say much then. . . . I want to pray. . . . So I'm telling you now. When you ask me that question on the final night, I'll simply say: Publish what I told you."

"O.K., lad. But stay where you are until I get this whole thing in writing. You men will act as witnesses."

Lady and Rankin nodded.

Two days later Penney was in Lexington. Three days later he was on the witness stand, which had just been vacated by Bob Anderson after the latter had said: "Tom Penney has told so many lies in this case, no one knows what to believe from him."

The tall, scar-faced prisoner looked neater and much more gentle than when he had taken that same stand fourteen months earlier. But despite the pronounced change in the aura he carried about him, despite the marked gentleness and kindliness in his whole mien, it was evident to all that Tom Penney was both nervous and very determined.

Cahill first questioned him. Tom readily admitted he had made conflicting statements, but when asked which statement was true, he electrified the Court by refusing to answer. Judge Adams' head turned and his eyebrows lifted in surprise. Park, the prosecuting attorney, allowed himself the shadow of a smile as he saw Frank Cahill frown and give a grimace of impatience and chagrin.

Before the Attorney could frame his next question Tom very

quietly but very convincingly said: "All I've got to say in connection with this case has been said. I made that clear before I left Eddyville."

"But tell us, did you disclose the truth in that deposition you made before you left Eddyville."

Tom shifted slightly in the witness box but very quietly replied, "I've got nothing to say."

Cahill paused, then turned to the Judge and requested a ten-minute recess. The request was granted. But the interval availed him nothing. Though Cahill peppered him with questions, the prisoner's only reply was the quiet: "I've got nothing to say." In exasperation and frustration the Attorney finally appealed to the Judge.

Judge Adams turned to the witness. "It is your duty to answer these questions unless you stand on your Constitutional rights."

Tom did not know just what his Constitutional rights were. He remembered Father George had said something about them, but what it was he could not recall. He did not know the Judge was referring to the right he had to keep silence when by speech he would be incriminating himself. He simply looked at His Honor and said: "I simply refuse to answer."

Cahill gave up in despair. Park took over for the State but got only: "I won't say," as reply to the many questions he fired at the man in the witness box. Tom gave one affirmative answer. It was to the question of the Court: "Do you refuse to testify in detail concerning the Miley Case?"

"I do," snapped Tom; and everyone in the courtroom knew he meant it.

The hearing lasted over a week, for Judge Adams, out of wise caution, was admitting much testimony he would ordinarily spurn. Penney was called to the stand three times and requested to be heard once. Yet, despite his four appearances, no one learned which statement: the one in the first trial in Lexington, or the deposition made recently at Eddyville, was true.

But Tom had a deeper concern than the hearing. As soon as he had arrived in Lexington he dashed off a note to his mother telling her to see Judge Adams and get an order to visit him in jail when the hearing was over. On January 27, after the first session in Court, Tom found a reply to his note awaiting him. He sat down immediately and wrote his mother:

> The lawyer said Mr. Adams would let him know when you can see me. I am pretty sure I will get to see you before I have to go back; for I think the Warden will grant me that privilege even if the Judge should refuse it.
>
> Please do not let anything trouble you about my conflicting statements. I know exactly what I have done, and I am not worried.
>
> Did you call the Sisters? I should have written to them, but there isn't much one can say just now, so I will wait until this thing is over. I would like to see Father Brian, too, but I am afraid of the publicity it might involve. I might write the Sisters a note tonight at that.
>
> Take care of yourself, and try, please, Mother, not to worry. . . .

He saw her Monday afternoon, February 1. Sisters Mary Laurentia and Robert Ann were in the visitors' room with Tom when his mother arrived. In her hands was a huge pie which she had baked that morning. Sister Mary Laurentia took it from her with a smile and nodded toward the tall, sparkling eyed man who was literally atremble. Sister Robert Ann turned away quickly and hunted for her handkerchief to wipe the tears which welled up as she saw an embrace in which was exemplified a love that is so like the love of God for His creature man.

The Sisters very gracefully withdrew. It made an easy farewell for both parties. The nuns had been with the prisoner over an hour and were delighted with his looks, his spirit. Tom had explained his contradictory statements to them; had assured them it was partly ignorance and partly anxiety to do all the good he could before he died that had prompted the deposition. He laughed as he said: "But here's proof that God still draws good from evil. If I hadn't been so stupid, I'd never have seen you again."

"You prophesied you would, Tom. The day we visited you at Eddyville . . . remember?"

"Call it a hunch, Sister Robert Ann; for I'm not a prophet nor a prophet's son."

"Tom," said the older Sister Mary Laurentia in her own direct way, "are you afraid to die?"

The head went back, the blue eyes opened wide and their sparkle emphasized the truth of his words as he said: "Afraid? Why, Sister, if that chair there," and he pointed to the one he should have been sitting on, "were the Electric Chair, gladly would I sit in it this moment. . . . And it makes me very happy to realize I am the same age as our Lord was when He died. Just another instance of His goodness to me. As you say, I'm spoiled. I only hope He takes my life as an offering."

"For whom, Tom?"

"For Bob as much as for anyone."

The parting with his mother was not so easy. The mother might never have loosed her arms from the embrace had not Tom assured her he felt positive he was going directly into the hands of God.

Early the next morning Penney and Baxter were on the road to Eddyville; Anderson remaining behind for the decision of the Court. That night Tom wrote to his mother:

> Arrived in Eddyville O.K. at 2:45 p.m. Left Lexington at 7:07 a.m. Had another beautiful day for traveling and enjoyed a splendid ride. Just another proof of God's goodness, Darling.
>
> Tommie came yesterday just after you left and stayed about an hour. I am so glad I got to see everyone. Tommie brought me a carton of Camels and the Warden let me bring them with me. I ate the candy on the way down and enjoyed your pie last night. It was delicious, Mother. . . .

The long drive up and back; the tense, nervous days on the witness stand; and the emotional drainings caused by his meeting with and final partings from those whom he loved so deeply, left Tom almost exhausted. But one night's sleep and the urgency of time brought him to his table the next day and set him writing energetically. He had but three weeks to live. He must reassure his friends and explain as much of the baffling situation as he could. Father Brian was the first to whom he turned. His explanation was not too clear, but the young Passionist was happy to read:

Father Libs will be here next Wednesday. I can hardly wait. He was not to blame for my errors, Father. I did not make the thing clear to him. That is why I wanted Father Donnelly — he already knew everything.

To Father Eugene he wrote an explanation which ended with a promise:

Be assured, Father, that Father Libs will know about everything. I stumbled but I did not fall, and I think you know, Father, that I am sincere when I say I had no evil intentions and that it was all my fault for not making it clear to my Confessor. I love God too much to offend Him intentionally, Father, and am as sorry as can be for what happened, and tell Him so, many, many times a day.

. . . I am also very sorry for all the publicity and the disturbance it caused you and others. I know you will forgive me and continue to pray for me. . . . Write any time, and if it so happens that you can be here the 26th, remember I want you!

On February 4 he wrote a full explanation to Father Donnelly at Turner Field, which ran in part:

Dear Father:

Came back from Lexington Tuesday, but thought I would wait until they had decided on Bob's case before I wrote you. Judge Adams denied him a new trial yesterday. I don't know what they will do now, Father, but whatever it is, you can be sure, I'm through with it. . . .

Please, Father, do not blame anyone but me. I did not explain the case thoroughly to Father Libs. I took it for granted that he knew more about it than he did. . . . Father Libs will be here Wednesday. I'll let you know about it all then.

I was permitted to see Mother, my sisters and brothers. The good nuns came Monday afternoon for about an hour. I am so thankful that I saw them, Father. They were so disturbed about the conflicting statements — as was only natural. I won't feel right until I see Father Libs and make everything right with him.

. . . I know you were hurt to think that I would do a deliberate deed so contrary to all your teachings. I have suffered from it, too, Father. But I want to suffer for it here. I won't complain. Nothing like it will ever happen again, you may be sure. . . .

Tom was tired and tempted to put his pen aside but his eyes fell on an envelope with an Owensboro postmark. He knew the handwriting and smiled: Sister Francesca's, the little Ursuline whom Father Brian had asked to write to Tom. He must write to her no matter how tired and tempted. She had replied so promptly and with such evident trust in the man the whole world was calling "liar" that he warmed at the very thought of her. From the very beginning he had found it easy to write to this nun, who was so direct, so optimistic, so full of fun. Scanning her latest Tom knew he must give her something worth while. He drew a bit of prison stationery to him and wrote:

Dear Sister Mary Francesca:

Don't know how many bars you were out, but you came in on the down beat! I arrived yesterday afternoon and received your letter this morning. I want to tell you, dear Sister, that more than you will ever know, I *do* appreciate your wonderful faith in me. . . .

The newspapers published my conflicting statements and thus disturbed you, all my friends, and even myself. I am sure, Sister, that you are entitled to know that my Confessor has been fully informed of the truth and now assures me all is well. Let me add that I stumbled but I did not fall. My soul is still intact. God is pleased; I am happy; and the devil is furious. Which makes everything perfect. He is not a nice playmate — the devil I mean. And as you say, he has many accomplices who appear in many forms and fashions.

Oh, by the way, I had many visitors last Monday afternoon and evening, after the sessions in Court were over. Did your ears burn? Sisters Robert Ann and Mary Laurentia came to the jail for about an hour and a half, then my mother, sisters, brothers, two nephews and others. Sister Robert Ann knows you. Oh why can't everyone be like you Sisters! Then everyone would love everyone else. There wouldn't be all this war; people would not have to, or would not want to lie, cheat, steal, rob, or kill.

Until next time I'll be asking our Lady to assist you in all you do. So you see, you cannot fail; for she has never failed me! Continue to remember me.

Your devoted friend in our Lord and our Lady . . .

Late Friday night the prison grapevine was at work spreading the news that Bob Anderson was back from Lexington after having been denied a new trial. Penney was still up on "the walk" so he did not see Bob, but the reports that reached him set his hand stroking the long scar on his cheek — a gesture that always accompanied strong emotion or deep thought. It was said that Anderson was bitterly cursing Penney, priests, and the whole Catholic Code.

Tom sought outlet for those thoughts and feelings by writing Sister Robert Ann:

Bob came back tonight. I am still separated from him. Perhaps it is best that way. I am doing fine up here. No one to bother me. Just me and Jesus. And you may be sure I pause every so often to tell Him how sorry I am for my error. Oh, Sister, ask Him to punish me here. . . . If I had listened to you, Sister, this thing would never have happened. But . . . it has taught me that His way is the only way; that there is no such thing as half right and half wrong. It is all for God or nothing!

Sister, you made me want to crawl into a hole Monday — and I deserved it. So don't feel bad about it. I am praying so hard that Bob will not be embittered. I do not care what he thinks of me. In fact, I am glad to bear his wrath if in the end it will save his soul.

Hurry and write to me. I will stop now and say my beads. Oh yes, Sister, I will take them with me. You will see that Mother gets a rosary when she is ready, won't you? I just know she will be some day. . . .

Early next morning Tom heard his name called by one of the inmates of the next cell. He knew Don and Alex Daugherty, two brothers, were there in "permanent lockup." He liked these burly lads, and when he heard that they were under instructions ever since Father Brian's Mission, he felt he was near friends. He answered their hail as cheerfully as he could.

Don cried: "I just got a look at today's paper. The Judge puts the blame exactly where it belongs."

"Where's that, Don?" said Tom with quickening interest.

"Right on Anderson's shoulders."

"How come?"

"He says Anderson could have and should have gone on the stand in the original trial and flatly contradicted your testimony. He didn't. So the Judge says his action now is utterly unconvincing. And of course he's right. So don't let Anderson's growls get you down, Tom. You did all you could for the guy."

"Thanks, Don, not only for the news but for the encouragement."

It proved more encouraging than Tom realized. It put him in the mood to write one of his most cheerful letters since January 21. He addressed it to Mother St. Clare and her Magdalens, telling them something of his most recent experiences:

> While I was in jail last week in Lexington, there were locked up with me 2 Chinese, 5 Mexicans, 1 Greek, 1 Canadian, and 2 American boys. They could not understand my cheerfulness or good humor, or how I could sleep. They had prepared a cell for me apart, and these men had orders not to talk to me or give me anything such as knives or razor blades, etc. That night they brought a dope addict in and locked him in with me. When preparing for bed I removed some articles from my pockets and laid them out. Pretty soon he said: "What do you have in that little purse?" It was one Sister Mary Holy Name sent me for Christmas. I handed him the purse. He opened it, took out the beads and stared at them. Soon two big tears rolled down his cheeks. I didn't say anything to him just then, but was conscious of the fact that it was the first time in my life that I was happy at the sight of tears. Later we had quite a talk and between his grunts and groans I learned that it was nearly six years since he had been to Church or Confession. The next morning they took him to the U. S. Public Health Service. As he was leaving I said to him: "Frank, what are you going to do when you get out there?" He said: "Tom, the first thing I do will be to call Father and go to confession. . . .

To that he added:

Then a very young boy who cursed something terrible was put in with me. Poor kid could not even read or write. Somehow I gained his confidence and, my dear Mother and Sisters, the last three days I was there I never heard him utter one bad word. . . .

On the last day, after Court was over, I was permitted to see many of my loved ones . . . my dear old mother, when I held her in my arms and kissed her good-by — perhaps for the last time — asked me . . . "if you will be able to see me from up there?" I said: "Mother, dear, my eyes will never leave you until you join me in heaven." I left her heartbroken, but happy. . . .

Mother, I have prattled on here with my personal pronoun until I have no room for personal messages, but tell my Echo I really got acquainted with J. Buchanan on the trip and learned a secret. He fell in love with a girl once and she turned nun on him. I said: "My, but she must have been very intelligent!" "How so?" said he. I replied: "Oh I was just judging from the preference she made." He is really a swell fellow, this giant J.B.

The days were flying now and, despite the fact that Tom spent most of his day and much of his night at his table writing, he could not seem to keep abreast of his mail. But God's hand is evident here perhaps more than anywhere else; for this correspondence with his mother, these nuns and priests kept the doomed man's mind focused on the great Reality beyond the last horizon and on Him whom someone has called "the Obvious Invisible."

It seems as if the thing that Tom had asked Sister Robert Ann to pray for in his letter of February 5 was being granted; for on the 10th of the month he wrote "Well, Sister, the thing I tried so hard to prevent has happened. Bob is very bitter toward Father Libs and sent word for him not to come down to see him today. I am sorry. It really hurts. It hurt Father, too. . . . Perhaps you can help with a letter, Sister. But don't mention me or let on that you know anything. I gave Father leave to reveal anything I have ever told him so that he could talk to Bob plainly.

It is my personal opinion that Bob will want to see him soon, and very soon. I hope and hope and hope. . . ."

But Anderson's bitterness was not the only source of anguish for the man in the little cement hole-in-the-wall up on "the walk." Letters from Lexington told him his mother was not well. On Lincoln's Birthday he wrote: "Oh, if God would only give me your pains and aches, how happy I would be!"

Tom gave Father Brian an insight into his aching heart in a letter dated February 16:

I am certainly happy that you will be able to visit your good parents, Father. Some of us never appreciate them until we lose them or come to the full knowledge of just how seriously we can injure them. . . .

On February 21 Tom was writing Sister Mary Laurentia, telling her how Anderson's lawyers had been down to Eddyville again and had had him summoned to the Warden's office where they told him Bob was to have a hearing in Louisville Wednesday before Judge Miller of the Federal Court. "But I had nothing to say to them, Sister, so I will not be called again. I thank God for sparing me that ordeal. I don't think Satan will bother me again, Sister; but I'll be on my guard." In closing he wrote: "I must get a letter out to Father Donnelly today. . . . Yes, Sister . . . there is no name for what he has been to me."

Tom immediately carried out his intention. He closed his letter to the priest with: "I understand that Bob has not given up hope yet, but for me it is still February 26. . . . I do hope that you can get up, but if you can't, well . . . you're in the army now!"

But Tom's hopes were high. Father George had thought nothing of risking bitter criticism in Lexington when he first entered the case; thought nothing of driving the hundred miles between Covington and Fayette County Jail two or three times a week to instruct the prisoner; thought nothing of making the wearying six hundred mile round trip between Eddyville and his parish house week after week in order to sustain the newly baptized.

He had thought nothing of risking his life in flying from Georgia with a very young cadet in order to be with Tom the day he was scheduled to die. The prisoner had reason to believe his faithful friend would be with him when he walked those last few steps from his cell to the room with only a single chair.

With eagerness, then, he tore open the envelope from Turner Field on Tuesday morning, February 23. He unfolded the letter with high expectations, but the very first sentence made him sit down and drew a groan of disappointment from him:

Dear Tom:

After all these months I am going to have to disappoint you. I had planned on coming down to Eddyville, but conditions here will not permit my absence. I'm sure you will understand.

However, Tom, in my disappointment, I have the consolation of knowing that you are one whom I am sure is going to enjoy the bliss of heaven. . . . What happiness is awaiting you, Tom!

Don't forget me when you come face to face with our Saviour. Remember we all need help and your influence will be great. You can obtain much for me. And don't forget those who have been so kind and helpful. You can rest assured they will not forget you.

I will write to Bob. . . . I wrote him last week, but have received no answer. If it were possible for me to talk to him, I know he would do what is right; but at present it seems impossible. I feel sure God will hear our prayers.

Sometime, Tom, I will see your mother and explain to her what I know you would like her to know; namely, that you are in the friendship of God and certainly one of His choice souls. May she have the grace to enjoy what you have enjoyed this past year before God calls her.

I am going to say good-by, Tom. Your example has meant much to me. I will never forget you and even though I shall pray for you always, I know you will never need my prayers. You have earned heaven yourself; I have only supplied the opportunity. . . .

I shall be with you in spirit Thursday night. God love you always, Tom.

Until we meet in heaven,
Father.

It was the last sacrifice God was asking of Tom Penney, and perhaps the greatest and the most beneficial. For the last time on this earth the prisoner had seen his mother, his sisters and brothers, the two Nazareth nuns; and now he knew he had seen for the last time the man he had so often confessed he all but adored. He was as naked now as Christ had been on Calvary . . . for a few moments he thought he was more naked and alone; for Christ did look down from the Cross on His Mother, on John, Magdalen, and the Holy Women. But then, Tom caught himself. No. He was not alone; for God seemed almost as tangible as his table, as intimate as his heartbeat; more real than any reality on earth. He placed the letter flat on his table, struck it with his large right hand and said: "If that's what You want, Lord, I want it too. Bless Father George for all he has been to me."

With that Act of Resignation a peace of soul came to Tom Penney that was not to leave him while he lived. He had taken all the setbacks as so much Purgatory, and now he suddenly saw how happy those suffering souls can be.

His thoughts were frequently in Lexington. But when he read how Sisters Mary Laurentia and Robert Ann visited his mother weekly and allowed her to come to the hospital as often as she liked; when he read how Tommie, the girl he now knew he should have married, was talking with his mother every day either face to face or over the phone; when he read how this same Tommie was consulting lawyers, writing judges, visiting Price and planning a call on the Governor; when he read how letters were arriving at 383 South Spring Street from priests and nuns and kind-hearted layfolk; Tom knew that God and His Blessed Mother were answering his prayers in a measure he never dared ask.

One week before the date of execution he wrote:

> Mother, dear, I could ask Mr. Davis to bring you down, but I can't bear the thought of seeing anyone who really cares about me here. . . .
>
> Mother, I want you to know I willingly accept whatever God, in His Infinite Wisdom, has ordained for me. . . . It is not easy to hold oneself in perfect resignation, but I have often wondered lately

if it doesn't require more grit and courage to want to live than it does to want to die. God has given me grace to carry on so far, Mother, and I know He will continue so long as I love Him. So whatever happens I will not murmur against Him. I only ask that His holy will be done! . . .

The only sad moments I have, Mother, are those in which I think of the ones who really love me and will hate to see me go. If I could only be sure that they would not worry or grieve, I would say that my last moment on this earth would be my happiest. . . .

In this last week of life Tom learned the limitations of human language when he tried to show his heart to the one from whose veins that heart had drawn its blood. But he was able to open the final week with:

How did you like the little spread I told Tommie to surprise you with, Mother. I was going to have two made for you but changed my mind when I realized you could hide one easier. You see, I know my mother pretty well. . . .

Tommie wanted to have my picture made and surprise you with it. But I can't get one made in here. I'm sorry for your sake and hers. Mother, I need not tell you that that girl's interest is much more than mere sympathy. And I think it will lighten her heart somewhat if some day you tell her that your Tom loved her and loved her for years!

I guess this will be the last letter you can answer, dear. And you must have that answer in the mail Tuesday night, or I won't get it. But do not worry yourself about it, Mother; for I know all the things you would like to say, so never worry about having left anything unsaid. . . .

The very next day he sent her a Mother's Day card, which had been sent him by Regene Unger, an invalid of Sauk Center, who had been corresponding with Tom since the appearance of the article in the *Register* concerning the Biblical Contest. Within the folds of the card, Mrs. Penney found a dollar bill, a short note from Regene to Tom, telling him to send the card and the bill to his Mother as a gift; finally there was a clipping with Msgr. Bougaud's inspiring message for those who mourn;

a message which insists on the very thing Mrs. Penney had asked Tom when she held him in her arms for the last time. "The great and sad mistake of many people," wrote the Monsignor, "is to imagine that those whom death has taken, leave us. They don't. They remain! Where are they? In darkness? Oh, no! It is we who are in the dark. We do not see them, but they see us. Their eyes, radiant with glory, are fixed on ours filled with tears."

On Wednesday morning Tom penned the last letter his mother could receive while he yet lived:

Will write now, and again tomorrow night.

I had a letter from the Sisters today and will write them some time tonight; for I want to have my mind as clear as possible tomorrow night. I'll tell you what I am going to do Mother: It is too painful to write to all my brothers and sisters, so I'm going to write one letter to you, and you can either read it to them or let them read it themselves. I am sure all will be together.

Then after detailing a few messages he wished her to pass on, he concluded:

Bye for now, Darling. Just keep your chin up and remember, Dear . . . I am going to my home in heaven to await your coming.

He signed it just as his second last day on earth ended.

CHAPTER THIRTEEN

Last Day on Earth

TOM PENNEY was up early on the 25th. He had much to do his last day on earth. But his first thought was of adoration. Down on his knees he went in his cold, dark cell and looked lovingly at a little round, white wafer of unleavened bread. It had come some days ago from Sister Magdalen of St. Gertrude, the aged contemplative whose office it was to bake the altar breads at the Detroit monastery. At the moment Tom recognized it for what it was: just a weightless wafer of wheat. But he knew that before many hours it would hold under its appearances of bread the Body and Blood, Soul and Divinity of Him who holds up the world.

Tears were in his eyes as he recalled what he had written to Sister Robert Ann the day it had arrived:

> Sister Magdalen of St. Gertrude just sent me the host for my last Holy Communion. So you see, in a way dear Sister, I have His precious Body right here in my cell with me, just waiting for the 25th when Father Libs will make it the Living God of my heart. Please do not divulge this to anyone save Sister Laurentia. I am sure it is all right, for Sister St. Gertrude obtained the permission of her Confessor and her Superioress to do this. You know I could not deprive her of the pleasure of knowing that she had made my last one. Believe me I shall not waste a single moment of that precious union with God.

191

Before beginning the letters he had planned, Tom took a look at the box he had packed for his mother. Some shoes, shirts, and trousers were on the bottom, but then came the treasures: books, pamphlets, holy cards, and those precious letters from nuns, priests, and layfolk. He gave a hasty glance around the cell to satisfy himself that everything was in the box that should be. Then he took a huge sheet of paper, measured it over the top of the box, tore it on the edge of his table, fitted it again, then in large, fat letters printed his farewell message to his mother:

GOOD-BY, MOTHER DARLING.

I LOVE YOU

and

WILL AWAIT YOU IN HEAVEN!

Your own Tom.

He slipped it in snugly, then closed the box and placed it to one side. The first chore of his last day on earth was done. Now for the others. He read the letter he had started to Sister Francesca the night before. In it he had been telling Sister about Regene Unger, his Sauk Center friend, advising her to give Regene notice whenever she was in trouble, and the girl would soon have "half the convents and monasteries in the country praying for you." He smiled now as he added:

> But why go to all that trouble? Are you not sending me to heaven to do your praying? I will have found your Friend even before you receive this letter perhaps, and when I get through telling Him about you — well, you just wait and see. I'm saying nothing of what I will have to tell our Lady.
>
> Sister, I am glad you are at last understanding *Mizpah*. I intended telling you about that, but forget. . . . You know there is a special reward for converts, but for such a convert as yours! Well, seriously you'll probably inherit a private Throne.
>
> Now let me confess that I was conceited enough to think of sending you a remembrance even before you asked for one. But now I am in a quandry just what to send. Most of my books and prayer books I have autographed and returned to the ones who sent them;

the beautiful little metal crucifix you gave me will stay right where it is: on my scapular chain around my neck; my rosary will be placed in my hand with my crucifix. So, as value doesn't count in this instance, I am sending you a little metal rose, the Little Flower's, with the Sacred Heart and Our Lady of Mt. Carmel attached to a badge that was made especially for me by Sister St. Clare of the Good Shepherd Convent in Detroit. . . .

Now, Sister, I won't say good-by, and I know you don't like praise, so I won't take advantage of this perfect opportunity, knowing that you cannot answer back. But I do say: Hold that old fighting spirit and keep that "sassy grin" (I wanted to say "sweet smile") and if I don't see you up there some day, I'll bet my socks and shoes it will be I who is absent! Thank all the dear people for their good prayers.

He had just signed his name when he heard steps outside his door. He listened as the long bolt was shot back, then watched his door open. It was the Warden.

"Good morning, Tom. You seem busy."

"I am, Mr. Buchanan. I'll never finish all I should today."

"Tom, is there anything you want to say before you die?"

"Not a thing about the case, Mr. Buchanan. But I do want to say thanks to you and all the officers of the prison. You've been very kind."

"Thanks, Tom. You've been a good boy. I'll do my best to see that you're not bothered today. There are a few things that can't be avoided. You need a haircut for one thing. Then I must come around twice more to ask this same question. But sit in and accomplish all you can. See you later, boy."

Tom "sat in," and wrote to Father Brian:

Doubtless you are wondering why I didn't answer your last letter. Well, Father, I knew that you would not receive it on time to write again, so I have taken my time. . . .

I am feeling fine, Father, and to change a few words, I will use a few sentences from your last letter: The love of God is so strongly embedded in my heart that knowledge of the "inevitable" has brought a resignation to me that makes the prospect pleasing — yes, even joyfully so. . . . My love of God still outweighs my love of life. I seek not the consolation of God, but the God of consolations; not the gift but the Giver. . . .

Bob just came back from Court — turned down, of course, as we all expected. I am sorry that nothing can be done for him. . . . He has finally decided, I think, to be baptized in the Baptist church. However, I shall not give up hope. . . . I think you know how I feel about you and how grateful I am for all you've done for me. I cannot begin to thank you enough, so God will do it for me. I will not forget you in my happiness, Father; be assured of that. Nor the other good friends you have made for me . . . the kind the world needs more of.

The time has come at last when I must say "Good-by." I've enjoyed your wonderful letters of encouragement and your friendship. Your efforts have not been in vain. I'll be there to witness your reward when your work is completed. "He will gently call you home. Oh, the rapture of that meeting. Oh, the joy to see you come!" Until then, may God bless you, Father, and all you hold dear. . . .

As soon as he had finished that, he turned to the one he always thought of when he thought of Father Brian and wrote in part:

Dear Father Eugene:

It may sound unreasonable, Father, for me to say that I have hardly had time to breathe the past few days. . . .

Let it be some measure of comfort to you, Father, to know that you have helped me with your wonderful letters of advice and encouragement. Without them I may not have been able to say with the great Apostle: "I have fought the good fight, and I have kept the Faith."

If the occasion ever arises, give my kindest regards to the Sister Magdalens and Mother Mary Holy Name of the 8th St. Good Shepherd Convent.

I will have Father send you the beautiful little prayer book. It has meant much to me.

At last the time has come for me to say "Good-by." But I won't say it. I'll say instead: "Until we meet in Heaven!"

They came with breakfast, but Tom waved it aside. "Not today, boys. For one thing, I haven't the time." His real reason, of course, was the little white wafer of wheat Father Libs had just taken to transubstantiate.

But the next interruption he had to accept. It was made by the Prison's barber. As the nuns had advised him, Tom thought of what had happened to Christ on another Thursday night. They had not cut His hair, they had crowned it with a crown of thorns. The barber was surprised at the calm of the man under his tools, and still more surprised when that man smiled and thanked him graciously when the task was completed.

Shortly after noon Warden Buchanan came along to ask the routine question. Tom did not even bother to answer. He just smiled at the big man. Then Jess said: "Here's a man I want you to talk to, Tom. He's from the kitchen. You can have anything you want for dinner: steak, chops, chicken. . . ."

"I'm not fussy, Mr. Buchanan. Let it be a steak."

"How about potatoes, sliced tomatoes, butter, hot biscuits, strong coffee, and cigarettes?"

"Sounds perfect. Did you get it all, waiter?" When the man smiled and nodded, Tom added: "Sorry I can't give you a substantial tip, but I just sent my last penny home to Mrs. Penney."

"O.K., Tom," said the Warden and walked off with the grinning guard.

Tom looked at his list. He had checked off a good many names since early morning, but the most important still remained. There was home, Father Donnelly, the Detroit Magdalens, Sisters Mary Laurentia and Robert Ann. He bent over his table again and decided to get the most difficult one of all written. He began: "My Darling Mother and all." Then his pen poised over the paper. What should his last words to his mother, brothers and sisters be? He sat there rejecting idea after idea until he was startled by a knock.

"Father Libs is coming," said the guard, then hurried along "the walk" to shoot the long bar that locked the entire tier of cells.

Tom fell on his knees. The priest came in silently. He opened a kit; arranged a miniature altar; lit two candles, then began to pray. Tom was still on his knees with head deeply bowed. God alone knows the thoughts that filled his mind during those sacred moments, but that he was as close to heaven as it is possible for a man to be while still on earth is suggested by the first letter he wrote after his long colloquy with Christ, sacramentally present in his heart. It was the letter he was about to begin before he had received what was to be his Viaticum.

February 25, 1943

My Darling Mother and All:

I have not sought the consolation of God, but the God of consolation.

So dear Mother, sisters and brothers, please, I implore you, give thanks, *everlasting* thanks to the good God who is present in my heart, for giving me the grace to die a happy death.

Keep your chins up. . . .

I'll be watching and waiting to greet you — do not let me down. I won't get mushy because I am too happy in my heart.

Remember dear ones, I love you all.

Tom

May God bless you and keep you!

With that final exclamation point he sat back and wept quietly. It was in this position those who served his last meal found him. When they entered he wiped his eyes and smiled sadly. "Thanks, boys," he said fairly cheerfully, "I think I can do justice to what you have brought." It was almost four in the afternoon and Tom had been up since before dawn.

He had just lit a cigarette to enjoy with his coffee when the Warden came again.

"Did you eat well, Tom?"

"There's the evidence, Mr. Buchanan," and he pointed to a plate that was almost empty.

"I'd call that eating moderately, Tom. Did you enjoy it?"

"Perfectly."

"Well, look. There's a man outside who would like a word with you."

"Who is he?"

"A reporter."

Tom's lips pressed together and his head shook in what Buchanan later called "a touch of indignation and impatience."

"For your sake I'll see him, Mr. Buchanan. But I'll have nothing to say."

He went to the door of his cell and met Bruce Temple, Staff Correspondent of the Louisville *Courier-Journal.* He quietly acknowledged the introduction and listened politely as Temple told his purpose in coming and related something of his interviews with Anderson and Baxter, who were down on Death Row. When he finished his account with "And now what have you to tell the world, Tom?" and stood with pencil poised over pad, Penney quietly answered: "I've said all I'm going to say, Mr. Temple."

"Well, Tom, will you tell the waiting world which of the stories you told is true?"

Penney just stared at the reporter in stony silence.

Before it became too embarrassing, Buchanan nudged Temple and started away with: "Come along, Bruce, Tom has some important work to do."

That was true enough. The prisoner went back to his table and studied the document he called his "Last Will and Testament." He read each sentence very carefully. When at last he felt satisfied, he put three copies aside, mentally naming those for whom they were intended.

It was 6 p.m. when the next interruption occurred. It was the Warden again. Not to ask a question this time, but to read the Death Warrant. Tom listened quietly. When Buchanan ended, Tom said: "Thank you. God's will be done. I'm a lucky man."

At seven o'clock Father Libs came into the tiny cell to spend the remaining hours with the doomed man. They chatted for a few moments. Tom assured the priest he was perfectly ready to go; had nothing on his mind; forgave everyone from the bottom of his heart; and if he could finish three letters he'd be happy.

"O.K., Tom. I'll pray my Office for you while you write."

"Perfect!" exclaimed Penney enthusiastically. "I've simply got to get these three letters off. They are to my best friends on earth."

The first was to Father Donnelly. It was begun at 8 p.m.

I have neglected you terribly, Fr., but I so counted on your being here tonight and thought I could tell you my appreciation personally, but it seems that our Lord has ordained otherwise, so now I am out on a limb, how can I write all the things I want to say. I have no secrets from you, Fr., unless it is that I have kept you in ignorance of the miracle that God has wrought in my soul.

It looks like I am going to have to cut this short, Fr. I have been interrupted several times already and I see that I am not going to [be] able to concentrate. I will ask Fr. Libs to finish for me, and God will have to thank you for me. Mere words may prove meaningless, but God will give the credit where it belongs. Fr., be assured in this case yours will be great. I will not forget you in my happiness. Keep up the good work and we know God will make all right some sweet day. Say Hello to Sr. Adelaide. I won't be able to answer her beautiful letter. Five more hours, dear Fr., I will meet our Lord and our Lady with all the Holy Saints and Angels. Bet your socks you'll get talked about too.

Until we meet

My love and fondest wishes,
Sincerely in our Lord and Lady,
Tom.

Am enclosing a copy of my Last Will. Father Libs will write you. "Mizpah" is the watchword.

Quickly he drew another sheet to him and wrote to Mother Clare and the Sister Magdalens:

Dear Mother and Sisters:

Thank you for your beautiful letters of yesterday.

I only have time for a note, but felt that I must have the last word. In that I am almost "feminine," eh?

I cannot say that I shall miss you, dear Mother and Sisters, because where I am going I'll be so happy and busy I won't have time to miss anyone, but you can bet your boots I won't be too happy and forget you, depend on me to deliver every message you have given me.

I have felt the effects of your prayers these last months, you know, or else how could I sit here with courage to face this thing so calmly. I feel fine and have no fear I will continue to the very end. I must stop now, dear Sisters and Mother. Father will be here any moment now.

So until God brings you home, I'll be watching for you. And oh, the joy to see you come.

May our suffering Saviour and Sorrowful Mother bless and guard you night and day. Remember I'll be watching and waiting and begging the necessary graces to attain the highest perfection.

I am always in our Lord and Lady, your loving Son and Bro.

Thomas Penney
At the right of the Holy Cross
God bless you.

As he signed his name he felt a qualm of conscience. There was one old Magdalen who deserved something more than this general letter. Tom asked Father Libs the hour. When he learned it was 9:30 he cried: "I can make it," and straightway began his last letter to Sister Magdalen of St. Gertrude.

Dear Sister:

I have let the time slip by on me and I am not going to have time for a letter, but I could not think of going without leaving you a message.

I am sending you my scapular and crucifix. I have worn it since my First Holy Communion and you may know that it witnessed my last one — the one that your own precious hands prepared. Be assured our little secret will be kept. Only the loving and tender heart of a Sister could think of those things. . . . Until we meet in heaven I'll be begging favors for you. I'll deliver all your messages, be assured of that. . . .

May God bless you always!
In our Lord and Lady,
Thomas Penney.

Tom had one more letter to write, but before he could get to it the guards came to lead him on the journey that gave the cement corridor its name. They took him on his "last walk." Down to Death Row he went to be greeted by a curse from Anderson. Tom answered with a quiet "God bless and help you, Bob," then went to the cell appointed him.

"Anything you want, Tom?" asked one of the guards kindly.
"Yes, I'd like a sheet of paper and re-fill for my pen."

The guard hurried away with the almost empty fountain pen.
Father Libs chatted while they waited and marveled inwardly at
the calm of the man so soon to die. When the guard returned
Tom sat down and wrote:

Dear Sisters M. L. and R. A.

It's now 11:20 p.m. dear Sisters, and I won't say much — but the
joy in my heart is unspeakable as I calmly await the approaching
end. Only then, dear Sisters, will my life begin!

Fr. Libs will write you later and tell you *all*. I am assured of
heaven, Sisters. I won't forget you in my happiness, be assured of
that. Thank you for all you have done. I will in a very short while
be repaying some of those favors.

So until we meet up there I'll be watching and waiting. Thank
Mrs. Campbell and God bless her charitable heart.

I have great hopes of many accomplishments.

May God bless and keep you under the protection of our Bl.
Mother.

In loving gratitude,
Tom P.

When he finished folding it he looked up and said: "Well,
Father, I am now ready to go into the hands of God."

It was three minutes to twelve.

Three minutes later the Death House came to life with an
excited start as the number of the guards along the corridor was
increased and the prison electricians hurried through their final
tests in that green and tan room, whose twenty foot square held
but one article of furniture — a chair that was awesome in its
awful emptiness.

Directly opposite this chamber, four cells held men whose
hourglass of life showed very few grains of sand — and these
were fast trickling through. By twelve-thirty everything was
prepared and the only sounds were those made by the shuffling
feet of the guards.

A weird rupture of the nervous silence came when Trent

attempted a hymn on a wheezy harmonica and Baxter sang the words in a thin, trembling tenor. Anderson cursed the interruption. Penney never noticed it.

As the long hand of the clock crept inexorably along, Baxter and Anderson drew more fiercely on their cigarettes. Penney, who had been in prayer for almost an hour, seemed to grow even calmer.

At two minutes to one the giant Buchanan led more than two dozen men — reporters, a doctor, a few ministers, and some extra guards — into the Death House. The same nervous silence gripped these usually talkative men as the Warden, with nods of his head, motioned them to their various places in the green and tan room. To every eye that empty chair was a magnet which pulled them irresistibly and from which they were wrested only by force. Despite the crowd of witnesses huddled there the room seemed filled with an eerie emptiness.

One o'clock rang out. A tingling expectancy filled the gathering. Every eye focused on the door through which men were to take their last few steps on earth.

At one minute past one, the chunky form of Anderson filled the opening. Through it he swayed. In obvious agitation his jaws worked vigorously as he nervously chewed some gum. A guttural curse of Tom Penney rang round the room as the prisoner swaggered up to the empty chair. He puffed angrily at his cigarette as he seated himself, then snapped it away with a flourish as he flashed a sneering smile on the all-male assembly. It was bravado at its nakedest. As he settled his arms for the strapping, the Warden asked the usual question. Anderson blew the wad of gum from his mouth and answered: "Gentlemen, all I can say is that I'm innocent of the thing I've been charged with." The black mask was slipped over his head, he kicked off his shoes as a Baptist minister began some prayer. Two shocks of electricity shot through his body — and Bob Anderson was dead.

At 1:14 another man walked into that drab room. It was tall Tom Penney. His hands were behind his back. His dark blonde head was bowed in recollected prayer. An aura of calm solemnity radiated from his person and enveloped the thirty men huddled in that eerie silence. With surprising absence of tremor the prisoner quietly seated himself and very deliberately placed his arms in position to be strapped.

"Tom," said the giant Buchanan, "there is something you want to tell?"

"Yes," came the resonant baritone. "Publish in the morning what I asked you to."

Sixty eyes focused on the Warden. Buchanan calmly went on: "What you told me is the truth and you want me to tell it?"

"That's right."

Before Tom could say more, the black mask fell over his head. Father Libs began the prayers for the dying. It sounded as if Tom was answering from behind the bit of black which covered his features. That he was listening intently was evident from the position of his head. Then his body was seen to jerk four distinct times. A doctor stepped up to the form in the chair, applied stethoscope, turned to Buchanan with a nod.

"Tom Penney is dead," said the Warden. "It took four shocks." It was exactly 1:22 a.m.

The Dead Live—and Work

IT WAS a restless group of reporters that watched the final execution. Raymond "Skeeter" Baxter had never been "copy"; but never less so than now. The two principals having been removed from the stage and Buchanan being in possession of some statement from the man who had given them so much to write about these past seventeen months, they were impatient with all formalities. But neither the Warden nor the doctor were to be hurried. The self-confessed drug addict was led in, asked the usual question, and methodically strapped into the chair. A few of the newsmen edged toward the door but Buchanan stopped them with a glance. A Protestant minister began to pray, the two Catholic priests — Father Libs and Father Boehmicke of Earlington, whom Father Libs had asked to come — were seen to make the Sign of the Cross in the direction of the hooded man; a signal was given and the little body beneath the black-hooded head shook violently twice. As the doctor moved toward the platform, a hoarse whisper from one of the reporters was heard: "He's gone. Let's go."

By quarter to two all had crossed the yard and crowded into the Warden's office. Buchanan seemed exasperatingly deliberate. But once seated he talked rapidly enough. He began by reminding them it was January the eleventh that Penney had made his long deposition exonerating Anderson. Nervous nods told him that

203

newsmen needed no reminders. "Well," said Buchanan, "on January twenty-second, the day he should have died, Penney begged me for another interview. I granted it on the twenty-third. . . . "

"That was the Saturday before they went to Lexington for the last hearing," put in one of the reporters.

"That's right," said the Warden, and went on to tell how Tom had confessed that he had gambled with his soul by making the long deposition a fortnight earlier, and now wanted to rectify the situation as far as possible by telling the truth.

"And what was that?" broke in an impatient reporter.

Buchanan eyed him coolly and said, "That Bob Anderson was with him at Lexington and participated in the robbery and murder."

That was enough for most of the newsmen. These bolted from the room and headed for the nearest telephone or telegraph. Those who remained heard the detailed confession: how Baxter had really hatched the plot; how Anderson had furnished the guns and fired first; how Tom had been knocked down in the dark and arose firing his own gun. Nothing new was contained in the confession, but it corroborated what had been told in the first Lexington trial and completely cleared the name of Buford Stewart. Penney had told the Warden that the plot to involve the lame bar tender was first concocted while they were still in Lexington — early in 1942. Porter B. Lady, one of Buchanan's assistants, broke in here to assert that Tom had said that Anderson knew then that Stewart was already dead.

As the Warden finished his narrative, one of the reporters asked what was to be done with the bodies of the deceased. Buchanan made immediate answer. "Anderson's goes to Louisville. Penney's and Baxter's go back to Lexington."

But the Warden did not know the charity he was hiding in that last sentence. Sister Mary Laurentia, faithful to the end — and beyond it — had suggested to Mrs. Penney that she allow the State to bury Tom in prison ground. The wise old nun knew something of the fee demanded by morticians and the condition of Mrs. Penney's bank account. But when the mother's eyes filled with tears, Sister Mary Laurentia's mind was made up.

When Mr. Kerr, a Lexington undertaker, next came to St. Joseph's Hospital, he was taken aside by a serious faced Sister Mary Laurentia and told much about charity. He heard so much that he ended the interview with a smile, saying: "Don't you worry any more, Sister. The body will be brought back, prepared properly for burial, and kept at my parlors until the interment. Have you any idea where and when that will be?"

It was the nun's turn to smile. "Can you keep a secret?" she asked.

"I can try."

"Tom Penney is to be buried from St. Paul's Church. He is to have a funeral Mass and will lie in blessed ground. Father McKenna, the pastor, has arranged everything. The plot is at Hill Crest."

Mr. Kerr smiled a wider smile. "Did you say Father McKenna had arranged everything? Would you be willing to swear that Sister Mary Laurentia had nothing to do with any of the arrangements? God bless you, Sister. It will be a pleasure."

And so Tom Penney came back to Lexington. The funeral was a very quiet affair. Some school children formed the choir. Mrs. Penney and her little family were there along with faithful Sister Robert Ann and two companions. Sister Mary Laurentia, who had kept the night watch with Tom Penney as February 26 grew into day, was too ill from emotional exhaustion, to attend. Thus she missed the touching tribute Father McKenna saw fit to pay to this man who had turned so completely to God once he had been converted. She missed also the warm comfort offered to the mother, who smiled through her tears as she heard a priest of God insist that "every death is a resurrection."

The following day Mrs. Penney received another word from another priest of God which produced the same effect. It was in a letter from Paducah, dated February 27, 1943:

Dear Mrs. Penney:

I am going to write something which I have never done before. I hardly know how to begin or what to say to a mother who has had to suffer so much because of her son. However, taking everything into consideration, I feel there is much to be thankful for. As your son once told me: "Father, if I had not gotten into this trouble, I don't believe I would have gone to heaven."

You know our Lord can get much good out of anything. And I don't think I have seen a more beautiful death, nor will I; for as far as it was possible to determine, he died as a good Catholic ought to die. He spent his last hours in a spirit of recollection concerning the things of God — and such sincere sorrow I have never seen. He was especially sorry for all the heartaches he caused you, and he asked me to write this letter to you and tell you how he died.

He was a wonderful character and only God knows how much good his death will do for souls. He also told me he believed firmly that you yourself would embrace the Catholic Faith before your time comes, and he prayed much for this for he wanted his mother to have all the joys and consolations which his Faith and the sacraments gave him.

Mrs. Penney, I want to apologize for opening again the wound in your heart, but I wanted to tell you about your son; for he was one of the saintliest souls I have met. His faith was as simple as a child's, and you know our Lord has said: "Unless you become as one of these, you cannot enter the Kingdom of Heaven." He was ready, and as I told him, I only hope I myself will be as well prepared as he was.

May God give you His choicest blessings in your trouble, and may I say God bless you for such a grand son and a holy man.

Sincerely,
Thomas Libs,
Chaplain, Eddyville.

P.S. I have said Mass for Tom and I will keep him and yourself in my prayers.

Faithful to his promise, the Chaplain also sent word to the nuns. In their letter he was briefer, but his very brevity was eloquence to the Sisters who could read between his very words, let alone between the lines. The note ran:

February 27, 1943

Sisters Mary Laurentia and Robert Ann
Dear Sisters:

Thomas Penney asked me to write to you and state that he died as a Catholic man should die and that Robert Anderson died unrepentant as far as human beings could determine. However, he may have repented while in the electric chair. We do not know.

Mr. Penney said it would be all right to write to both of you in the same letter, as it would be passed around anyway.

Sincerely,
Thomas Libs,
Chaplain, Eddyville.

The following week the Chaplain was able to view the scene with greater calm and in his review gave a completer picture. On March 8 he wrote to Father Brian.

I know you want to hear how Tom Penney took the execution. Well, here are some of the facts. I went up to the Pen on Thursday afternoon and gave Penney Holy Communion. This was about 3:30. . . .

After dinner we went back to Death Row. . . . I took Father Boehmicke along because Anderson was angry at myself and Penney, and I thought Father might be able to do Anderson some good. . . .

When time came for the boys to die, Anderson was in first and cursed Tom Penney, cigarette in mouth, and as far as we could tell, died unrepentant. Father Boehmicke had worked hard with him, but no success. . . .

Tom Penney was next, and even the Preacher remarked on the recollected way he died. He walked in, hands behind his back and his eyes cast down. While they strapped him in the chair, the Warden asked him if he had anything to say, and Tom replied: "Publish in the morning what I asked you to." (It was concerning Anderson's part in the murder.) Then I began the prayers. After the execution I got Father B. to hold the oils while I anointed Tom conditionally.

Baxter, the other man of the trio, went saying: "I am going home to Jesus." The Preacher prayed while Father B. and I read the prayers for the dying and gave him conditional absolution.

After the last was gone, Father B. and I wasted no time in getting out of there. We went to Father B.'s place in Earlington, arriving about 4 a.m. It was the end of the hardest day I have ever had, and I hope never to have another like it. Knowing that one of the preachers who had been present has a radio program at eleven every morning, I got up on time to hear what he had to say. Generally he gives the priests and nuns "hell" — but he didn't this day. He even went so far as to say: "When Penney died I heard the angels singing and the harps playing." My ears, unfortunately, were not able to hear so keenly; but he (Tom) died a wonderfully Catholic death. . . .

A few days later Father Brian was hurriedly getting off a note to Sister Francesca. He was anxious that she see the last letter Tom had written him. Then he bethought himself and wrote: "I don't believe you have read the last several letters I received — if I can find copies I will enclose them, too. One of them — the one written after he returned from Lexington might prove very interesting to you."

He sat for a few seconds before his paper then set forth the truth: "A very interesting case is closed . . . and I feel that some of us have a friend in heaven. That Tom was a rat in his early days cannot be doubted — but that only lends luster to the work of grace, and what a work that was! I have never had the least reason to doubt his sincerity since first meeting him. And his gratitude to you for your kindnesses should tide you over some of the rough spots in life."

At this point in his composition a letter was handed to him bearing an Eddyville postmark. With mounting curiosity he opened it and read:

Dear Father:

We wish to take this opportunity to acknowledge your most kind and welcome letter. We had been expecting one all along, but did not know when it would arrive. Tom Penney was telling us sometime ago that he had asked you to drop us a few lines.

Tom thought the world of you, Father. After receiving one of your cheerful letters one day he said: "Boys, there is a real man!"

Naturally we had to agree with him, for even though our meeting through the Mission period was short, you certainly made a hit with us. We celled next door to Tom and he always seemed cheerful and full of fun. The evening they took him down below to the "Death House" his face seemed to drop for the first time. He stopped in front of our cells and said: "Good-by, boys." I could hardly see him for the tears in my eyes. All I could say was: "God bless you, Tom. We'll be praying for you tonight!" That was my only regret in getting acquainted with him. I knew it would hurt deep when he had to leave us and go down to the "Death House."

He sent word that same evening to get all his books and pamphlets out of his cell and give them to us. What Tom gave us is about all the Catholic literature we have. I didn't know you were sending books to the library. I will send up tomorrow and see what they have there. Tom gave each of us a prayer book with his name and the date we received it on the inside. We promised him we would keep them as long as they lasted. . . .

Father Brian could not resist any longer; he had to turn the paper over to glimpse the signature. He found a double one awaiting him. It read "Don and Alex." He placed them immediately — the Daugherty brothers who were in prison for life. They were taking instructions — at least they were supposed to be. The young Passionist shook his head. "Tom," he said, "you were the greatest missionary Eddyville ever had!"

But there was a priest further south who was even more affected by his contact with the man who had just died in the electric chair. Father George T. Donnelly sat in his chaplain quarters on Turner Field, Georgia, numb with wonder and gratitude as he read again and again the last thing he had received from Tom. With exceptional care and neatness the prisoner had written:

My Last Will

In the name of the Most Holy Trinity. Amen.

I, Thomas Penney, while I have the full use of my powers, wish to publish and declare before the Most Holy Trinity and all the Court of Heaven, this my last will: how I wish to live and die.

I give Thee highest and everlasting thanks that Thou hast made me Thy creature, hast regenerated me in holy baptism, and sanctified me with the holy sacraments of Thy grace.

I firmly believe and profess the true Faith, which I received in my baptism, and all and every one of the articles thereof in such manner and form as the One Holy Catholic Church believes and professes them.

O my God, in my last hour may my act be found whole and intact. I detest all the sins from my youth to this hour. I most humbly ask pardon of all and everyone whom I have ever grieved or offended by word or action. I do also from my heart forgive and pardon every injury, insult, or action whereby any person has offended me, even as my loving Jesus, while He hung suffering on the Cross, forgave His enemies.

Lastly, I profess that I desire to die as a true Catholic and to partake of the most holy sacraments. I desire to have my part and portion in all the Masses, prayers, and sufferings which shall be offered for all the faithful until the Day of Judgment.

O my dear Jesus, I implore Thee to send forth for my soul, one of those sighs which burst from Thy loving heart while hanging on the Cross, and to sprinkle my soul with one drop of Thy Precious Blood (the sealing).

I beseech Thee, O most tender Jesus, that Thou wouldst deign to register this, my last will, publicly in the Court of Heaven, and to witness it with the signature of Thy holy name, and to seal it with the impress of Thy five most sacred wounds.

O Precious Lord, be it known to all men whose creature I am, body and soul. This I, Thy most unworthy child, now sign and seal with my own hand.

Thomas Penney

"O God," murmured the priest, "how wonderful Thou art! And how mysterious are Thy ways!" For Father George had heard how Anderson had ended and how Baxter had faced the last moments. He was thinking of the poem:

Three men shared death upon a hill,
    But only one man died;
The other two —
    A thief and God Himself —
Made rendezvous.

Three crosses still
    Are borne up Calvary's hill,
Where Sin still lifts them high:
    Upon the one, sag broken men
Who, cursing, die;

Another holds the praying thief,
    Or those who penitent as he,
Still find the Christ
    Beside them on the tree.

† THE END †

DATE DUE

PRINTED IN U.S.A.